A New Perspective on the Use of Paul in the Gospel of Mark

This volume presents a detailed case for the plausible literary dependence of the Gospel of Mark on select letters of the apostle Paul.

The book argues that Mark and Paul share a gospel narrative that tells the story of the life, death, resurrection, and second coming of Jesus Christ "in accordance with the scriptures," and it suggests that Mark presumed Paul and his mission to be constitutive episodes of that story. It contends that Mark self-consciously sought to anticipate the person, teachings, and mission of Paul by constructing narrative precursors concordant with the eventual teachings of the itinerant apostle—a process Ferguson labels Mark's 'etiological hermeneutic.' The book focuses in particular on the various (re)presentations of Christ's death that Paul believed occurred within his communities—Christ's death performed in ritual, prefigured in scripture, and embodied within Paul's person—and it argues that these are all seeded within and anticipated by Mark's narrative.

Through careful argument and detailed analysis, *A New Perspective on the Use of Paul in the Gospel of Mark* makes a substantial contribution to the ongoing debate about the dependence of Mark on Paul. It is key reading for any scholar engaged in that debate, and the insights it provides will be of interest to anyone studying the Synoptic Gospels or the epistles of Paul more generally.

Cameron Evan Ferguson is a Writing Specialist at the University of Chicago and serves as adjunct faculty at McCormick Theological Seminary in Chicago, Illinois, USA. He completed his graduate work at the University of Chicago Divinity School, from which he graduated in August 2019.

Routledge Studies in the Early Christian World

Routledge Studies in the Early Christian World offers monographs and edited collections which explore the most cutting-edge research in Early Christianity. Covering all aspects of the world of early Christianity, from theology, archaeology, and history to urbanism, class, economics, and sexuality and gender, the series aims to situate these early Christians within the wider context of Late Antiquity.

Comprising both regional studies and broader thematic surveys, this series explores what changed with the advent of Christianity, what remained the same, and how early Christians interacted with, made sense of, and shaped the world around them. Aimed at early Christian scholars, classicists, and historians alike, *Studies in the Early Christian World* is an invaluable resource for anyone researching this fascinating period.

Jewish Glass and Christian Stone
A Materialist Mapping of the 'Parting of the Ways'
Eric C. Smith

The Slave Metaphor and Gendered Enslavement in Early Christian Discourse
Double Trouble Embodied
Marianne Bjelland Kartzow

Between Jews and Heretics
Refiguring Justin Martyr's 'Dialogue with Trypho'
Matthijs den Dulk

The Silencing of Slaves in Early Jewish and Christian Texts
Ronald Charles

A New Perspective on the Use of Paul in the Gospel of Mark
Cameron Evan Ferguson

For more information on this series, visit: https://www.routledge.com/Routledge-Studies-in-the-Early-Christian-World/book-series/SECW

A New Perspective on the Use of Paul in the Gospel of Mark

Cameron Evan Ferguson

Routledge
Taylor & Francis Group

LONDON AND NEW YORK

First published 2021
by Routledge
2 Park Square, Milton Park, Abingdon, Oxon OX14 4RN

and by Routledge
52 Vanderbilt Avenue, New York, NY 10017

Routledge is an imprint of the Taylor & Francis Group, an informa business

British Library Cataloguing-in-Publication Data
A catalogue record for this book is available from the British Library

Library of Congress Cataloging-in-Publication Data
A catalog record has been requested for this book

ISBN: 978-0-367-54910-7 (hbk)
ISBN: 978-1-003-09268-1 (ebk)

Typeset in Minion Pro
by KnowledgeWorks Global Ltd.

For Calvin Roetzel

Table of contents

List of tables

Modern Abbreviations

AB	Anchor Bible
AGAJU	Arbeiten zur Geschichte des antiken Judentums und des Urchristentums
ANTC	Abingdon New Testament Commentaries
BBR	*Bulletin for Biblical Research*
BECNT	Baker Exegetical Commentary on the New Testament
BETL	Bibliotheca Ephemeridum Theologicarum Lovaniensium
BHTh	Beiträge zur historischen Theologie
BIS	Biblical Interpretation Series
BNT	Die Botschaft des Neuen Testaments
BNTC	Black's New Testament Commentaries
BPC	Biblical Performance Criticism
BR	*Biblical Research*
Bsac	*Bibliotheca Sacra*
BTB	*Biblical Theology Bulletin*
BZNW	Beihefte zur Zeitschrift für die neutestamentliche Wissenschaft
CBNT	Commentaire Biblique: Nouveau Testament
CBQ	*Catholic Biblical Quarterly*
CGTC	Cambridge Greek Testament Commentary
CRINT	Compendia rerum Iudaicarum ad Novum Testamentum
CSC	Concepts for the Study of Culture
CUF	Collection des Universités de France
ÉBib	Études Bibliques
EF	Erträge der Forschung
EKK	Evangelisch-katholischer Kommentar zum Neuen Testament
ExpTim	*Expository Times*
GCS	Die griechischen christlichen Schriftsteller
GNS	Good News Studies
HNT	Handbuch zum Neuen Testament
HNTC	Harper's New Testament Commentaries
HTA	Historisch Theologische Auslegung
HThKNT	Herders theologischer Kommentar zum Neuen Testament
HTR	*Harvard Theological Review*

HUTh	Hermeneutische Untersuchungen zur Theologie
ICS	*Illinois Classical Studies*
Interpretation	Interpretation: A Bible Commentary for Teaching and Preaching
IRT	Issues in Religion and Theology
JBL	*Journal of Biblical Literature*
JR	*The Journal of Religion*
JSHRZ	Jüdische Schriften aus hellenistisch-römischer Zeit
JSJSupp	Supplements to the Journal for the Study of Judaism
JSNT	*Journal for the Study of the New Testament*
LCL	Loeb Classical Library
LD	Lectio Divina
LDC	Lectio Divina Commentaires
LNTS	Library of New Testament Studies
NCBC	New Cambridge Bible Commentary
NEB	Neue Echter Bibel
Neot	*Neotestamentica*
NIBCNT	New International Biblical Commentary on the New Testament
NICNT	The New International Commentary on the New Testament
NIGTC	New International Greek Testament Commentary
NovT	*Novum Testamentum*
NTL	New Testament Library
NTS	*New Testament Studies*
NTSupp	Novum Testamentum Supplements
NTT	New Testament Theology
OTS	Old Testament Studies
PNTC	The Pillar New Testament Commentary
RBén	*Revue Bénédictine*
RBS	Resources for Biblical Studies
SLR	Saarbrücker literaturwissenschaftliche Ringvorlesungen
SP	Sacra Pagina
ST	*Studia Theologica*
ThLZ	*Theologische Literaturzeitung*
TS	*Theological Studies*
VC	*Vigiliae Christianae*
WBC	Word Biblical Commentary
WGRW	Writings in the Greco-Roman World
WUNT	Wissenschaftliche Untersuchungen zum Neuen Testament
ZNW	*Zeitschrift für die neutestamentliche Wissenschaft*

Acknowledgments

It is with great difficulty that I compose these acknowledgments, not because I cannot think of persons to whom I owe my thanks (quite the contrary!), but because, in order to express my thanks truthfully, I must present myself in as painfully honest a fashion as possible. The University of Chicago, where I did my doctorate work, is a place of immense learning, but it is also a place where I sometimes struggled to feel at home (two realities enshrined, perhaps fittingly, in the brutalist architecture of the massive Regenstein library, where I spent much of my time). During the 2018–19 academic year, I graduated from its Divinity School. It was during that same year that I gave any consideration to taking my own life.

This is not the appropriate venue to share my story, though I will include my contact information at the end of this section in the hopes that, if there are others struggling with mental health during their graduate studies, my experiences might be of some help or comfort to them. Instead, I want to take this opportunity to express my thanks to those who kept me going during the final year of the composition of my dissertation (upon which this book is based) and to those who encouraged me to pursue its publication. Were it not for these persons, this book would not exist—indeed, *I* might not exist—and I want to highlight their great contributions to my life in the paragraphs that follow.

First and foremost, I express my love and gratitude to my parents and godparents (Tauron and Richard, Tom and Jeanne), my siblings (Renick and Brennan), and all of my extended family (too many to name here) for their love and encouragement. You have been and will continue to be constants in my life. Without you, I do not know what or where I would be.

Second, I thank Cal Roetzel, to whom this book is dedicated. Cal, you have been my mentor and my friend for many years. Your kindness, love, generosity, and your indefatigable faith in my academic abilities have sustained me in my darkest moments, even if you were not always aware of the demons that I faced. Had you not encouraged me to send my dissertation out after I graduated, I suspect I never would have. When I met you as an undergrad some 14 years ago, I saw in you the person that I wanted to be. That is no less true today.

Third, I express my gratitude to all of the friends made during my time at the University of Chicago—Christina, Aaron, Kelli, Doug, Emily, Richard, Caroline, Nathan, Matthew, Jonathan S., Jonathan W., Allison, Zach, Sam, Russell, Charissa,

Emily, Kyle, Marisa, Ryan, Katya, and so many others. Leaning on and commiserating with you has helped me to understand that I am not alone. Perhaps the greatest gift I have received from the Divinity School is all of you. And to those friends I have known forever (J.T., Hans, Shayna, Sean, Joe), you too buoyed me in my darkest hours, even if you did not always know it. Thank you for being there for me.

Fourth, I would like to express my thanks to Bret Lewis at Loyola University Chicago, Anna Souchuk at DePaul University, Sofía Torallas Tovar and David Nirenberg at the University of Chicago, and Steed Davidson and Sarah Tanzer at McCormick Theological Seminary for helping me to put food on my table as I pursued the publication of this monograph. In order to keep my head above water, I worked five different jobs at four different institutions, and these are the persons who took various chances on me. Particular thanks must go to Sofia and Steed. Sofia, you tried to figure out small ways to aid me, both financially and professionally, during this period and I will always be grateful for that. Steed, I do not know where I would be without the help of McCormick. With COVID-19, there was so much institutional uncertainty, especially financial, and McCormick went out of its way to try to protect me. There are no words to express my gratitude.

Fifth, I send my thanks to Amy Davis-Poynter at Routledge for gambling on my book, as well as my external reviewers—Drs. Elizabeth E. Shively, Martin Meiser, and Troels Engberg-Pedersen—for reading it and providing substantive feedback. When I received from each of you your kind words and your final recommendations for publication, I began to cry. I have done my very best to take all of your feedback into account and incorporate it as thoroughly as possible. If I have failed in any way, please accept my sincerest apologies.

Sixth, I express my gratitude to my dissertation committee (Profs. Margaret M. Mitchell, Calvin Roetzel, Sofia Torallas Tovar, and Richard Rosengarten) for their aid in turning a jumbled mess of ideas into a thesis that is cogent and, I hope, compelling. The process was not always easy for me, but I and the work are stronger for it.

Finally, to the general reader of this monograph, thank you for engaging with my work. If there are any gaps, shortcomings, or failures in its reasoning, I take full responsibility for them. If this book has any strengths, know that I am indebted to far better persons than myself for those insights.

With love,
Cam Ferguson
cferguson@uchicago.edu)
June 27, 2020

1   The relationship of Mark to Paul

As the theologians say, we "live from the end," even if the world should be endless. We need ends and kairoi and the pleroma, even now when the history of the world has so terribly and so untidily expanded its endless successiveness. We re-create the horizons we have abolished, the structures that have collapsed; and we do so in terms of the old patterns, adapting them to our new worlds. Ends, for example, become a matter of images, figures for what does not exist except humanly. Our stories must recognize mere successiveness but not be merely successive … In the middest, we look for a fullness of time, for beginning, middle, and end in concord.[1]

This monograph tells the (hi)story of the relationship of the Gospel of Mark to the apostle Paul. In the quote above, Frank Kermode, one of the great exemplars of 20th-century literary criticism, speaks of modern fiction. It is unlikely that he would admit that, for the evangelist or apostle, "time has so terribly and so untidily expanded its endless successiveness," or that "Ends" are simply "figures for what does not exist except humanly." Instead, for him, Mark's and Paul's conceptual horizon is that of apocalyptic, and their narrative constructions presume the imminent approach of the final moments of this world.[2] Yet, according to Kermode, it is from such presumptions that Western fictions are born and upon such that they pattern themselves, consciously or otherwise. He explains,

We seek to repeat the performance of the New Testament, a book which rewrites and requites another book and achieves harmony with it rather than questioning its truth. One of the seminal remarks of modern literary thought was Eliot's observation that in the timeless order of literature this process is continued. Thus, we secularize the principle which recurs from the New Testament through Alexandrian allegory and Renaissance Neo-Platonism to our own time. We achieve our secular concords of past and present and future, modifying the past and allowing for the future without falsifying our own moment of crisis. We need, and provide, fictions of concord.[3]

At a most basic level, then, modern humankind is no different than ancient. For Kermode, it is the universal experience of the sons and daughters of Adam to find themselves in the "middest," torn between bygone eras to which they do not have access and those murky futures played out in anticipation and imagination. Through recourse to narrative, human beings make consonance from distension, and they impose concordance upon an unstable and unpredictable world.

In the case of the Gospel according to Mark, Kermode would say that the "rectilinear" narrative structure of the Bible is presumed—a structure which extends from one end of historical time to the other—and Mark reworks and "requites" it in the service of a new apocalyptic vision.[4] He is, in a general sense, an author concerned with the *longue durée*. Yet, practically speaking, his engagement with the Bible's narrative structure is witnessed within the *courte durée* of a 16-chapter narrative set only a few short decades prior to Mark's composition, one which must speak to a real community living in the shadow of that duration's impending end. This temporal positioning invites exploration of how Mark uses the limited time within the narrative to help make sense of the time *between* the narrative and his community, a time of "transition" (to use Kermode's terminology) that does not belong to the End but immediately precedes it. One might label this the period of the mission, during which "it is necessary *first* [πρῶτον] that the gospel be proclaimed [κηρυχθῆναι τὸ εὐαγγέλιον] amongst all the nations [εἰς πάντα τὰ ἔθνη]" (Mk. 13:10).[5] If narrative concordance is to exist at the macro level of cosmogony and End, there should be some concordance at the micro-span that runs from the death of the messiah to the Markan community, as well. Were it otherwise, one could not expect either Mark or his readers to admit a meaningful and active space for themselves *within* that narrative, as the words and deeds of its heroes would be unfamiliar to them, and they would be reckoned mere passive vessels in and for events, if any reckoning was made of them at all. In other words, for the community to put their hopes in the story as a whole (which runs from one end of time to the other), there must be some significant way(s) in which it speaks to them directly and intertwines with their own lived experiences. In what follows, I will suggest that it is precisely in the investigation of the limited period that Mark's relationship to Paul comes into full relief.

Part I: Project overview

In his seminal article, "Mark—Interpreter of Paul," Joel Marcus makes the programmatic assertion that Mark's work is influenced by the thought of the apostle Paul.[6] To demonstrate this, Marcus suggests a list of potential theological, Christological, and ecclesiological overlaps between the two authors, and he then analyzes the apostle's and evangelist's shared emphasis on the cross. Interestingly, despite Marcus' provocative assertion, in his comprehensive *Mark* commentary—the first volume of which was published the same year as his article—only three short pages in his introduction discuss Mark's potential familiarity with Paul, and an argument for dependence is never sustained.[7] Moreover, Marcus nowhere claims that Mark had access to Paul's letters. My monograph will pursue what Marcus does not: a sustained case for the plausible literary dependence of the Gospel of Mark on select letters of the apostle Paul. I will suggest the historical possibility of Mark's and his community's knowledge of the person, teachings, and epistles of the apostle, and I will argue that Mark has self-consciously anticipated Paul and his mission within his story.

To state my thesis forthrightly: I contend that Mark adopts what I am calling an "etiological hermeneutic" vis-à-vis Paul. Mark's story is a story of origins (see Mk. 1:1: "The beginning [ἀρχή] of the gospel [τοῦ εὐαγγελίου] of Jesus Christ, the Son of God"), one which establishes continuity between the earthly life of Jesus, the contemporary situation of the Markan community, and the final ending of the world (see Mk. 13). Between the life of Jesus and Mark's historical moment, I presume that the evangelist knows that Paul is located, and I use "etiological" to suggest that one of Mark's primary literary goals is to create, within his narrative of the earthly life of Jesus Christ, historical precedent for the mission and teachings of Paul that occur subsequently to the conclusion of his narrative but prior to his composition of it. The evangelist's goal is not to repeat that which Paul has said (that is, to lift Paul from his letters and throw him some thirty years back into the past), but rather to *anticipate* him. Mark seeks to seed the apostle and his teachings into his text.

Mark's project is therefore both proleptic and synecdochical: he always presumes, though he does not narrate in full, the entirety of a salvation-historical narrative that extends from one end of historical time to the other (the "gospel" [εὐαγγέλιον], an episodic narrative he shares with Paul[8]), and his purpose is to tell a story that anticipates and concordantly connects with episodes subsequent to his 16 chapters. Believing that the mission of Paul is a part of this narrative, Mark seeks to create logical and concordant episodic precursors that will bind the missionary activity of the earthly Christ to the eventual teachings of the itinerant apostle, teachings that are themselves carried on within Mark's community. Depending on the particular Pauline phenomena Mark seeks to seed into his story, his literary strategies may be adapted, but his etiological hermeneutic remains fundamentally the same.

This chapter will be dedicated to setting out the historical presuppositions and methodological underpinnings of my thesis. In lieu of a comprehensive *Forschungsbericht* that situates the question of Mark's dependence on Paul within its modern historical context, I will offer a brief overview of the works of Gustav Volkmar and Martin Werner, two exegetes whose now-classic arguments have set the terms of the debate surrounding Mark's Paulinism for over a century, and I will summarize their exegetical legacies.[9] Following this review, I will chart a new path forward by building upon the contributions to Mark and Paul studies by C. H. Dodd, Richard B. Hays, Joel Marcus, and Margaret M. Mitchell. The hermeneutical road I propose to pave runs straight through Mark's perception of himself as one 'in the middest,' both at the macro level of universal (narrative) history, and at the micro level of transition. He is, on one hand, a storyteller living in a moment postdating the earthly career of the messiah and the missionary activity of the apostle but *preceding* the fulfillment of that mission and the consummation of the End. On the other, he is a storyteller anticipating the End and beginning to see the limits of historical time collapse upon themselves. It is through the composition of his gospel that he seeks to bring these tensive realities into a concordant and meaningful whole, and he does so, I suggest, by creating a retrospective narrative that *prospectively* engages the Pauline mission, anticipating the teachings of the apostle and seeding them into the earthly life of Jesus Christ.

Part II: Historical presuppositions, scholarly approach, and the genre of Mark

(A) Historical presuppositions

Any argument for Mark's familiarity with and use of Pauline traditions must begin by presenting a case for Mark's plausible *access* to them. Though Pauline letters and traditions were known throughout the ancient Mediterranean world at a very early date (before the middle of the second century C.E.),[10] the extent to which those letters were disseminated prior to 69–71 C.E.—the period during which Mark is generally thought to have been composed[11]—is unclear, and final judgment upon Mark's familiarity with Paul's epistolary correspondence is dependent, at least in part, upon where one imagines Mark's gospel was originally composed. Scholars have argued for both the Eastern and Western halves of the Roman empire,[12] but I am convinced by the contributions of Brian Incigneri and Michael P. Theophilos, both of whom place the composition of Mark at Rome. Incigneri argues comprehensively that Mark's rhetoric reflects a historical situation in which Vespasian rules the Roman empire and Titus has recently returned to the capital city carrying the spoils of the Second Temple (71 C.E.),[13] and Theophilos, building upon Incigneri's work but dating the gospel earlier (late '60s C.E.), emphasizes the number of Latinisms found in the text (10 of 18, "a frequency which is higher than any other Greek literary text of the period") and notes that several of those Latinisms are unattested in any Greek text prior to the first century.[14] Theophilos also underscores the observation made by Martin Hengel: only a Roman provenance would necessitate Mark's designating the Gentile woman of Mk. 7:26 a "*Syrophoenician*" (Συροφοινίκισσα) rather than simply a Phoenician (Φοῖνιξ), as it implies Mark's making a clear distinction between eastern Phoenicians and the "Carthaginians" (Λιβυφοινίκες), with whom the Romans would have been more familiar.[15] In my judgment, the arguments of these scholars, coupled with the Patristic evidence that places Mark in Rome as an interpreter of Peter,[16] suggests a Roman provenance for the composition of Mark's gospel and the inauguration of the synoptic literary tradition as a whole.

Should one adopt Rome as the place of composition for Mark's gospel, Mark's familiarity with Paul's letters circa 70 C.E. becomes significantly more probable, and it is possible that the evangelist had copies or knew the contents of as many as *three* Pauline epistles in the capital city: (1) Romans, (2) 1 Corinthians, and (3) Galatians. Rome is, of course, the destination of the first letter in this list (Rom. 1:7), and it is a text with which Mark shares significant thematic overlap.[17] Clement of Rome, writing sometime around the end of the first or beginning of the second century, had access to 1 Corinthians (and possibly Hebrews), which attests to the location of the second.[18] (To be sure, Clement was writing some

20 years after Mark, but he nevertheless demonstrates the arrival of 1 Corinthians in Rome at a very early date, and there is no reason to think it could not have been there earlier.[19]) Galatians presents the greatest challenge. Though there is no explicit evidence for the letter's reception at Rome in the first century, Arland Hultgren, Thomas Tobin, and Calvin Roetzel have all suggested that Paul's letter to the Romans was written—at least in part—to correct Roman misunderstandings about what the apostle had said in his contentious correspondence with the Galatian communities.[20] If true, even without a copy of Galatians, Mark may have been sufficiently familiar with the letter's *contents* (or characterizations of its contents [see Rom. 3:8; 6:15]) to incorporate elements of it into his gospel. One should not underestimate Mark's potential knowledge of Paul disseminated through a variety of media, including summary, hearsay, and rumor.

Thus, if the Gospel of Mark was written circa 70 C.E. in Rome, it is reasonable to imagine that the evangelist had access to Pauline letters and traditions. It would also mean that seismic shifts had recently occurred upon the early Christian landscape (both at home and abroad), which would have influenced the Markan composition in some profound ways. Over the previous two decades, not only had Jewish Christ believers been driven out of and allowed to return to Rome (see Suetonius, *Claud.* 25.3; Acts 18:2–3; Rom. 12–16), but Roman Christians, as a whole, had also been forced to endure a devastating persecution under Caesar Nero in 64/65 C.E. (Suetonius, *Nero* 16; Tacitus, *Ann.* 15.44.)—a persecution which, according to tradition, claimed the lives of both Peter and Paul (Eusebius, *H.E.* 2.25.1–8; Ignatius, Rom. 4.3; 1 Clem. 5.4–6.1). Moreover, in the East, the disciple James had been martyred (Acts 12:1–2; Eusebius, *H.E.* 2.9.1–4), as had James, the Lord's brother (Josephus, *A.J.* 20.9.1; Eusebius, *H.E.* 2.23). Finally, the Second Temple had been (or was about to be) razed to the ground and its spoils brought to Rome for all to see.[21] This cataclysm—one that would have reverberated with eschatological implication across the Mediterranean[22]—was the probable catalyst for Mark's composition. The fall of the Second Temple would have been seen as an epiphany of God's imminent second coming, and, in response to this imminence, Mark attempts to craft an epiphany of his own, one that combines traditional legends about Christ with the teachings of the apostle Paul in order to make manifest the truth of the gospel to which both bear witness but for which Paul is no longer available as an epiphanic stand-in.[23] I will return to this suggestion in more detail below.

(B) Scholarly approach

First and most important, I analyze Mark and Paul using the comparative and philological tools of "historical criticism."[24] It is my assumption that there is a historical milieu from which Mark comes, there are historical figures about whom Mark writes, there are historical sources with which he interacts, and, because I am interested in *how* Mark (the author) absorbs and accommodates certain source materials (the Pauline letters), I assume that there is a real author whom I can reconstruct with some accuracy, and that said author possesses creativity and exegetical autonomy of his own.

Second and relatedly, I presuppose that Mark's composition is logical, consistent, and complete, and that properly understanding the narrative requires interacting with it as such. To this end, my approach to the text is influenced by narrative critical methods.[25] I am attuned especially to the internal coherence of the Markan plot, and I closely analyze its characters, settings, and rhetoric in an effort to grasp how the story constructs its meaning. It is only through such careful literary analysis that one can trace the threads of Paul woven throughout.

Because I am using narrative criticism to aid in the reconstruction of a real historical author and community, I am cognizant of the so-called intentional fallacy and the related challenges associated with reconstructing a real historical community on the basis of literary implications.[26] For the purposes of this monograph, I do not utilize Seymour Chatman's famous interpretive matrix consisting of "real author," "implied author," "implied reader," and "real reader," where the "real author" and "real reader" remain "outside the narrative transaction" and, to a greater or lesser degree, beyond the reach of the literary critic.[27] Instead, I adopt what Mark Allan Powell has designated an "author-oriented" narrative criticism. According to Powell, this approach presumes an exegete's ability to speak concretely about a text's real author or real audience on the basis of the following logical inferences:

1   Narrative critics are able to discern how an imaginary implied reader would be expected to respond to Mark's story; this is the response that the narrative itself solicits or invites.
2   It is reasonable to assume that the original readers of Mark's gospel would have been expected to respond in a similar fashion; at the very least, the responses that we may infer for an imaginary implied reader may be taken as an index that approximates the actual response that would have been anticipated for original readers.
3   Since there is a logical connection between expected responses and inferred intent, the expected response attributable to Mark's implied reader may be taken not only as indicative of the response expected of the Gospel's intended audience but also as definitive of the historical author's actual intent.[28]

Presuming that Mark is not an unreliable or untrustworthy narrator who presents a distorted version of the real author's beliefs through the telling of the story, Powell's inferences are sound, and it thus becomes possible to reconstruct the plausible intention of a real author using narrative critical methods.[29]

Third and finally, I presume that ancient Mediterranean society was saturated with performance in various forms,[30] and Paul's letters would not only have been read out loud in performance, but particular phenomena within his letters would have been recognized as ritual or typological performances of specific episodes of his gospel narrative (baptism, Eucharist, scripture). Similarly, I presume that Mark's story would have been read and performed in front of his Roman community. Though I am not primarily concerned with the mechanics of Markan performance (the processes of memorization, the number of actors, its stagecraft, etc.), my readings of Mark and Paul have been influenced by performance criticism, particularly its emphasis on a performance's power to transform its viewers.[31] According to David Rhoads,

> With performance we ask in fresh ways not only what a composition *means* but what it *does* in performance. What is the impact of performance in terms of persuasion—subversion of cultural values, transformations of worldview, impulse to action, change in behavior, emotional effect, ethical commitment, intellectual insight, political perspective, re-formation of community, the generation of a new world? Put another way, what does a story or letter lead the audience to *become*—such that they are different people in the course of and as a result of experiencing the performance? [emphasis original].[32]

For the purposes of this monograph, I define "performance" in the following broad terms: any oral or embodied (re)telling of a tradition in the context of a gathered community by either trained or untrained performers.[33] I take it as a given that Mark's story would have been read or acted in front of a community of auditors and that its reader(s)/actor(s) would have been somewhat practiced in doing so. This has important implications for how the story of Mark would have been *experienced* in the ancient world, and, as I will demonstrate below, that experience is not only indebted to Paul, but it is also used to bind the Markan narrative of Jesus' mission to the teachings of the itinerant apostle.

(C) The genre of Mark

The Gospel of Mark is difficult to classify. Scholars have long debated whether it should more properly be categorized as a biography, a history, or a work that is some type of *sui generis* literary hybrid.[34] Indeed, so uncertain is its genre that one scholar has recently suggested that Mark's gospel is not, in fact, a narrative (διήγησις) at all. Rather, it is a collection of unfinished notes (ὑπομνήματα).[35] Though genre is not the focus of my study, because my argument for Mark's use of Paul is integrally bound up with the intended effects of Mark's performance on a listening audience (namely, the audience's internal connection of the missionary activity of Jesus to the teachings of the apostle Paul), it is necessary that I provide a sketch of what I take the Gospel of Mark to be, as well.

I begin with an assessment of the suggestion, put forth by Matthew Larsen in his *Gospels before the Book*, that Mark's gospel is a collection of unfinished notes. This thesis is largely incompatible with my own, and, because it has garnered significant scholarly attention in recent years, it requires comment.[36] Larsen's monograph is laudable for the new and important insights it provides into the possible ways in which the Gospel of Mark may have been received by various Christ-believing communities of the first and second centuries C.E.[37] Many of its exegetical conclusions vis-à-vis the text of Mark itself, however, are difficult to sustain. I will here provide one example: Larsen's reading of Mk. 5:21–6:6 (a section of Mark to which I will have occasion to return at the end of this chapter).

In his brief engagement with the text of the Gospel of Mark (21 pages of a 154-page monograph[38]), Larsen focuses on inconsistencies within the gospel that he takes to be demonstrative of Markan disunity. One example he brings forth is the apparent contradictions in Jesus' miraculous abilities: "Sometimes Jesus can do tremendous miracles and is aware of his power. Other times, though, the text is clear that he is not able to do miracles. Yet, still other times Jesus comes off as confused about the specifics of how or for whom he has performed a miracle."[39] Larsen uses the trio of stories found in Mk. 5:21–6:6—the raising of Jairus' daughter (Mk. 5:21–24, 35–43), the hemorrhaging woman (Mk. 5:25–34), and Jesus' unwelcome reception in his hometown (Mk. 6:1–6)—to make his case. In the raising of Jairus' daughter, Larsen supposes that Jesus is able to perform a miracle *despite* the fact that he is mocked, ridiculed, and encounters disbelief. Alternatively, in his hometown, so comprehensive is the disbelief that Jesus *cannot* perform miracles (see Mk. 6:5–6). Finally, in the case of the hemorrhaging woman, Larsen claims that Jesus does not seem to have any control over his miraculous powers at all.[40]

Though Larsen is correct to point out that belief or disbelief plays a vital role in Jesus' ability to perform miracles, Mark nowhere implies that, with a critical mass of disbelieving persons around Jesus, the messiah's miraculous power suddenly becomes ineffective. Jesus encounters disbelief throughout the narrative, and Mark repeatedly makes it clear that healing is accomplished on the basis of the belief of the *individual* who is asking for it, whether for his or her own sake (Mk. 5:34; 10:52) or for the sake of others (Mk. 2:5; 5:36; 9:23–24; see also Mk. 7:24–30), regardless of how many disbelieving persons might be in the immediate vicinity. It is therefore irrelevant whether or not the people in Jairus' home believe in Jesus; it only matters whether or not Jairus *himself* believes in the messiah ("Do not be afraid [μὴ φοβοῦ]. Only believe [μόνον πίστευε]" [Mk. 5:36]). Similarly, when Jesus comes to his hometown, it is not that the collective disbelief (ἀπιστία) of the people is so overwhelming that he cannot perform a deed of power (δύναμις). Rather, the problem is that there are so few there who have the necessary faith to receive it. Importantly, however, there are a few who do, and this is why Mark adds, "[Jesus] healed a few people sick with fever [ὀλίγοις ἀρρώστοις ... ἐθεράπευσεν]" (Mk. 6:5).

In the case of the hemorrhaging woman, whose restoration also operates on this faith-to-healing template, *pace* Larsen, the manner in which she is healed is neither unique nor inconsistent. Healings resulting from Jesus' being touched by a believer (with or without his knowledge) occur at Mk. 3:10 ("... with the result that they fell upon him in order that, as many as had afflictions [ὅσοι εἶχον μάστιγας] might touch him [αὐτοῦ ἅψωνται] ..."); Mk. 6:56 ("and they were beseeching him in order that they might even touch the fringe of his garment [κἂν τοῦ κρασπέδου τοῦ ἱματίου αὐτοῦ ἅψωνται]. And so many as touched him [ὅσοι ἂν ἥψαντο αὐτοῦ] were saved [ἐσῴζοντο]"); and, possibly, Mk. 8:22 ("And they carried to him a blind man and were beseeching him in order that he might touch him [ἵνα αὐτοῦ ἅψηται]"[41]). Within the larger context of Mark's narrative, the manner of the woman's healing is unsurprising. Jesus is a fount of divine energy that provides healing to all who come to him in faith.[42] Far from being incongruous, these stories stand in continuity with and add texture to the how and why of miracles across Mark's narrative.

The evidence Larsen here musters to argue that Mark should be classified as "unfinished notes" (ὑπομνήματα) is thus unconvincing. Because many of Larsen's other conclusions can be similarly challenged,[43] it is best to consider Mark a narrative (διήγησις), whether one chooses to designate it a history, a biography, or something *sui generis*. In my own judgment, Mark ought to be classified as the evangelist himself classifies it: it is "gospel" (εὐαγγέλιον [Mk. 1:1]). That is, though the story shares some generic features with historiography and biography, with Willi Marxsen I take Mark's primary literary purpose to be a textualization of the proclamation by which "the Risen Lord re-presents his own life on this earth."[44] Mark's principal goals are not historical or biographical; they are, like Paul's, theological and kerygmatic. The Gospel of Mark plays on the features of tragic drama to create an experience naively analogous to Aristotle's famous and enigmatic assertion that tragedy, "through pity and fear [δι᾽ ἐλέου καὶ φόβου], effects the catharsis [κάθαρσιν] of such emotions."[45] In and through the performance of Mark's gospel, the Markan audience would see the death of Christ (re)presented before their eyes, and they would experience the pain and fear elicited by that event from an external and (comparatively) safe vantage. As the story is not yet complete at Mk. 16:8, however, that (re)presentation would also necessitate the full recollection of the sacred story beyond its 16 chapters. Through this process, not only is the messiah (re)presented and proclaimed, but Kermode's periods of "transition" and "End" would be brought together, and, as I will argue, Paul and his mission—seeded into Mark's gospel—would be validated within the minds of the Markan auditor.

Part III: Gustav Volkmar and Martin Werner—settling the question?

Before advancing my thesis further, I will take a step back and sketch the origins of the debate surrounding the Paulinism of the Gospel of Mark and its effects on modern scholarship. The story begins some 150 years ago, with the work of Gustav Volkmar, a 19th-century German philologist and biblical critic.[46] Volkmar took up the subject of the relationship of Mark to Paul in two substantial monographs. The first, a popular work entitled *Die Religion Jesu und ihre erste Entwickelung nach dem gegenwärtige Stande der Wissenschaft*, was published in 1857 and introduced his thesis that Mark is a self-consciously crafted allegorical defense of Paul and his mission. Volkmar's second work, *Die Evangelien, oder Marcus und die Synopsis der kanonischen und ausserkannonischen Evangelien nach dem ältesten Text mit historisch-exegetischem Commentar*, was published in 1870 as a comprehensive commentary that furthered his earlier thesis.[47]

To understand Volkmar, one must recognize that, as the last great member of the Tübingen School, he was indebted to F. C. Baur's famous *Tendenzkritic* and his conviction that much of early Christian literature could be explained on the basis of the conflict(s) between a Petrine "Jewish Christianity" and a Pauline "Gentile Christianity." Volkmar's particular contribution was to argue that that conflict began in earnest with the Book of Revelation. He understood this text to be a challenge to Pauline Christianity and its message of salvation for all, and he considered the Gospel of Mark to be its direct, literary rebuttal.[48]

At the same time, Volkmar was a committed Protestant, and his project had an overtly theological tone. For him, the gospel narratives were allegorical (German: "sinnbildlich") models of the "one gospel" ("des Einen Evangeliums") of Jesus Christ and his apostle, Paul. During the first two centuries, prior to the imposition of Catholic traditionalism, Volkmar assumed that early Christian authors were well aware of the true didactic content ("Lehrgehalt") of the gospel stories; indeed, they were able to modernize while simultaneously remaining true to that content. But, as time passed, this didactic material was buried, and the gospels increasingly came to be recognized as "historical narratives" ("Geschichts-Erzählung") penned by the hands of the apostles themselves, or, in the case of Mark, by an apostle's amanuensis. Thus, they ceased to be primarily allegorical or figural and instead became historical. An awareness of the underlying spiritual sense ("geistigen Sinn") implicitly persisted alongside this external conception ("äusserlichen Auffassung"), however, and, with the coming of the Protestant reformers, the spiritual sense of the gospels was elevated to the surface once more.[49] Volkmar viewed his own project as contiguous with his Reformation predecessors: he sought to provide a means by which the gap between reason-based historical criticism and spirit-driven didactics could be bridged, and, in the process, the teachings of Protestant Christianity vindicated.[50]

For Volkmar, then, the Gospel of Mark is not properly a "history." Rather, it is a "self-conscious didactic-poetic composition [Lehr-Poesie] on historical ground."[51] He explains,

> [Mark's] whole work is an apology for the apostle to the Gentiles [eine Apologie des Heidenapostels], a defense [Vertheidigung] for the legitimacy [Rechtes] of the community of Gentiles in the name of Jesus Christ and the Old Testament, which is, through him, fulfilled and surpassed [erfüllt und übertreffen sei] …. Indeed, throughout the whole gospel the life of Jesus, as also the life, work, and suffering of Paul, is in view [durch das ganze Ev. hin ist das Leben Jesu, wie das Leben, Wirken, und Leiden Pauli mit im Auge].[52]

Volkmar imagined the Gospel of Mark to be a text in which spiritual truths were concealed within a historiographical "shell" ("Hülle"). The evangelist had access to oral traditions and various literary sources, including four of Paul's letters, but Mark's primary concern was to portray Christ as Paul's revealed and ascended Son of God.[53] Thus, the historical traditions standing behind the narrative were transformed by the evangelist into allegories that (re)present the theological convictions and experiences of Paul.[54] Anne Vig Skoven helpfully summarizes Volkmar's project as follows:

> Mark's Gospel is to be seen as an odyssey in which the reader travels with the historical Jesus, with the Apostle Paul and with the risen Christ (or the Christ-Spirit) …. Whereas the author of Luke and Acts chose to allocate these travel

narratives to two separate volumes, Mark's single two-level story encompasses both. Volkmar regards the Markan Jesus as a literary character who is based upon several literary and historical figures—including, of course, the historical Jesus. However, when speaking of Christ, the author often has Paul in mind. Apparently, Mark has projected Paul and his Gentile mission—as we know it from Paul's letters and the Acts of the Apostles—back into Jesus' life.[55]

On Volkmar's reading, Mark's layering of narratives necessitates the careful delineation of complex and ubiquitous external referents to what he believed were various Markan symbols. For example, in his discussion of Mk. 9:33–50, which Volkmar takes to be superlative proof of Mark's Paulinism, the German scholar asserts that the foreign exorcist must be a symbol for Paul on the basis of the following exegetical inferences: (1) the disciples' question "who is greater?" (τίς μείζων [Mk. 9:34]) refers not to an internal dispute but an external one (the disciples are judging themselves over and against outsiders); (2) the "child" (παιδίον [Mk. 9:36]) that Jesus embraces stands as a symbol for the Gentiles who bear Christ's name (ἐπὶ τῷ ὀνόματί μου [Mk. 9:37]); and (3) the exorcist is opposed by none other than John (Mk. 9:38), the author of the Book of Revelation and Paul's greatest opponent.[56] On the basis of these three speculative observations, Volkmar claims that Mk. 9:33–50 is written in support of Paul and warns about the dangers of excluding Gentile converts from the early Christian mission.

In response to Volkmar, Martin Werner, a 20th-century Protestant theologian, published a monograph in 1923 entitled, *Der Einfluss paulinischer Theologie im Markusevangelium: eine Studie zur neutestamentlichen Theologie*.[57] In addition to offering a thoroughgoing challenge to what he deemed the flawed and arbitrary allegorical approach of his German predecessor, Werner sought to institute specific criteria and a stable method for comparing Mark to Paul.[58] Instead of relying on Markan symbols, Werner compared the apostle and evangelist on essential themes that could be considered expressly "Pauline."[59]

As might be expected, Werner's hermeneutic differed significantly from that of Volkmar. Indebted for his thought to the work of Albert Schweitzer (to whom his monograph is dedicated), Werner formed a part of the so-called first quest for the historical Jesus (*Leben-Jesu-Forschung*), and his early monograph on Mark should be considered a contribution to that research.[60] For Werner, as for Schweitzer, the best hermeneutic for understanding the development of early Christianity was a "Consistent-Eschatological" ("Konsequent-Eschatologische") one, an approach that "seek[s] to interpret the essentials of the teaching of Jesus, of the first apostles, and of Paul ... consistently from the viewpoint of that sense of eschatological expectancy, current in late-Jewish apocalyptic, which dominated the whole of Primitive Christianity."[61]

As Werner saw it, the great benefit to viewing early Christianity through this lens was, on one hand, that it contextualized Jesus within, and understood him to be representative of, Second Temple Jewish apocalyptic and eschatology. On the other, and consequently (if not a bit circularly), exegetes could have a "high confidence" in the trustworthiness of the synoptic tradition that depicted Jesus in such a manner.[62] Indeed, in Werner's judgment, analyzing the synoptic gospels through the lens of "Consistent-Eschatology" not only preserved the historicity of the narratives, but provided a means by which a reader could make sense of literary problems he or she might encounter in the course of reading one of the texts.[63]

An essential consequence of engaging the gospels from this "Consistent-Eschatological" point of view was that the direction of influence had to run *from* the gospels *to* Paul and not the other way round. For Werner, to invert that sequence would be to call the entire hermeneutic into question. Paul did not know the historical Jesus (see Gal. 1:15–17), and, were he shown to have had a significant influence on synoptic literary tradition, the historical character of those texts would become far more difficult to discern.

Thus, in 1923, Werner published a book that systematically refuted Volkmar's claims. Reading through a "Consistent-Eschatological" lens, Werner sought to demonstrate on one hand that there was no rhyme or reason to Volkmar's allegories, and on the other that Volkmar had consistently misread or distorted the real historical data provided by biblical texts. As a result, Werner came to the exact opposite conclusion of Volkmar on nearly every point. At the close of the monograph, he summarizes his findings as follows:

1　Where Mark agrees with Paul, it is always a matter of general early Christian assumptions [um allgemein-urchristliche Anschauungen].
2　Where, in the letters, beyond this common ground [über diese gemeinsame Basis], characteristically Pauline assumptions happen to emerge [charakteristisch paulinische Anschauungen zutage treten], either Markan parallels are entirely lacking [fehlen … vollständig], or Mark represents downright opposite attitudes [geradezu entgegengesetzte Standpunkte].
3　Thus, the argument [die Rede] for an influence of Pauline theology on the Gospel of Mark [einem Einfluss paulinischer Theologie im Markusevangelium] cannot in the least be sustained.[64]

For nearly 100 years, these conclusions—with a few exceptions[65]—have been accepted by scholars, and they are still regularly assumed or explicitly (re)affirmed today.[66] Yet, Werner's monograph displays the problematic tendency to read evidence one-sidedly in an effort to preserve historical Jesus traditions from subsequent and external Pauline theological reflection.[67] For example, using the Parable of the Vineyard (Mk. 12:1–11), Werner reasons that the death of Christ in Mark runs directly contrary ("direkt zuwiderlaufend") to God's divine plan. This implies, according to Werner, that the gospel presents a Jesus whose earthly actions demonstrate his divinity despite his death and resurrection rather than because of it, which contrasts sharply with Paul, for whom Christ's messianism is dependent upon the crucifixion.[68] Yet, *pace* Werner, for Mark, *the* event towards which all those others build, and in light of which they must be understood, is Christ's death (see Mk. 2:18–20; 8:31; 9:31; 10:32–33, 45). A good reading of the text must deal both with Jesus' messianic demonstrations during his earthly life and the absolute salvation-historical necessity of the cross, and Werner has attempted to make the two Markan ideas mutually exclusive.[69]

Interestingly, amongst the various reactions to Werner that have arisen in the wake of Marcus' work (more on his article in Part IV below), methods of reading that bear some similarity to Volkmar's allegorical exegesis have seen a resurgence, perhaps due to William R. Telford's provocative suggestion in 1999 that, "With the development of narrative-critical tools and an increasing sensitivity on the part of scholars to the nuances of narrative theology, Volkmar's original suggestion that Mark is an allegorical presentation of Pauline teaching in the form of a narrative may be due, therefore, for a comeback."[70] Scholars who adopt such an approach generally make use of the intertextual methods of Gérard Genette, W. G. Müller, or Dennis R. MacDonald, and they analyze the ways in which the Gospel of Mark (a "hypertext") has systematically transformed and incorporated select Pauline epistles ("hypotexts") into its body.[71] These approaches to Mark's Paulinism have not persuaded the majority of the scholarly community, however. Because an exegete adopting a hypertextual reading might claim that, if there is clear thematic overlap between the two texts under examination, it is because the hypertext is commenting in a relatively straightforward fashion upon the hypotext; and, alternatively, if there are tensions or disagreements between the two writings, it is because the hypertext has *transformed* the hypotext, the interpretive malleability of their intertextual methods shields these scholars from critical examination.[72] Rather than counter-evidence leading to the questioning of starting assumptions, that counter-evidence is incorporated and transformed into evidence *for* the starting assumptions.

Thus, though Werner's conclusions are increasingly recognized as flawed, a sustained and convincing assessment of Mark and Paul's relationship still remains a *desideratum*. That assessment must on one hand provide a clear and historically plausible account of Mark's approach to Pauline materials, while on the other present a replicable methodological model for testing its conclusions. At the same time, it must avoid overly symbolic readings, and it must challenge Werner's recourse to "general early Christian assumptions" (allgemein-urchristliche Anschauungen) that can be used to explain away any overlaps. As I will demonstrate, reading Mark's gospel as an etiological narrative goes far in satisfying all of these requirements. Mark is not writing an allegory for the apostle; rather, he is writing a historically circumscribed portion of the gospel narrative that he and Paul share. Because the story he tells is not the whole story, however, he is careful to anticipate (not "incorporate") those episodes that will occur after the conclusion of his 16 chapters, one of which is Christ's revelation to Paul himself.

Part IV: Joel Marcus—reopening the question

No scholar has done more to reinvigorate the question of Mark's Paulinism than Joel Marcus. His essay, "Mark—Interpreter of Paul," is now generally accepted as the catalyst for a new investigation into the relationship between the two authors.[73] Recognizing the great challenge posed by Werner's assertion that a common tradition stands behind the evangelist and apostle, Marcus attempts to refute Werner's claim by comparing Mark with idiosyncratic or characteristically Pauline teachings. According to Marcus, the strongest case for establishing Mark's dependence on the apostle is made by demonstrating that the evangelist agrees with the apostle at points where others on the early Christian landscape would not, and he suggests that fruitful areas of potential investigation include Paul's theological use of the term "gospel" (εὐαγγέλιον), his insistence on the crucifixion as the apocalyptic turning point of the ages, his negative portrayal of the pillar apostles, his dualistic understanding of "faith," his insistence on the priority of the Jews (Ἰουδαίῳ πρῶτον [Rom. 1:16]), his apocalyptic reformulation of the law, his emphasis on the "ungodly sinners," Christ's victory over the demonic in death, and Christ as a "new Adam," all of which Marcus suggests are (re)presented within Mark's narrative.[74]

For the purposes of his article, Marcus focuses narrowly on how Paul and Mark understand the cross. Marcus not only highlights the problematic bifurcation Werner creates on the subject of crucifixion theology (discussed above); he also demonstrates that Mark and Paul share a belief that the death of Christ is the turning point of the ages, and it necessitates the adoption of a new epistemology that sees God's eschatological power and glory displayed in the form of human flesh and weakness.[75] Because there is evidence within Paul's letters that these beliefs were not, in fact, universally accepted at the time of the earliest mission, Marcus suggests that Werner's argument for a common tradition standing behind the two authors cannot be sustained.[76]

I am indebted to Marcus for both the attention he has drawn to the flawed conclusions of Werner and the comprehensive list of themes shared by Mark and Paul that require further investigation, and one of the goals of this monograph is to build upon Marcus' work in positive new directions. His investigation into the evangelist's and apostle's theology of the cross has correctly identified significant overlap between the two authors. That said, Marcus does not explore Mark's broader hermeneutics vis-à-vis Paul, and he provides no explication of *how* Mark envisions the shared themes he has identified interacting with one another. This is the goal of my monograph. I contend that Mark's literary purpose in integrating Pauline theology into his narrative is consistent and methodologically predictable: Mark looks to establish literary continuity between the missions of Christ and Paul, both of which form a part of the same gospel narrative that the evangelist and apostle share. Mark thus tells a story that is self-consciously crafted to anticipate episodes of the gospel that occur subsequently to his 16 chapters, within which Paul and his mission must be included.

Importantly, I am not suggesting that Mark's project functions *solely* to anticipate Paul. An etiological approach to the mission and teachings of the apostle is, rather, an aspect of a much grander literary endeavor. The Markan community lives in the period of the mission to the ends of the earth that immediately precedes the end times (Mk. 13:10), and, in the wake of a persecution that claimed the lives of Peter and Paul and the war in Judaea that razed the Second Temple to the ground, Mark composes that portion of the gospel narrative wherein the earthly Jesus can be encountered—a figure who, like Paul, experienced rejection, suffering, and death and who forecasted a vision of the world's ending—in order to provide an epiphanic bridge between the period of the charismatic authority of the apostles and the final ending of this world. It is to an explanation of this larger project that I now turn.

Part V: The synecdochical poetics of Mark and Paul

For Paul, the "gospel" (εὐαγγέλιον) is an episodic narrative that tells the story of the life, death, resurrection, and second coming of Jesus Christ "in accordance with the scriptures" (see 1 Cor. 15:3–8). This was first outlined by C. H. Dodd in his important monograph, *The Apostolic Preaching and Its Developments*, wherein Dodd compares narrative elements in the letters of Paul to the speech complexes of Acts in an effort to triangulate back to and reconstruct the earliest apostolic kerygma.[77] Though Paul nowhere lays out his gospel in all its episodic detail, Dodd's work establishes its skeletal outline by culling from Paul's letters its central episodes. The following is the narrative Dodd was able to reconstruct:

1 The prophecies are fulfilled, and the new age is inaugurated by the coming of Christ.
2 He was born of the seed of David.
3 He died according to the Scriptures, to deliver us out of the present evil age.
4 He was buried.
5 He rose on the third day according to the Scriptures.
6 He is exalted at the right hand of God as Son of God and Lord of quick and dead.
7 He will come again as judge and savior of men.[78]

Dodd's outline is revealing, though it is noteworthy that Jesus' resurrection appearances are not included, as they are explicitly presented as episodes of Paul's kerygma (1 Cor. 15:5–8), which Dodd himself notes.[79] Because it is through the experience of the risen lord that Paul comes to believe he is entrusted with stewardship of the Gentile mission (see Gal. 1:15–16; 2:7, 9), the resurrection vision of Christ is crucial to Paul's gospel: it provides the warrant for the Gentile mission he takes to be an essential element of the story (Rom. 11:11–32). I will return to this omission in Part VI of this chapter.

Building upon Dodd's work, Richard B. Hays has suggested that "any attempt to account for the nature and method of Paul's theological language must reckon with the centrality of *narrative* elements in his thought" (emphasis original).[80] In his provocative and influential work, *The Faith of Jesus Christ: The Narrative Substructure of Galatians 3:1–4:11*, Hays affirms that Paul's letters allude to and reflect a gospel which originates as a "sacred story"—a story about the life, death, and resurrection of Jesus Christ—and he argues that it is upon the "foundational substructure" of that narrative that Paul's occasional arguments build. The episodes of the sacred story are the "constant" elements within the framework of which Paul's "variable" elements (his historical and rhetorical circumstances) must be interpreted, and the letters that the apostle writes reflect his attempts to draw out the theological, Christological, and ecclesiological significances of that story for his scattered communities.[81]

Margaret M. Mitchell has since expanded upon the work of Hays and Dodd by composing two interrelated essays that argue Paul employs a "synecdochical hermeneutic" in relation to the gospel story.[82] Like Hays and Dodd before her, Mitchell contends that the "gospel" (εὐαγγέλιον) is, for Paul, an episodic narrative only partially represented through the apostle's occasional letters, and the parts that are represented are always rhetorically determined. She builds upon their insights, however, by arguing that, through the use of ancient rhetorical short-hand (βραχυλογία), Paul "is able to allude to the gospel and incorporate it into particular argumentative contexts without reciting the whole all over again each time."[83] For example, in 1 Cor. 1:17–2:5, where Paul seeks to combat the factional-ist boasting of the Corinthians by claiming that his own weak demeanor is exem-plary of Christomorphic humility, the apostle appeals to the gospel narrative and pulls forward the cross ("the word of the cross [ὁ λόγος ὁ τοῦ σταυροῦ]" [1 Cor. 1:18]) as a means to undermine Corinthian posturing. Paul clearly assumes (and expects his readers to assume) the whole story, but, for the purposes of his argu-ment, he underscores what he considers its most important episode in modeling upright behavior for God's eschatological community: Jesus' humble, obedient, and humiliating death upon a cross.[84]

Additionally, Paul's ability to evoke the narrative synecdochically is not limited to epistolary argumentation. The apostle also asserts that he *embodies* the narra-tive, taking his person to be a "rhetorical abbreviation" of the gospel.[85] Mitchell analyzes the interpretive difficulties associated with Paul's claim in Galatians that God revealed his Son ἐν ἐμοί (Gal. 1:16), and she points out that, on one hand, ἐν ἐμοί could be translated "*to me*," thereby making Paul the recipient of an epiph-any. On the other, it could be translated "*in me*," with Paul understanding himself to be "*the epiphanic medium* through whom God's son, Jesus, is revealed to oth-ers" (emphasis original).[86] Mitchell argues that the double meaning is deliberate, and Paul presents himself as a walking synecdochical epiphany of the deity. When Paul claims at various points throughout the letter to embody the death of Christ (Gal. 3:1; 2:19–20; 4:14; 6:17), he is in fact presenting himself as an icon of Jesus Christ crucified, and facilitating an epiphanic encounter with the deity via the rec-ollection of the whole gospel story through the synecdochical manifestation of one of its parts.[87] Through the (re)presentation of a particular episode, there occurs an autonomous "filling in" of the remainder of the narrative, which serves to confirm the story and validate the apostle's authority. This process is articulated explicitly at 2 Cor. 4:10: Paul carries around the "dying process of Jesus" within his body (τὴν νέκρωσιν τοῦ Ἰησοῦ ἐν τῷ σώματι [2 Cor. 4:10a]), in order that the "life of Jesus" might also be made manifest in his body (ἡ ζωὴ τοῦ Ἰησοῦ ἐν τῷ σώματι ἡμῶν φανερωθῇ [2 Cor. 4:10b]). According to Mitchell, "Paul contends that the necrotic epiphany currently on display in his body actually signals the resurrection epiph-any to come."[88] Thus, an essential element in the Pauline epiphanic experience is this synecdochical process by which the whole sacred story is recalled via the iconic display of one of its parts.

For Mitchell, this epiphanic process is also essential for understanding the Gospel of Mark. Though it is a fuller narrative in both form and purpose, Mitchell argues that Mark is, nevertheless, synecdochical: it presumes the whole sacred story, but it only tells a portion of it (the missionary activity and death of Jesus Christ) and points to the remainder through prophetic prediction (Mk. 8:31; 9:31; 10:32–34, 45, 13; etc.).[89] Neither Jesus' resurrection, nor his resurrection appearances, are narrated. They are prophesied, but it is up to Mark's audience to recall them as a part of the larger story. Similarly, the miraculous events occurring throughout the narrative (baptismal and transfiguration epiphanies [Mk. 1:10–11; 9:2–9], nature miracles, healings, exorcisms, etc.) are also synecdochical. At the level of the story, characters consistently encounter yet do not comprehend Jesus' true identity, but, because Mark's audience knows the full gospel plot, they are able to import that external knowledge into the text.[90] Thus, the Gospel of Mark, by knowing and making use of the same theological poetics as Paul, functions as a literary epiphany: "The oral gospel has become text, a literary icon of the crucified messiah. Mark (the text) is (incorporeal) Paul for all time: Jesus Christ crucified can be seen there."[91]

It is important to note here that the sacred story of which I am speaking is, for both Paul *and* Mark, flexible. Mitchell points out that Paul is able to expand the gospel by composing new "episodes" that respond to challenges facing believers in the present moment. In 1 Cor. 15, for example, as a result of Paul's having provided little in the way of concrete detail about the resurrection of the body when he first preached in Corinth, the apostle finds himself addressing members of the community who have come to doubt the resurrection of the dead. In order to respond to their concerns, Paul composes an expanded narrative of the End wherein the resurrection of the dead is made a constitutive part of the gospel story (see 1 Cor. 15:22–28; see also 1 Cor. 15:51–55).[92] While a certain narrative scaffolding of the gospel thus subsists (mission, death, resurrection, and resurrection appearances, second coming, etc.), Paul's theological poetics allows new episodes to be composed and made a part of it.

For Mark, things are no different. The composition of any literary work involves a deliberate process of selection and arrangement of events that necessarily excludes some and requires the configuration of others such that an order is imposed that is both contextual and, to a greater or lesser degree, contestable.[93] Mark's gospel, in other words, has a combined historical and fictive nature: the episodes of the story have been conceived or selected (from a range of possible options), reworked, and ordered in accordance with Markan literary or theological ideals.[94] For the evangelist, a narrative foundation exists that includes the mission, death, resurrection, resurrection appearances, and second coming of the messiah, but, as with Paul, Mark exercises creative control over this foundation. He builds out the story of Jesus' earthly life, including some episodes he shares with the apostle (e.g., the Last Supper [Mk. 14:22–25; 1 Cor. 11:23–26]), while adding numerous others that he has either composed himself or learned from tradition (e.g., the Baptism of Jesus by John [Mk. 1:2–11]). The result is that, though Mark's gospel is fully concordant with Paul's, it is not the same in all of its episodic detail, as Mark seeks to present a fuller accounting of that part of the story upon which Paul spends little time: the earthly career of Jesus Christ.

Part VI: Markan etiological hermeneutics

The etiological hermeneutic I am suggesting Mark employs vis-à-vis Paul should be considered a feature of this larger synecdochical hermeneutic that Mitchell argues the evangelist and apostle share. Mark's text is designed to facilitate an epiphanic encounter with the crucified and resurrected messiah through his audience's recollection of the full sacred story via the narrativization of a circumscribed portion of it. Because, for Mark, Paul and his mission are a part of the gospel narrative, the evangelist has composed his story such that the teachings of the apostle are anticipated within his narrative in order to facilitate their inclusion by his audience in the synecdochically evoked remainder.

Thus, my monograph argues that Mark's consistent hermeneutical principle vis-à-vis Paul is etiological: the evangelist seeks to seed the apostle and his teachings into his text. Mark's goal is to anticipate Paul, and his project is both proleptic and synecdochical: he always presumes, though he does not narrate in full, the entirety of the gospel of which Paul and his mission form a part, and his purpose is to tell a story that logically anticipates and concordantly connects with episodes subsequent to his 16 chapters.

In order to demonstrate my thesis, I will use the arguments of Mitchell as a starting point, but I will expand upon them in two ways. First and most important, as I have already suggested, I assume not only that Mark and Paul share a sacred story, but also that their common narrative shares at least one all-important *episode*: the epiphany of Jesus Christ to Paul himself. At 1 Cor. 15:3–8, Paul writes,

> 3. For I have handed over to you in the first place that which I also received: that Christ died on behalf of our sins [Χριστὸς ἀπέθανεν ὑπὲρ τῶν ἁμαρτιῶν] in accordance with the scriptures [κατὰ τὰς γραφάς], 4. and that he was buried [ἐτάφη], and that he was raised on the third day [ἐγήγερται τῇ ἡμέρᾳ τῇ τρίτῃ] in accordance with the scriptures [κατὰ τὰς γραφάς], 5. and that he appeared to Cephas and then to the twelve [ὤφθη Κηφᾷ εἶτα τοῖς δώδεκα]. 6. Then he appeared to over 500 brothers at once [ὤφθη ἐπάνω πεντακοσίοις ἀδελφοῖς ἐφάπαξ], of whom the majority live to this day, but some have fallen asleep. 7. Then he appeared to James [ὤφθη Ἰακώβῳ] and then to all of the apostles [τοῖς ἀποστόλοις πᾶσιν]. 8. Last of all [ἔσχατον δὲ πάντων], as if to an abortion, *he appeared also to me* [ὤφθη κἀμοί] (1 Cor. 15:3–8).

This is the fullest recitation of the gospel narrative that is to be found in any one place in Paul's letters, and in its final verse Paul writes himself into, and understands his person and his mission to be constitutive episodes of, the sacred story.[95] If Mark shares this narrative with Paul, it has profound implications for how he engages Paul and his teachings and how he tells the story about Jesus. In narrating more fully the gospel of Jesus Christ crucified—known to him in and through Pauline theological poetics—Mark must deal with the place of Paul within it.

Second, I expand upon Mitchell's work by suggesting that the media by which the death of Christ is made manifest should be multiplied. Mitchell focuses upon the epiphanic manifestations of Christ's death that occur in Paul's person, but there are other epiphanic media to be found in Paul's letters: the death of Christ made manifest for Paul in baptism, in the Last Supper celebration, and in the communal performance of select scriptural passages. To see Paul, read scripture, or partici-pate in one of these rites is to encounter an epiphanic performance of the cross that synecdochically evokes the apostle's whole gospel plot.

Beginning, then, with the thematic overlap with which Marcus began—the cen-trality of the cross for Mark and Paul—I will test my thesis by exploring on the one hand the ways in which Jesus' death is constructed and epiphanically performed in Pauline communities, and on the other how Mark has sought to anticipate and justify those Pauline performances within his own story. I contend that Mark has not only crafted a narrative that is dependent upon and functions as a Pauline mediated epiphany, but also that Mark has taken up those mediated epiphanies of Christ's death found within Paul's letters to which he is indebted for the creation of his own story and adapted them to his narrative. For example, Christ's baptism by John proleptically performs Jesus' death, something to which the reader is cued by the epiphanic manifestation of God's voice from heaven and the typological asso-ciation of Jesus with the binding of Isaac (Mk. 1:9–11; see also Gen. 22:2, 12, 16). Similarly, the Eucharist proleptically performs the cross, signaled overtly by Jesus' prophetic words (Mk. 14:22–25) and subtly by Mark's associating the messiah with the Passover lamb (see Mk. 14:12). Even the manifestation of Christ crucified in Paul's person finds itself incorporated into and adapted to Mark's story: Jesus pro-leptically performs the effects of his sacrificial death in and through his various healings and exorcisms.

In the chapters that follow, I will demonstrate that, for both Paul and Mark, per-formances of the cross are synecdochical and proleptic, but the purpose and ref-erent of the prolepsis predictably differ as a result of their different genres (letters vs. narrative) and the historical perspective they adopt in relation to the events. If, for Paul, a performance of the death of Christ is not *itself* an episode of the gospel that predates the cross, but it is rather a new medium subsequent to Jesus' death by which the gospel is epiphanically made manifest (e.g., the death of Christ displayed in Paul's person or the death and resurrection of Christ performed by believers in baptism), Mark's concern is to establish sufficient literary precedent within his own story to create concordance between the episodes of Jesus' mission, his death upon the cross, and the unique significances attached to the new performances of that death by the apostle. Alternatively, if for Paul a particular performance of Christ's death *is* a part of the sacred story prior to the cross (e.g., typological manifestations of Jesus' death within scripture or the episode containing the Last Supper), Mark's project is more synthetic: he both includes within his narrative those performances Paul has assumed, and adapts them so as to accommodate the unique significances Paul has attached to them. Taking the Eucharist as an example, it is on the one hand a gospel episode anterior to and anticipatory of the cross in Paul's thinking (see 1 Cor. 11:23), and as such Mark incorporates the episode into his narrative with little literary modification. On the other hand, as a new and timeless rite celebrated by early Christian communities and a retrospective performance of Jesus' death to which Paul attaches a particular ecclesiological significance (namely, communal unity), Mark anticipates that significance by embedding within his narrative logical literary precursors for it (in this case the miraculous feeding narratives).

The chapters that follow will explore each of the media by which the cross of Christ is performed in Paul's letters and the means by which that performance is adapted to and anticipated in the Gospel of Mark, beginning with baptism, then examining the Eucharist, and concluding with scripture. This sequence allows me to follow the emplotted order of Mark. It also results in the systematic backwards movement through the temporal perspectives Pauline performances adopt in relation to the cross. For Paul, baptism is a retrospective performance of the death and resurrection of Christ, but it is one that has prospective consequences for the baptizand: namely, death to sin and proleptic resurrection in imitation of the messiah [Rom. 6:4–5]). Eucharist, as a timeless rite performed by Pauline communities, is retrospective, but, as itself an episode of the gospel narrative that proleptically performs Jesus' impending death ("the night on which the Lord was handed over" [1 Cor. 11:23]), it is prospective and communally unifying. Finally, scriptural exemplars, as biblical witnesses to and proofs of the cross, are always prospective and proleptic literary performances, but they can only be recognized as such from the retrospective vantage of one who believes that the cross is the hermeneutic key to unlocking the meaning of these sacred texts.[96] Each of these observations will be unpacked in detail in the chapters that follow, but, before doing so, I will conclude this chapter with a brief example, one for which the necessary foundation has already been laid in the analyses I have set out above.

Part VII: Death in the body of Paul and salvation in the body of Jesus

Within the Gospel of Mark, despite his frequent miraculous actions, Jesus' identity is consistently misunderstood at the level of the characters within the story. For the knowing audience, however, Jesus is recognized as the savior of the world, the messiah of Israel who must die and rise for the sake of the many (Mk. 8:31; 9:31; 10:32–34, 45) in order that the people's sins might be forgiven (see Mk. 1:4; 2:1–12) and believers attain the resurrected life (see Mk. 12:18–27). If Paul claimed to be the walking iconic embodiment of the death of Christ, and his person created an epiphanic encounter with the deity through the synecdochical (re)presentation of one of the parts of his gospel, then the same poetic operation is at work within the person of Jesus in the Gospel of Mark. The miracles that Christ performs iconically and synecdochically manifest the salvation he has come to offer through his death upon the cross. This is most clearly perceived in the language Mark uses to characterize the effect of Jesus' various healings.

When the Markan Christ performs a curative action in the gospel, the evangelist regularly uses one of the following verbs to describe the event: "save" (σῴζω [Mk. 3:4: 5:23, 28, 34; 6:56; 10:52]), "raise" (ἐγείρω [Mk. 1:31; 2:9, 11–12; 5:41; 9:27]), or "arise" (ἀνίστημι [Mk. 5:42; 9:27]). In addition, there is only ever one prerequisite for effective healing—"faith" (πίστις [Mk. 2:5; 5:34, 36; 9:23–24; 10:52; cf. 6:5–6]). In the raising of Jairus' daughter and the intercalated story of the hemorrhaging woman (Mk. 5:22–43), Mark uses all of this language in close proximity. When Jesus travels to Jairus' home and the cloak of his garment is surreptitiously grasped along the way, the verb "save" (σῴζω) occurs twice: first, in the hemorrhaging woman's internal justification for her action ("If I but touch his garments, I will be saved [σωθήσομαι]" [Mk. 5:28]) and second, in Jesus' authoritative pronouncement, "Daughter, your faith [ἡ πίστις σου] has saved you [σέσωκέν σε]" (Mk. 5:34). In this latter verse, "faith" (πίστις) also occurs. Then, when Jesus' company arrives at the home of Jairus, and the death of his daughter is announced (Mk. 5:35), faith occurs again, this time as a verbal command on the lips of Jesus: "Do not be afraid; only have faith [μόνον πίστευε]!" (Mk. 5:36). Finally, when Jesus interacts with the little girl, "raise" (ἐγείρω) and "arise" (ἀνίστημι) both occur in quick succession: upon expelling all but his picked disciples and the girl's parents from the home (Mk. 5:37–40), Jesus speaks to the body of the child and says, "Little girl, I say to you, rise up [ἔγειρε]!" (Mk. 5:41), and the reader is informed that "the little girl immediately arose [ἀνέστη] and walked about" (Mk. 5:42).

Importantly, Mark self-consciously employs *all* of this language to describe resurrection and eschatological deliverance. "Save" is Mark's preferred term for the end-times salvation of all believers (see Mk. 8:35; 10:26; 13:13; 13:20), while "arise" and "raise" describe both the resurrection of Jesus (ἀνίστημι: Mk. 8:31; 9:9–10, 31; 10:34; ἐγείρω: Mk. 16:6) and the general, future resurrection of all believers that will occur at his second coming (ἀνίστημι: Mk. 12:25; ἐγείρω: Mk. 12:26). Thus, for Mark, the same theological poetics embodied in the person of Paul are now embodied in the character of Jesus: he is the walking synecdochical epiphany of the effects of his cross. *Pace* Werner, the faith-based miracles that the messiah performs within the narrative do not demonstrate Jesus' status despite the cross. Rather, they point to it and anticipate the salvation that comes through it (see Mk. 10:45), but it is only the Markan audience (and not the characters within the story) that recognize this, as it is only they who know the full story and are able to recall the whole through the iconic manifestation of its part. Through the use of Paul's theological poetics, Mark has adapted a body of miracle traditions about Jesus to create gospel concordance between the earthly life of the messiah and a particular element of the missionary activity of the apostle. The death of Christ iconically made manifest in the body of Paul now has historical antecedent in the salvation made manifest in the body of Jesus. As I will demonstrate in the chapters that follow, the creation of literary precursors that bind the earthly life of Jesus concordantly with the mission and teachings of Paul is a fundamental aspect of Mark's project. Indeed, it can be seen in the very first episode of Mark's gospel: the baptism of Jesus by John.

Notes

1 Frank Kermode, *The Sense of an Ending: Studies in the Theory of Fiction* (Oxford: Oxford University Press, 1966), 58.
2 Kermode, *Sense of an Ending*, 5–14.
3 Kermode, *Sense of an Ending*, 59.
4 See Kermode, *Sense of an Ending*, 6–7. That Mark's own text looks to an end times modelled upon Jewish prophecy and Second Temple apocalyptic need not be argued here, but it is worth stating that Mark's text also presumes the "beginnings" as narrated in Genesis, and it recapitulates them accordingly (see esp. Mk. 1:12–13) to bring them into concord with the salvific work which Christ performs and the new end-times scenario that is to occur subsequently. For a thorough argument, see Joel Marcus, "Son of Man as Son of Adam," *RB* 110 (2003), 38–61, 370–86.
5 The Greek text of the New Testament used in this monograph is taken from *Nestle-Aland: Novum Testamentum Graece* (28th edition; eds. Barbara and Kurt Aland et al.; Stuttgart: Deutsche Bibelgesellschaft, 2012). All translations of ancient languages (Greek, Latin, Hebrew) are my own, unless otherwise noted.
6 Joel Marcus, "Mark—Interpreter of Paul," in *New Testament Studies* 46 (2000) 473–87. All subsequent references to and citations of Marcus' article are taken from its updated publication in *Mark and Paul: Comparative Essays Part II, For and Against Pauline Influence on Mark* (eds. Eve-Marie Becker, Troels Engberg-Pedersen, and Mogens Müller; BZNW 199; Berlin: de Gruyter, 2014), 29–49. The contents of this article will be discussed in more detail below.
7 See Joel Marcus, *Mark: 1–8* (AB 27; New York: Doubleday, 2000); and idem, *Mark 8–16* (AB 27a; New Haven: Yale University Press, 2009). His discussion of Pauline influence can be found on pages 73–5 of the first volume.
8 By "episodic," I mean a narrative with a series of discrete and flexible episodes. For discussion of the essential contents of Paul's gospel narrative, see Part V of this chapter. The temporal span it covers is witnessed in 1 Cor. 15, where the story begins with Adam (1 Cor. 15:21–22, 45), and it ends with God being "all in all" (πάντα ἐν πᾶσιν [1 Cor. 15:28]).
9 Numerous surveys of the historical scholarship have recently been written. See, for example, the late Anne Vig Skoven, "Mark as an Allegorical Rewriting of Paul: Gustav Volkmar's Understanding of the Gospel of Mark," in Becker et al., *Mark and Paul*, 13–27; Heike Omerzu, "Paul and Mark—Mark and Paul: A Critical Outline of the History of Research," in Becker et al., *Mark and Paul*, 51–61; W. R. Telford, "Introduction: The Gospel of Mark," in *The Interpretation of Mark* (ed. William Telford; IRT 7; Philadelphia, Fortress, 1985), 20–27 (and idem, *The Theology of the Gospel of Mark* [NTT; Cambridge: Cambridge University Press, 1999], 164–9); Bartosz Adamczewski, *The Gospel of Mark: A Hypertextual Commentary* (Frankfurt am Main: Peter Lang, 2014), 17–22; Johannes Wischmeyer, "Universalismus als Tendenz und Entwicklungsmoment: Die Frage nach Markus und Paulus in der historisch-kritischen Geschichtsschreibung des Urchristentums von 1850–1910," in *Paul and Mark: Comparative Essays Part I, Two Authors at the Beginnings of Early Christianity* (eds. Oda Wischmeyer, David C. Sim, and Ian J. Elmer; BZNW 198; Berlin: de Gruyter, 2014), 19–42.
10 There is a huge selection of locatively disparate texts that betray familiarity with Paul's letters. Colossians, for example, is thought to have been written in Ephesus or the Lycus Valley as early as 70 or 80 C.E. (e.g., Paul Foster, *Colossians* [BNTC; London: T&T Clark, 2016], 61–80), with Ephesians written somewhere in western Asia Minor shortly thereafter (e.g., Andrew T. Lincoln, *Ephesians* [WBC 42; Nashville: Thomas Nelson Publishers, 1990], lxxiii–lxxxvii). Hebrews is thought to have been sent from (or to) Rome during the latter half of the first century C.E. (for good discussions of the options, see David A. deSilva, *Perseverance in Gratitude: A Socio-Rhetorical Commentary on the Epistle "to the Hebrews"* [Grand Rapids: Eerdmans, 2000], 20–23;

William L. Lane, *Hebrews 1–8* [WBC 47a; Dallas: Word Books, 1991], lviii–lxvi; Gareth Lee Cockerill, *The Epistle to the Hebrews* [NICNT; Grand Rapids: Eerdmans, 2012], 34–41). The Pastoral Epistles were composed at the beginning of the second century either in Ephesus or Rome (see Arland J. Hultgren, "The Pastoral Epistles," in *The Cambridge Companion to St. Paul* [ed. James D. G. Dunn; Cambridge: Cambridge University Press, 2003], 142–4; Raymond E. Collins, *I & II Timothy and Titus* [NTL; Louisville: Westminster John Knox, 2002] 3–11). Acts was written in Ephesus around 115 C.E. (Richard I. Pervo, *Dating Acts: Between the Evangelists and the Apologists* [Santa Rosa: Polebridge, 2006], *passim* and *Acts* [Hermeneia; Minneapolis: Fortress, 2009], 5–7). Finally, James—whether one considers his letter anti-Pauline or not—may have been written from Antioch anytime between the last quarter of the first century to the first quarter of the second (see C. Freeman Sleeper, *James* [ANTC; Nashville: Abingdon, 1998], 31–41; Martin Dibelius, *James* [trans. Michael A. Williams; Hermeneia; Philadelphia: Fortress, 1964], 45–7. On James' relationship to Pauline traditions, see Joachim Jeremias, "Paul and James," in *ExpTim* 66 [1955], 368–71; C. Ryan Jenkins, "Faith and Work in Paul and James," in *BSac* 159 [2002], 62–78; Wiard Popkes, "Two interpretations of 'Justification' in the New Testament Reflections on Galatians 2:15–21 and James 2:21–25," *ST* 59 [2005], 129–46; and Margaret M. Mitchell, "The Letter of James as a Document of Paulinism?" in *Reading James with New Eyes: Methodological Reassessments of the Letter of James* [eds. Robert L. Webb and John S. Kloppenborg; London: T&T Clark, 2007], 75–98).

11 Marcus (*Mark 1–8*, 37–9) suggests that Jesus' prophecy of the destruction of the Temple (Mk. 13:1–2), together with his reference to an "abomination of desolation" (βδέλυγμα τῆς ἐρημώσεως) and the Judeans' flight to the mountains (Mk. 13:14), points to a date of composition for the Gospel of Mark sometime during the Jewish War of 66–73 C.E., very near to the fall of the Temple in 70 C.E.

12 For a good survey of the history of scholarship on this question, see John R. Donahue, "The Quest for the Community of Mark's Gospel," in *The Four Gospels: Festschrift for Frans Neirynck* (vol. 2; eds. F. van Segbroek et. al.; BETL 100; Leuven: Leuven University Press, 1991), 817–37. The major commentaries in the Hermeneia and Yale series both place Mark near Antioch (see Adela Yarbro Collins, *Mark* [Hermeneia; Minneapolis: Fortress, 2007]), 96–102 and Marcus, *Mark 1–8*, 30–37.

13 See Brian J. Incigneri, *The Gospel According to the Romans: The Setting and Rhetoric of Mark's Gospel* (BIS 65; Leiden: Brill, 2003), 59–207, where the author covers challenges to a Roman setting (chapter 2), makes a sustained case for the destruction of the Second Temple as having already occurred by the time Mark writes (chapter 3), and describes the "climate" of Rome shortly thereafter (Chapter 4—in my judgment, Incigneri's most convincing analysis).

14 Michael P. Theophilos, "The Roman Connection: Paul and Mark," in Oda Wischmeyer et al., *Paul and Mark*, 51–2. The citation comes from page 50.

15 Martin Hengel, *Studies in the Gospel of Mark* (Eugene: Wipf & Stock, 1985), 28–30.

16 Most important is the attestation of Clement of Alexandria (Eusebius, *H.E.* 6.14.5–6), who, writing in the last decades of the second century, says,

> When Peter had preached the word publicly at Rome [ἐν Ῥώμῃ κηρύξαντος τὸν λόγον] and by the Spirit had proclaimed the gospel, those present, who were many, exhorted Mark [παρακαλέσαι τὸν Μάρκον], as someone who had followed him from long ago [πόρρωθεν] and remembered the things he had spoken [μεμνημένον τῶν λεχθέντων], to write down the things [Peter] had said [ἀναγράψαι τὰ εἰρημένα]. And [Mark], having done so, handed the gospel over to those who asked it of him.

The Greek text is taken from Eusebius, *Ecclesiastical History, Books 6–10* (trans. J. E. L. Oulton; LCL; Cambridge: Harvard University Press, 1932). See also Irenaeus, *Adv. Haer.* 3.1.1 and the testimony of Papias (Eusebius, *H.E.* 3.39.15). Though neither explicitly locates Mark's composition at Rome, they both reflect a tradition that Mark is Peter's interpreter, and it is likely that they imagine a Roman provenance for Mark's scribal activity. Finally, the Anti-Marcionite prologue to Mark, composed as early as 160–180 C.E., introduces the gospel with the following words: "[Mark] was the interpreter of Peter [*Iste interpres fuit Petri*]. After the death of Peter himself, [Mark] wrote down this same gospel in the regions of Italy [*in partibus Italiae*]" (The Latin text is taken from Dom Donatien De Bruyne, "Les plus anciens prologues latins des Évangiles," *RBén*, XL [1928], 193–214).

17   For a survey of the overlaps between the Gospel of Mark and Paul's letter to the Romans, see Theophilos ("The Roman Connection," 53–67, esp. 66–7). He notes, amongst other correspondences, the importance and meaning of the term "gospel" (εὐαγγέλιον), the emphasis on the Gentile mission, the priority of Israel, the use of the Hebrew Bible to rationalize and condemn Jewish obduracy to Christ, the abrogation of food laws, and the economic responsibility of the state.

18   On Clement's date and provenance, see Andreas Lindemann, "The First Epistle of Clement," in *The Apostolic Fathers: An Introduction* (ed. Wilhelm Pratscher; Waco: Baylor University Press, 2010), 64–5, and Michael W. Holmes, *The Apostolic Fathers: Greek Texts and English Translations* (3rd ed.; Grand Rapids: Baker Academic, 2007), 33–38. See also L. L. Welborn, "The Preface to 1 Clement: The Rhetorical Situation and the Traditional Date," in *Encounters with Hellenism: Studies on the First Letter of Clement* (eds. Cilliers Breytenbach and Laurence L. Welborn; AGAJU 53; Leiden: Brill, 2004), 197–216, who problematizes the traditional dating of 1 Clement to the persecution of Domitian.

Clement's access to 1 Corinthians is demonstrated at 1 Clem 47.1–5, where, in his effort to shame the Corinthian community, not only does Clement mention Paul by name ("Take up the epistle of the blessed Paul the apostle [τὴν ἐπιστολὴν τοῦ μακαρίου Παύλου τοῦ ἀποστόλου]!)," but he also summarizes a portion of the letter's contents (see 1 Cor. 1:12–13; 3:4–9). A citation of Heb. 1:3–5, 7, 13 likely occurs at 1 Clem. 36:2–6 (for a thorough discussion of the evidence, see Andreas Lindemann, *Die Clemensbriefe* [Tübingen: J.C.B. Mohr {Paul Siebeck}, 1992], 17–20). The Greek text of 1 Clement is taken from Clement, *Épître aux Corinthiens* (ed. A. Jaubert; SC 167; Paris: Les Éditions du Cerf, 1971).

19   On this point, I am influenced by the hypothetical reconstruction of Harry S. Gamble (*Books and Readers in the Early Church: A History of Early Christian Texts* [New Haven: Yale University Press, 1995], 99–100), who argues that the production of pseudonymous letters in Paul's name shortly after the apostle's death presupposes a situation in which (authentic) letters by him were collected, circulated, and valued as sources of instruction (see Col. 4:15–16). Only a reality of this sort would allow an author writing in Paul's name to presume that his or her newly "discovered" letter of Paul would find a broadly receptive readership and not be judged an anomaly and subject to repudiation. Should one adopt Gamble's reconstruction, Paul's martyrdom in Rome—which would have left Christ believers there bereft of one of their apostolic founders—when coupled with the testimony of Clement for 1 Corinthian's reception in the capital city at an early date, transforms Rome into a prime candidate for the early solicitation and accumulation of copies of Paul's letters.

20   Arland J. Hultgren, *Paul's Letter to the Romans* (Grand Rapids: Eerdmans, 2011), 14–15; Thomas H. Tobin, *Paul's Rhetoric in its Contexts: The Argument of Romans* (Peabody: Hendrickson, 2004), 53–78 esp. 70–8; Calvin J. Roetzel, *Paul: The Man and the Myth* (Minneapolis: Fortress, 1999), 121–5.

21   See Incigneri, *Gospel to the Romans*, 116–55 for a comprehensive argument that Mark knows that the Second Temple has fallen. In my own exegesis, I see additional evidence for the Temple's destruction in Mark's tiered prophecy/fulfillment schema that is integral to the gospel's rhetorical strategy. To explain: in reading the gospel, one notices that there are prophecies made by Jesus that are fulfilled *within* the narrative

(as, for example, his prediction that the disciples will find an upper room ready for Passover supper [Mk. 14:12–16] or Jesus' predictions of his impending passion and resurrection: Mk. 8:31; 9:31; 10:32–4); there are prophecies that are fulfilled externally to the narrative but *prior* to the composition of Mark's gospel (most famously, Jesus' resurrection appearances [Mk. 14:28; 16:8]); and there are prophecies that *will be* fulfilled during the time of the Markan community (such as the end times [Mk. 13]). This temporally variegated pattern is one of the means by which Mark demonstrates that Jesus is the Messiah: his prophecies have been and will continue to be fulfilled. On my reading, then, Jesus' prediction of the Second Temple's destruction should be understood as functioning like the prophecy of his resurrection appearances: it is an event external to the narrative but one which *has occurred* for Mark's community, and it serves as further proof that that which Jesus has said is yet to occur (his parousia) *will* occur for those who believe.

22 Prophecies that predict the destruction or replacement of the Jewish Temple as a necessary component of or prerequisite for the end times are well attested in Hebrew Bible and Second Temple Jewish literature. See, for example, Dan 9:24–7; 11:31; Jer. 7:3–15; 9:1–16; Ezek. 40–43; Micah 3:11–4:8; 1 En. 89.51–67; 90.20–29; Sibyl Or. 3.273–94; 4.115–129; Tob. 14:3–7; Josephus, *B.J.*, 6.300–309.

23 This is, in essence, the thesis of Margaret M. Mitchell, "Epiphanic Evolutions in Earliest Christianity," in *Paul and the Emergence of Christian Textuality* (WUNT 393; Tübingen; Mohr Siebek, 2017) 237–55; repr. from *ICS* 29 (2004), 183–204. See also Willi Marxsen, *Mark the Evangelist: Studies on the Redaction History of the Gospel* (trans. James Boyce et al.; Nashville: Abingdon, 1969), 147 and 216.

24 On this method, see the still-useful presentation by Edgar Krentz (*The Historical-Critical Method* [Philadelphia: Fortress Press, 1975]). For an important recent discussion of and corrective to the method, see John Barton, *The Nature of Biblical Criticism* (Louisville: Westminster John Knox, 2007), esp. 31–116. On the various methods utilized in the interpretation of Mark throughout history generally, see Janice Capel Anderson and Stephen D. Moore, "Introduction: The Lives of Mark," in *Mark and Method: New Approaches in Biblical Studies* (2nd edn.; eds. Janice Capel Anderson and Stephen D Moore; Minneapolis: Fortress, 2008), 1–27.

25 Here, I am thinking of biblical narrative criticism as defined and demonstrated in such works as David Rhoads, Joanna Dewey, and Donald Michie, *Mark as Story: An Introduction to the Narrative of a Gospel* (3rd edn.; Minneapolis: Fortress, 2012); Elizabeth Struthers Malbon, "Narrative Criticism: How Does the Story Mean?" in eadem, *In the Company of Jesus: Characters in Mark's Gospel* (Louisville: Westminster John Knox, 2000), 1–40 (repr. from Anderson and Moore, *Mark and Method*, 23–49); and Robert C. Tannehill, "The Disciples in Mark: The Function of a Narrative Role," *JR* 57 (1977), 386–405.

26 The "intentional fallacy" is a concept made famous by W. K. Wimsatt, Jr. and Monroe C. Beardsley, *The Verbal Icon: Studies in the Meaning of Poetry* (New York: The Noonday Press, 1954), 3–18, and it is used in relation to poetry and not narrative. For a good introduction to reconstructing Mark's audience, see Robert M. Fowler, "Reader-Response Criticism: Figuring Mark's Reader," in Anderson and Moore, *Mark and Method*, 59–93.

27 See Seymour Chatman, *Story and Discourse: Narrative Structure in Fiction and Film* (Ithaca: Cornell University Press, 1978), 146–151 for this famous schematization and the reasoning behind it (the quoted words come from pg. 151). See also Malbon, "How Does the Story Mean?" 7.

28 Mark Allan Powell, "Narrative Criticism: The Emergence of a Prominent Reading Strategy," in *Mark as Story: Retrospect and Prospect* (eds. Kelley R. Iverson and Christopher W. Skinner; RBS 65; Atlanta: Society of Biblical Literature, 2011), 28.

29 For an introduction to unreliable narration in literary studies today, see Vera Nünning, "Conceptualizing (Un)reliable Narration and (Un)trustworthiness," in *Unreliable Narration and Untrustworthiness: Intermedial and Interdisciplinary Perspectives* (ed.

Vera Nünning; Narratologia 44; Berlin: de Gruyter, 2015), 1–30; eadem, "Reconceptualizing Fictional (Un)reliability and (Un)trustworthiness from a Multidisciplinary Perspective: Categories, Typology, and Functions," in Nünning, *Unreliable Narration*, 83–108.

30 Theatre, ritual, athletics, litigation, lecture, debate, etc. On Graeco-Roman performance culture generally, see Richard P. Martin, "Ancient Theatre and Performance Culture," in *The Cambridge Companion to Greek and Roman Theatre* (eds. Marianne McDonald and J. Michael Walton; Cambridge: Cambridge University Press, 2007), 36–54.

31 On performance criticism, see David Rhoads, "Performance Criticism: An Emerging Methodology in Second Testament Studies—Part I," *BTB* 36 (2006), 118–33, and idem, "Performance Criticism: An Emerging Methodology in Second Testament Studies—Part II," *BTB* 36 (2006), 164–84. On Mark in performance, see Antoinette Clark Wire, *The Case for Mark Composed in Performance* (BPC 2; Eugene: Cascade Books, 2011); Holly E. Hearon, "From Narrative to Performance: Methodological Considerations and Interpretive Moves," in Iverson and Skinner, *Mark as Story*, 211–32. For Pauline letters in performance, see Bernhard Oestreich, *Performance Criticism of the Pauline Letters* (trans. Lindsay Elias and Brent Blum; BPC 14. Eugene: Cascade Books, 2016); and for the performance of scripture in early Christian worship more generally, see Gamble, *Books and Readers*, 2011–31.

32 Rhoads, "Performance Criticism: Part I," 130.

33 Compare this with the definition of Rhoads, "Performance Criticism: Part 1," 119: "I am defining performance in the broadest sense as any oral telling/retelling of a brief or lengthy tradition—from saying to gospel—in a formal or informal context of a gathered community by trained or untrained performers." I add "embodied" to my own definition because, as will become clear, words need not be spoken for particular episodes of the gospel narrative to be "performed." Regardless, this expansion does not strike me as particularly divergent from Rhoads' way of thinking about performance, as he will later suggest that the performer "embodies" the text or tradition he or she seeks to manifest and becomes "*the medium* that bears the potential meanings and impacts of the story upon the audience in a particular context" ("Performance Criticism: Part I," 128 [emphasis original]).

34 For Mark as biography, see Richard A. Burridge, *What are the Gospels: A Comparison with Graeco-Roman Biography* (2nd edn.; Grand Rapids: Eerdmans, 2004); for Mark as history, see Eve-Marie Becker, *The Birth of Christian History: Memory and Time from Mark to Luke-Acts* (New Haven: Yale University Press, 2017), who understands the gospels to add a new "subgenre" to the field of history-writing (71–2). Collins' understanding of Mark as an "eschatological historical monograph" (*Mark,* 42–3) can be taken as exemplary of a *sui generis* approach.

35 Matthew D. C. Larsen, *The Gospels before the Book* (Oxford: Oxford University Press, 2018), *passim*, but see esp. 133–4.

36 On its back cover, one eminent scholar lauds the work as "the best book on the Gospel of Mark and the synoptic Gospels in general, since they were written" (!).

37 This is one of the stated contributions of the book, though the degree to which Larsen ultimately advocates this approach is difficult to discern. On one hand, he states that he is not making a claim about the nature of the Gospel of Mark *per se*: "My claim is more modest: the Gospel of Mark was regularly described and received by its earliest readers and users as less finished, more rough, open, revisable, unpublished, and not very 'bookish'" (*Gospels before the Book,* 122). As such, Larsen invites his readers to approach Mark as an unfinished collection of notes in order to better understand the nature of Mark's reception history (see *Gospels before the Book,* 149). Yet, Larsen also has ideas about what Mark *is*. In his view, it is not simply hermeneutically fruitful to think about the Gospel of Mark *as* a collection of notes in order to gain insight into how some early Christian thinkers might have

engaged it; the Gospel of Mark *is* notes: "I have argued that the Gospel according to Mark was unfinished, fluid, and prone to alteration" (*Gospels before the Book,* 151); "the producer(s) of the textual tradition we now call the Gospel according to Mark seems (seem) to have collected sets of notes to be mediated upon, to be reread, to be rewritten, to be used, to be taught and preached" (*Gospels before the Book,* 147). Larsen appears to invite his readers to think of Mark as notes because he takes it to be notes. What may have been true of some circles of Markan readers in the first and second centuries has become normative of all Markan readers of the period and down to the present day.

38 Larsen, *Gospels before the Book,* 107–8, 114–120 [focusing on Mark's endings], 128–35, 138–44. Indeed, Larsen states that a close reading of Mark is not the project of his monograph: "An entire book would be needed to do a closer reading of the whole Gospel according to Mark from the perspective of an unfinished note collection. But for the present it is sufficient to note that once one is dislodged from presupposing narrative logic as the only possible form of organization, a different kind of logic emerges within the Gospel according to Mark" (*Gospels before the Book,* 135). Interestingly, this quote seems to contradict Larsen's own language on the facing page, where he explicitly states that Mark has "some narrative logic to it" (*Gospels before the Book,* 134).

39 Larsen, *Gospels before the Book,* 140.

40 Larsen, *Gospels before the Book* 141–2.

41 The Greek is here ambiguous. Jesus could either be the subject or the object of the purpose clause. If he is the latter, it is the blind man who is brought to touch *him*.

42 For a good discussion of this phenomenon, see Candida Moss, "The Man with the Flow of Power: Porous Bodies in Mark 5:25–34," *JBL* 129 (2010) 507–19, esp. 516–18.

43 In Chapter 5, for example, when engaging patristic understandings of Mark, Larsen argues that, because Luke views Mark as in need of significant literary modification, the second gospel should not be considered an internally coherent narrative (Larsen, *Gospels before the Book,* 86). Though it is historically plausible that Luke found Mark's gospel literarily deficient, Larsen glosses the important fact that Luke also refers to Mark *as* a narrative (διήγησις), precisely that which Larsen claims the second gospel is not (see, *Gospels before the Book,* 133–4). Lk 1:1 reads, in part, "Inasmuch as many have tried to arrange in order the narrative [διήγησιν] of the things that have been fulfilled among us …". It is particularly striking that, in his translation of Luke's preface on pg. 84, not only does Larsen render διήγησις as "story" instead of "narrative," but he does not provide a transliteration of the Greek word (I am indebted to a workshop conversation with Prof. Margaret M. Mitchell for this observation).

Similarly, in his chapter on the earliest "users" of Mark (chapter 6), it is Larsen's contention that Mark ought to be classified as a collection of unfinished notes because Matthew "clarifies" the second evangelist at various points (a procedure that, according to Larsen, should not be necessary of polished narrative). Larsen points out, for example, that Mark's statement, "the disciples did not understand about the loaves [ἐπὶ τοῖς ἄρτοις] because their hearts were hardened" (Mk. 6:52), is unexpected in the context of Jesus' walking on water (Mk. 6:46–52). According to him, "nothing in the story is about bread, so the comment hangs there without explanation" (*Gospels before the Book,* 113). This results in Matthew's clarifying the narrative by removing the bread entirely (see Matt 14:22–33). To be sure, there is nothing about bread in Mk. 6:46–52 (other than Jesus' statement, of course), but the story that *immediately* precedes it is the feeding of the five thousand (Mk. 6:34–45), where bread plays an immensely important role (see Mk. 6:38, 41–2). Matthew's failure to understand the significance of the bread in Mk. 6:46–52 should not be taken as evidence that, for Mark, there was none.

44 Marxsen, *Mark*, 131: "Through the event of this proclamation the Risen Lord actualizes himself … In and by his gospel, the Risen Lord re-presents his own life on this earth. And the goal is that he himself becomes contemporaneous with his hearers in the proclamation."

45 Jeff Jay (*The Tragic in Mark: A Literary-historical Interpretation* [HUTh 66; Tübingen: Mohr Siebeck, 2014]) has convincingly argued that Mark is written in a tragic "mode." It is not by generic definition a "tragedy," but it clearly plays upon the themes and motifs of tragedy in the unfolding of its plot. In terms of Aristotle's famous definition (*Poetics*, 1449b 27–8. The Greek text is taken from Aristotle, *Poetics* [trans. Stephen Halliwell; LCL; Cambridge: Cambridge University Press, 1995]), modern scholarship tends to understand Aristotle to mean by these words that, because universal patterns of human action are represented in the theatre, tragic catharsis helps to train a person to feel emotion in the right or appropriate way. See, for example, Richard Janko, "From Catharsis to the Aristotelian Mean," in *Essays on Aristotle's Poetics* (ed. Amélie Oksenberg Rorty; Princeton: Princeton University Press, 1992), 346–7. See also Martha C. Nussbaum, "Tragedy and Self-sufficiency: Plato and Aristotle on Fear and Pity," in Rorty, *Essays*, 280–3; Stephen Halliwell, "Pleasure, Understanding, and Emotion in Aristotle's *Poetics*," in Rorty, *Essays*, 241–60; David Wiles, "Aristotle's *Poetics* and Ancient Dramatic Theory," in McDonald and Walton, *Greek and Roman Theatre*, 98–100. Cf. Jonathan Lear, "Katharsis," in Rorty, *Essays*, 315–40. While not entirely separate, I take Mark's intent to be more metaphysical. The pedagogical aspects of his gospel are directed towards recognizing Jesus as the messiah of the world and preparing his audience for the end times that will soon occur at his second coming.

46 For a survey of his life and intellectual background, see Bernd Wildemann, *Das Evangelium als Lehrpoesie: Leben und Werk Gustav Volkmars* (Kontexte 1. Frankfurt am Main: Peter Lang, 1983); see also Vig Skoven, "Mark as Allegorical Rewriting," 13–16; Horton Harris, *The Tübingen School: A Historical and Theological Investigation of the School of F. C. Baur* (Grand Rapids: Baker, 1990), 127–33.

47 The full bibliographical information for the two works is as follows: Gustav Volkmar, *Religion Jesu und ihre erste Entwickelung nach dem gegenwärtige Stande der Wissenschaft* (Leipzig: F. A. Brockhaus, 1857); idem, *Die Evangelien, oder Marcus und die Synopsis der kanonischen und ausserkannonischen Evangelien nach dem ältesten Text, mit historisch-exegetischem Commentar* (Leipzig: Fues's Verlag [R. Reisland], 1870).

48 Volkmar, *Evangelien*, VIII–XI, 646; Wildemann, *Lehrpoesie*, 8, 314–19. For a good introduction to Baur, see Harris, *Tübingen*, 10–54.

49 Volkmar, *Evangelien*, VII–XI.

50 Wildemann notes Volkmar's indebtedness to 19th-century Protestant idealism and neatly encapsulates his project as follows: "Das wesen des Christentums, wie es in Paulinismus am besten auf den Begriff gebracht und in der Reformation erneuert worden ist, will in der Gegenwart durch die historisch-kritische Forschung erkannt und verteidigt werden" (*Lehrpoesie*, 10). For a more detailed overview of Volkmar's "sense of mission" (his "Sendungsbewsstsein"), see Wildemann, *Lehrpoesie*, 336–43.

51 Volkmar, *Die Evangelien*, 643.

52 Volkmar, *Die Evangelien*, 645.

53 Volkmar, *Religion Jesu*, 263. For Volkmar's judgments on Mark's sources, see *Der Evangelien*, VII and 646.

54 See Wildemann, *Lehrpoesie*, 346.

55 Vig Skoven, "Mark as Allegorical Rewriting of Paul," 21. See also Wildeman, *Lehrpoesie*, 319.

56 Volkmar, *Evangelien*, 464–75, esp. 464–7. See als Volkmar, *Evangelien*, 645, where the pericope is given pride of place in his concluding list of proofs for the Paulinism of Mark's Gospel.

57 Martin Werner, *Der Einfluss paulinischer Theologie im Markusevangelium: eine Studie zur neutestamentlichen Theologie* (Giessen: Verlag von Alfred Töpelmann, 1923).

58 Werner, *Einfluss*, 7–8.

59 These themes include the Jewish law, the "gospel" ("Evangelium"), faith, sin, flesh and Spirit, baptism and Eucharist, Eschatology, and Jews and Gentiles (Werner, *Einfluss*, 31–2).

60 See Werner, *Einfluss*, IV–VI; see also Albert Schweitzer, *Von Reimarus zu Wrede: Eine Geschichte der Leben-Jesu-Forschung* (Tübingen: J.C.B. Mohr [Paul Siebeck], 1906). For an English translation, see idem, *The Quest of the Historical Jesus* [ed. John Bowden; Minneapolis: Fortress, 2001].

61 Martin Werner, *The Formation of Christian Dogma: A Historical Study of its Problem* (trans. S. G. F. Brandon; New York: Harper & Brothers, 1957), 9.

62 Werner, *Formation*, 12–13.

63 Werner, *Formation*, 18–19.

64 Werner, *Der Einfluss*, 209; see also Marcus, "Interpreter of Paul," 32.

65 In the intervening period between Werner and Marcus, there have been occasional authors who have suggested Mark's close relationship to Paul, but none of their arguments have carried the day. See, for example, Benjamin W. Bacon, *The Gospel of Mark: Its Composition and Date* (New Haven: Yale University Press, 1925); J. C. Fenton, "Paul and Mark," in *Studies in the Gospels: Essays in Honor of R. H. Lightfoot* (ed. D. E. Nineham; Oxford: Basil Blackwell, 1955), 89–112; Marxsen, *Mark*, 117–50; Joseph B. Tyson, "The Blindness of the Disciples in Mark," *JBL* 80 (1961), 261–8; Michael D. Goulder, "Those Outside (Mk. 4:10–12)," *NovT* 33 (1991), 289–302; Wolfgang Schenk, "Sekundäre Jesuanisierungen von primären Paulus-Aussagen bei Markus," in Van Segbroek et al., *The Four Gospels*, 2.877–904; and C. Clifton Black, "Christ Crucified in Paul and Mark: Reflections on an Intracanonical Conversation," in *Theology and Ethics in Paul and His Interpreters: Essays in Honor of Victor Paul Furnish* (eds. Eugene H. Lovering, Jr. and Jerry L. Sumney; Nashville; Abingdon, 1996), 184–206.

66 Werner's conclusions are taken for granted by Markan commentators who do not engage Mark's Paulinism at all (see, for example, the introduction to Collins' commentary [*Mark*, 1–125], where Paul plays no significant role in her lengthy discussion, but Mark's access to early Jesus traditions is assumed), or, where the debate is entered and Pauline influence found wanting, it is presumed that Werner's judgments about a common tradition are, in the main, correct (see, for example, Michael Kok, "Does Mark Narrate the Pauline *Kerygma* of 'Christ Crucified?' Challenging an Emerging Consensus on Mark as a Pauline Gospel," *JSNT* 37 [2014], 139–57. See also the various scholars who doubt the conclusions of Marcus in the de Gruyter volumes: Omerzu, "Paul and Mark—Mark and Paul," 51–61; Ole Davidsen, "Adam-Christ Typology in Paul and Mark: Reflections on a *tertium Comparationis*," in Becker et al., *Mark and Paul*, 243–72; Jan Dochhorn, "Man and the Son of Man in Mark 2:27–28: An Exegesis of Mark 2:23–28 Focusing on the Christological Discourse in Mark 2:27–28 with an Epilogue Concerning Pauline Parallels," in Becker et al., *Mark and Paul*, 147–68; Kasper Bro Larsen, "Mark 7:1–23: A Pauline Halakah?" in Becker et al., *Mark and Paul*, 167–87 [though he disagrees with Werner's own reading of the passage under discussion]; Florian Wilk, "'Die Schriften' bei Markus und Paulus," in Wischmeyer et al., *Paul and Mark*, 189–211; Oda Wischmeyer, "Konzepte von Zeit bei Paulus und im Markusevangelium," in Wischmeyer et al., *Paul and Mark*, 361–89; Andreas Lindemann, "Das Evangelium bei Paulus und im Markusevangelium," Wischmeyer et al., *Paul and Mark*, 313–56).

67 This has been rightly noted by both Marcus, "Interpreter of Paul," 29–49 and Vig Skoven, "Mark as Allegorical Rewriting," 25.

68 Werner, *Einfluss*, 61–2.

69 The famous formulation of Martin Kähler, that the gospels are "passion narratives with extended introductions" (*The So-Called Historical Jesus and the Historic, Biblical Christ* [trans. Carl E. Braaten; Philadelphia, Fortress, 1964], 80 n. 11) is particularly

true of the Gospel of Mark, where the cross is again and again emphasized. For a fuller discussion of Werner's one-sided focus on Markan Christology, see Marcus, "Interpreter of Paul," 34–43.

70   Telford, *Theology of the Gospel of Mark,* 164–5.

71   See Gérard Genette, *Palimpsestes: La Littérature Au Second Degré* (Paris: Seuil, 1982); W. G. Müller, "Interfigurality: A Study on the Interdependence of Literary Figures," in *Intertexuality* (ed. H. E. Plett: Berlin: de Gruyter, 1991), 101–21; Dennis R. MacDonald, *The Homeric Epics and the Gospel of Mark* (New Haven: Yale University Press, 2000); idem, *Does the New Testament Imitate Homer?: Four Cases from the Acts of the Apostles* (New Haven: Yale University Press, 2003). The most prolific scholarly advocate for a reading of this sort vis-à-vis Mark's relationship to Paul is Bartosz Adamczewski (*Gospel of Mark*; see also idem, *Hypertextuality and Historicity in the Gospels* [Frankfurt am Main: Peter Lang, 2013]; idem *The Gospel of Luke: A Hypertextual Commentary* [Frankfurt am Main: Peter Lang, 2016]), but he is by no means the only proponent. Similar approaches to Mark's gospel have been adopted by Paul Nadim Tarazi, *The New Testament Introduction: Paul and Mark* (New York: St. Vladimir's Seminary Press, 1999); Tom E. Dykstra, *Mark, Canonizer of Paul* (St. Paul: OCABS Press, 2012); and Thomas P. Nelligan, *The Quest for Mark's Sources: An Exploration of the Case for Mark's Use of First Corinthians* (Eugene: Pickwick Publications, 2015).

72   See, for example, the critical review of Adamczewski's *The Gospel of Luke: A Hypertextual Commentary* by Dieter T. Roth in *ThLZ* 1 (2018), 57–9. See also Margaret M. Mitchell, "Homer in the New Testament?" *JR* 83 (2003), 244–60, esp. 251–4.

73   Virtually every author in Becker et al., *Mark and Paul,* gives some credit to Marcus, and such a formative influence is explicitly reflected in the editors' introductory statement: "In his seminal essay, 'Mark—Interpreter of Paul,' Joel Marcus *brought the Mark/Paul debate to scholarly attention once again*" (Eve-Marie Becker, Troels Engberg-Pedersen, Mogens Müller, "Mark and Paul—Introductory Remarks," in Becker et al., *Mark and Paul,* 3 [emphasis added]). Though many of the essays provided in this volume present significant contributions to the Mark/Paul debate, and the arguments contained therein have informed my own conclusions in numerable important ways, no one argument has proved decisive for demonstrating Mark's dependence upon Paul. This results from the fact that particular essays that explore specific themes only ever present a partial picture, and, because no two exegetes share the same understanding of Mark's approach to the Paul, their conclusions when dealing with similar subjects do not always result in reciprocally informative expositions of the source material. Indeed, two works may argue that Mark is Pauline, but they may end up reading the same evidence so differently that it becomes impossible for both to be right, and this, in turn, calls into question the accuracy of either (I will return to an example of this phenomenon at the conclusion of my monograph). Thus, the "part" has not, as yet, been embedded successfully within the "whole"; that is, a larger explanation of Mark's project vis-à-vis Paul.

74   Marcus, "Interpreter of Paul," 30–2. For an expanded list of overlaps, see Theophilos, "The Roman Connection," 53–61. See also Telford, *Theology of the Gospel of Mark,* 169.

75   Marcus, "Interpreter of Paul," 36–8.

76   Marcus points to the pre-Pauline traditions preserved in Paul's letters (which generally do not emphasize Christ's crucifixion), Paul's opponents ("who take their cues from the glory and strength of the resurrected Christ rather than from the lowliness and weakness of the Crucified One"), and the ways in which the other gospels seek to attenuate the weakness of Christ as it is portrayed in the latter half of Mark's gospel (particularly the Garden of Gethsemane [Mk. 14:32–42; cf. Matt. 26:36–46; Lk 22:40–46; Jn 18:1, 12:27] and the cry from the cross [Mk. 15:34; cf. Lk. 23:46; Jn 19:28–30]). (See Marcus, "Interpreter of Paul," 38–41; the quotation comes from p. 39.)

77 C. H. Dodd's *The Apostolic Preaching and Its Developments: Three Lectures* (Chicago: Willett, Clark & Company, 1937), 1–49. Due to Acts' late date and dependence upon both Paul's letters (Pervo, *The Dating of Acts,* 51–147) and the gospel of Mark, I am hesitant to ascribe to Acts a kerygma distinct from, but shared in common with, Paul. Should one conclude that the episodes are shared in common, however, the ways in which Paul interfaces with that story throughout his letters are uniquely his own, and I will argue that they have had a profound effect on the way Mark has composed his story, as well.

78 Dodd, *Apostolic Preaching*, 18.

79 Dodd calls the appearance to Peter an explicit portion of "that which [Paul] had preached at Corinth" (Dodd, *Apostolic Preaching,* 7. See also *Apostolic Preaching*, 2–3, where Dodd equates "preaching" in the ancient church with gospel proclamation).

80 Richard B. Hays, *The Faith of Jesus Christ: The Narrative Substructure of Gal 3:1–4:11,* (2nd edn.; Grand Rapids: Eerdmans, 2002), 6. For his indebtedness to Dodd, see pp. 60–4.

81 Hays, *Faith of Jesus Christ,* xxiv and 6–7.

82 Margaret M. Mitchell, "Rhetorical Shorthand in Pauline Argumentation: The Functions of 'the Gospel' in the Corinthian Correspondence," in eadem, *The Emergence of Christian Textuality,* 111–32; repr. from *Gospel in Paul: Studies on Corinthians, Galatians, and Romans for Richard N. Longenecker* (eds. L. Ann Jervis and Peter Richardson; Sheffield: Sheffield Academic Press, 1994), 63–88; and eadem, "Epiphanic Evolutions," 237–55.

83 Mitchell, "Rhetorical Shorthand," 112. Indeed, according to her, the term εὐαγγέλιον is itself a "'superabbreviation' of the whole, functioning as a title which both characterizes its full contents and interprets its meaning for the hearer" (Mitchell, "Rhetorical Shorthand," 112).

84 Mitchell, "Rhetorical Shorthand," 117.

85 Mitchell, "Rhetorical Shorthand," 123; see also Paul Brooks Duff, "Apostolic Suffering and the Language of Processions in 2 Cor. 4:7–10," *BTB* 21 (1991) 158–65; idem, "Metaphor, Motif, and Meaning: The Rhetorical Strategy Behind the Image 'Led in Triumph' in 2 Corinthians 2:14," in *CBQ* 53 (1991), 79–92.

86 Mitchell, "Epiphanic Evolutions," 241–2. For a similar conclusion regarding Paul's self-perception, see Morna Hooker, "A Partner in the Gospel: Paul's Understanding of His Ministry," in Lovering and Sumney, *Theology and Ethics in Paul,* 83–100.

87 According to Mitchell, "Paul saw himself as a one-man multi-media presentation of the gospel of Christ crucified. The message (τὸ εὐαγγέλιον) and the messenger (Paul the ἀπόστολος) were indivisibly united in re-presenting to the audience an aural–visual icon of Christ crucified, which is the gospel" ("Epiphanic Evolutions," 242–3).

88 Mitchell, "Epiphanic Evolutions," 244–5.

89 Mitchell, "Epiphanic Evolutions," 246–7.

90 Mitchell, "Epiphanic Evolutions," 247–8.

91 Mitchell, "Epiphanic Evolutions," 194.

92 Mitchell, "Rhetorical Shorthand," 119–20. See also Mitchell, "1 and 2 Thessalonians," in Dunn, *Cambridge Companion to Saint Paul,* 51–63 for a discussion of a similar type of expansion in a different letter.

93 For varied discussions of this process, see Hayden White, *Metahistory: The Historical Imagination of Nineteenth-Century Europe* (Baltimore: John Hopkins University Press, 1975), 1–42; Paul Ricoeur, *Time and Narrative* (3 vols.; trans. Kathleen McLaughlin and David Pellauer; Chicago: University of Chicago Press, 1983), 1.52–87, esp. 64–70; Ansgar Nünning, "Making Events—Making Stories—Making Worlds: Ways of Worldmaking from a Narratological Point of View," in *Cultural Ways of Worldmaking: Media and Narratives* (eds. Vera Nünning et al.; CSC 1; Berlin: De Gruyter, 2010), 191–214; Vera Nünning, "The Making of Fictional Worlds: Processes, Features, and Function," in Nünning, *Cultural Ways of Worldmaking,* 215–43.

94   See Martin Meiser, "Evangelien als faktuale Erzählungen—Narration und Geschichte," in *Literatur und Geschichte* (eds. Sikander Singh and Manfred Leber; SLR 7; Saarbrücken: Universitätsverlag des Saarlandes, 2018), 9–36.

95   See David C. Sim, "The Family of Jesus and the Disciples of Jesus in Paul and Mark: Taking Sides in the Early Church's Factional Dispute," in Wischmeyer et al., *Paul and Mark*, 76–7.

96   Throughout this monograph, when Mark or Paul refer to scripture (whether by allusion or citation), I presume that they have in view a Greek translation of the Hebrew Bible rather than the Hebrew scriptures themselves. Paul's primary reliance on Greek is well known (see, for example, Dietrich-Alex Koch, *Die Schrift als Zeuge des Evangeliums: Untersuchungen zur Verwendung und zum Verständnis der Schrift bei Paulus* [BHTh 69; Tübingen: Mohr Siebeck, 1986]; Florian Wilk, "The Letters of Paul as Witnesses to and for the Septuagint Text," in *Septuagint Research: Issues and Challenges in the Study of the Greek Jewish Scriptures* [eds. Wolfgang Kraus and R. Glenn Wooden; SCS 53; Atlanta: Society of Biblical Literature, 2006], 253–71). The case for Mark is more complicated, as the evangelist works extensively with inherited narrative traditions. Some of these traditions no doubt originated in Greek, but others have their origins in Aramaic or Hebrew and were only later translated into Greek (possibly by Mark himself). As a result, Mark's use of a Greek or Hebrew source is generally determined on a case-by-case basis, with Greek being the more frequent conclusion (e.g., Howard Clark Kee, "The Function of Scriptural Quotations and Allusions in Mark 11–16," in *Festschrift für Werner Georg Kümmel zum 70. Geburtstag* [eds. E. Earle Ellis and Erich Gräber; Göttingen: Vandenhoeck & Ruprecht, 1975], 166–75; John S. Kloppenborg Verbin, "Egyptian Viticultural Practices and the Citation of Isa. 5:1–7 in Mark 12:1–9," *NovT* 44 [2002], 134–59; Daniel M. Gurtner, "LXX Syntax and the Identity of the NT Veil," *NovT* 47 [2007], 344–53; Kurt Queller, "'Stretch Out Your Hand!' Echo and Metalepsis in Mark's Sabbath Healing Controversy," *JBL* 129 [2010], 737–58; C. Clifton Black, *Mark* [ANTC; Nashville: Abingdon Press, 2011], 33. For a more thoroughgoing discussion, see Rikki E. Watts, "Mark," in *Commentary on the New Testament Use of the Old Testament* [eds. G. K. Beale and D. A. Carson; Grand Rapids: Baker Academic, 2007], 111–250). In the end, whatever Mark's source(s), the community for which the evangelist wrote was Greek-speaking, and I presume that Mark's allusions to scripture (no matter how free) were designed to point his auditors to texts written in their common tongue (for a similar judgment, see Stephen Ahearne-Kroll, "Abandonment and Suffering," in Kraus and Wooden, *Septuagint Research*, 293–4). Thus, throughout this monograph, unless otherwise noted (and despite the historical complexities involved in its compilation), the "scriptures" to which I refer are those presented in the Septuagint (hereafter LXX), and all citations of this text are taken from *Septuaginta* (eds. Alfred Rahlfs and Robert Hanhart; Stuttgart: Deutsche Bibelgesellschaft, 2006). For a good general study on the historical evolution of the LXX as Christian scripture, see Martin Hengel, *The Septuagint as Christian Scripture: Its Prehistory and the Problem of Its Canon* (OTS; Edinburgh: T&T Clark, 2002); for Mark's and Paul's use of scripture in comparison [and further bibliography] see Wilk, "Die Schriften," 201–7.

2 Baptism into death

In the previous chapter, I argued that the content of the gospel is, for both Paul and Mark, an episodic narrative that covers of the life, death, resurrection, post-resurrection appearances, and second coming of Jesus Christ "in accordance with the scriptures" (see 1 Cor. 15:3–8), and that the messiah is (re)presented for the community in the synecdochical evocation of the whole story through the iconic manifestation of one or more of its parts. I also suggested that Mark makes use of this synecdochical poetics to anticipate and justify the mission and teachings of the apostle (constitutive episodes of the gospel narrative [see 1 Cor. 15:8]). Mark's hermeneutical approach to Paul is, in other words, etiological. The goal of this chapter is to demonstrate that Mark's etiological project is operative in the very first episode of his story: Jesus' baptism by John in the River Jordan (Mk. 1:4–11).

This chapter falls into three parts. First, I will establish that baptism for Paul is the synecdochical evocation of his entire gospel narrative through the retrospective performance of Christ's death and resurrection by the believer. In undergoing the rite, believers symbolically put themselves to death and proleptically anticipate their coming salvation (see Rom. 6:3–8). Through it, their lives are grafted onto the "meta-plot" of Christ's death and resurrection, and as a result they are incorporated into the gospel narrative and become a part of the communal body of Jesus Christ (they "put on" Christ [Gal. 3:27–8] and thereby become members *of* Christ [see Rom. 12:4–8; 1 Cor. 12:12–27]).[1]

Second, I will show that, for Mark, John's "baptism of repentance for the forgiveness of sin" (Mk. 1:4) is a rite that looks forward to and proleptically performs a key episode of the gospel narrative—Jesus' death "on behalf of the many" (ἀντὶ πολλῶν [Mk. 10:45])—and that the forgiveness sought through John's baptism is anticipatory of the forgiveness and salvation Jesus offers through the cross. At the same time, I will suggest that Jesus' baptism in Mark is also synecdochical. In order to recognize the prolepsis inherent to John's baptism, readers must know and recall later episodes within the story (Mk. 10:38–39; 12:6–8; 15:37–39). Without doing so, the full significance of John's baptism cannot be perceived.

Third and finally, I will argue that Mark has deliberately composed his narrative such that literary concordance is established between the baptismal experience of Jesus, his death upon the cross, and a rite that is performative of that death within the Pauline mission. To anticipate the conclusions of this chapter: if Paul looks back to the cross in order to establish the patterning of believers' fates on that of their messiah, and, through the performance of Jesus' death, Paul claims that believers have been gifted with the Spirit, adopted as sons and daughters of God (Rom. 8:15–17; Gal. 3:27–4:6), and proleptically anticipate their coming resurrections (Rom. 6:5, 8), then Mark's story claims that Paul's rite and its attendant significances have historical precedent within the earthly life of Christ. In undergoing "a baptism of repentance for the forgiveness of sins" (Mk. 1:4), Jesus too performs his own death, albeit proleptically. For Mark, through Jesus' death, which the messiah conceptualized *as* baptism (Mk. 10:38–39; 15:38–39), that which *was* localized in Jesus at baptism prior to his death (sonship, Spirit [Mk. 1:9–11]) becomes accessible to all Pauline believers in their retrospective performances of the cross that occur in their own ritualized washings (Rom. 6:3–8; 8:15; see also Gal. 3:27–4:6). The baptism Christ undergoes is a proleptic performance of the cross, the baptisms in which believers participate are retrospective performances of it, and the patterning of the life narrative of the believer onto the life, death, and resurrection of Jesus Christ becomes all the more acute as a result.

Part I: Baptism in Paul

Baptism is, for Paul, a complex ritual performance replete with eschatological significance. It is, first and foremost, a ritualized (re)presentation of the gospel narrative: in baptism, believers are symbolically put to death, buried, and, in their emerging from the waters, proleptically raised to walk about in the newness of life (see Rom. 6:4–8). This is done in imitation of their messiah who has also died, been buried, and raised to eternal life (1 Cor. 15:3–4). Through this gospel performance, the baptizand is infused with the Spirit and transformed into a child of God and sibling to Christ (see Gal. 3:26–4:6). Thus, by becoming coheir with the messiah (see Rom. 8:15–17), the believer is incorporated into the sacred story of Christ's death, resurrection, and second coming. He or she is infused with eschatological energy (see 1 Cor. 12:3–7), transformed into a member of Christ's body (1 Cor. 12:12–13), and promised future attainment to eternal life (Rom. 6:22–23).

Paul's conception of baptism as a ritualized performance of Christ's death is expressed most clearly in his letter to the Romans. As a part of a larger discussion about believers' new life in Christ (Rom. 5:1–8:39), Paul dilates on the redemptive work of the messiah for the whole human race (Rom. 5:12–21).[2] During this discussion, Paul claims that grace triumphs over sin in and through the salvific action of Jesus (Rom. 5:17–19), but because he also makes the astounding assertion that, where there was sin, grace abounded all the more (Rom. 5:20–21), the apostle asks of himself an ostensibly logical question: "What then will we say? Should we persist in sin in order that grace may abound [χάρις πλεονάσῃ]?" (Rom. 6:1; see also Rom. 6:15).[3] Paul's answer resounds in the negative (μὴ γένοιτο! [Rom. 6:2]). For him, "those who have died do not live in sin and, consequently, do not behave in sinful ways."[4] To demonstrate this, the apostle launches into a point-by-point exposition of the baptismal rite:

> 3. Or do you not know that, as many of us as were baptized into Christ Jesus [ὅσοι ἐβαπτίσθημεν εἰς Χριστὸν Ἰησοῦν], we have been baptized into his death [εἰς τὸν θάνατον αὐτοῦ ἐβαπτίσθημεν]? 4. We have therefore been buried together with him [συνετάφημεν ... αὐτῷ] through baptism into death [διὰ τοῦ βαπτίσματος εἰς τὸν θάνατον] so that, just as Christ has been raised from the dead [ὥσπερ ἠγέρθη Χριστὸς ἐκ νεκρῶν] through the glory of his father, we too will walk about in the newness of life [ἐν καινότητι ζωῆς περιπατήσωμεν]. 5. For, if we have become united to the likeness of his death [σύμφυτοι γεγόναμεν τῷ ὁμοιώματι τοῦ θανάτου αὐτοῦ], we will also be [united to the likeness] of his resurrection [τῆς ἀναστάσεως ἐσόμεθα] (Rom. 6:3–5).

Though Paul presumes that Roman Christ-believers already practice baptism, scholars generally recognize that the apostle has here expanded the significance of the rite in some fundamental ways.[5] Through the apostle's teaching, the Romans are to recognize that to be baptized is to be baptized "into Christ's death" (εἰς τὸν θάνατον αὐτοῦ), which means on one hand that they perform retrospectively the death, burial, and resurrection of the messiah—three key episodes of Paul's gospel narrative (1 Cor. 15:3–4)—while on the other (and at the same time) they effect their own deaths and burials, and they proleptically perform their future resurrections. The idea of imitation is here essential. Because the messiah has been raised, and the gospel promises that believers are conformed to his type as adopted brothers and sisters (see Rom. 8:14–17; Gal. 3:27–4:6; 1 Cor. 15:14–22), the resurrections they proleptically anticipate at baptism are assured.[6] The ritual is thus an embodiment of Paul's larger theological poetics: a portion of the story is put on display, the rest is evoked synecdochically, and, in the course of one's "filling in" that narrative, the believer experiences an epiphanic and transformative encounter with the deity.

That baptism is, in fact, a transformative experience is confirmed by the role that the Holy Spirit plays within it. Paul claims that, through the rite, a decisive rupture from one's former life occurs (Rom. 6:6–11), and those once enslaved to sin (δοῦλοι τῆς ἁμαρτίας [Rom. 6:20]) are liberated as they await the final ending of the world.[7] This liberation is granted by the Spirit, which transforms believers into adopted "children of God" (τέκνα θεοῦ [Rom. 8:16]). Though Paul does not mention either "Spirit" (πνεῦμα) or "adoption" (υἱοθεσία) in Romans 6, in chapter 8, where baptism serves as a backdrop to Paul's extended discussion of the Spirit's eschatological power (esp. Rom. 8:12–17), the apostle makes the connection explicit: "For as many as are led by the Spirit of God [πνεύματι θεοῦ], these are sons of God [υἱοὶ θεοῦ]. For you did not receive the spirit of slavery [leading] again into fear, but you received the Spirit of adoption [πνεῦμα υἱοθεσίας] in which we cry out, 'Abba! Father! [αββα ὁ πατήρ]'" (Rom. 8:14–15).[8] The cry, "Abba! Father!" is a baptismal one; it signals the ritual's successful transformation of a believer into a son or daughter of God.

The connection between baptism, spiritual insorcism, and adoption that is assumed in Romans is fleshed out more fully in Paul's letter to the Galatians. In that contentious epistle, Paul finds himself struggling to justify a Gentile mission that has come under attack by the pillar apostles or those who claim their authority.[9] For his opponents, part of what it means to be a Christ believer is to be law observant, with particular emphasis placed on the necessity for circumcision (see Gal. 2:3; 5:2–3, 6, 11; 6:12–13, 15; see also Gal. 2:11–14; 4:9–10). These Judaizing interlocutors have managed to convince Paul's communities that, to be true heirs to the promises of Abraham, they must be circumcised and adopt a Jewish mode of life. Thus, in Galatians 3, the apostle finds himself exegeting anew the Abrahamic narrative. Paul's counterclaim is that it is the faith(fulness) demonstrated by the patriarch *prior* to circumcision that secures for him God's blessing (Gal. 3:6–9, 16–18; see also Gen. 12:1–3; 15:1–6).[10] Subsequent to the Christ event, the obligation to emulate Abraham does not go beyond imitating his initial trust in God's promise. Baptism is introduced into Paul's argument in order to demonstrate that the adoption occurring during that rite counters his rivals' claims to additional ritual or practical requirements for election:

> 27. For as many of you as have been baptized into Christ [εἰς Χριστὸν ἐβαπτίσθητε], you have put on Christ [Χριστὸν ἐνεδύσασθε]. 28. There is neither Jew or Greek, slave or free, male and female; for you all are one in Christ Jesus [ὑμεῖς εἷς ἐστε ἐν Χριστῷ Ἰησοῦ]. 29. But if you belong to Christ [εἰ δὲ ὑμεῖς Χριστοῦ], then you are the seed of Abraham [Ἀβραὰμ σπέρμα ἐστέ], heirs according to the promise [κατ᾽ ἐπαγγελίαν κληρονόμοι.] … 4. And when the fullness of time came, God sent his own son, born from a woman, born under the law, 5. in order that he might redeem those under the law [τοὺς ὑπὸ νόμον ἐξαγοράσῃ], in order that we might receive adoption [τὴν υἱοθεσίαν ἀπολάβωμεν]. 6. And since you are sons [ὅτι δέ ἐστε υἱοί], God sent the Spirit of his Son [τὸ πνεῦμα τοῦ υἱοῦ αὐτοῦ] into our hearts crying out [κρᾶζον], "Abba! Father!" [αββα ὁ πατήρ]. 7. And so, you are no longer a slave but a son [οὐκέτι εἶ δοῦλος ἀλλὰ υἱός]. And if you are a son, you are also an heir through God [κληρονόμος διὰ θεοῦ] (Gal. 3:27–9; 4:4–7).[11]

According to Paul, baptism is the process of "putting on" Christ (Gal. 3:27–8).[12] Through identification with Christ, and in imitation *of* Christ, baptizands become the "seed of Abraham" (Ἀβραὰμ σπέρμα) and "heirs according to the promise" (κατ᾽ ἐπαγγελίαν κληρονόμοι [Gal. 3:29]). It is "in Christ Jesus" (ἐν Χριστῷ Ἰησου [Gal. 3:28]) that the promises to Abraham find their fulfillment.[13] Because the neuter singular participle κρᾶζον can only refer to the neuter and accusative singular noun πνεῦμα, the Greek syntax of Galatians 4:6 requires that the Spirit be responsible for the baptismal cry, rather than the believer: "God sent the Spirit of his Son [τὸ πνεῦμα τοῦ υἱοῦ αὐτοῦ] into our hearts, crying out [κρᾶζον], 'Abba! Father! [αββα ὁ πατήρ].'" The agency of the individual baptizand is thus momentarily subsumed as he or she is insorcized with the Spirit of Christ, and, in assigning such autonomous activity to the Spirit, Paul's insistence on a singular transformative moment of entry into the community is complete.[14] The Spirit's cry to the father affirms both for the baptizand and all who are present that the believer truly has become coheir with Christ (see Rom. 8:17). In Galatians, then, the baptismal ritual is far more than the (re)presentation of individual episodes of Paul's gospel narrative. In the course of this performance, divine energy seizes control of baptizands' bodies and iconically displays for all who are present (including the participant) the eschatological promises of that narrative.

Finally, it is important to note for a comparison with Mark's gospel that, after believers' ritualized performance of Christ's death and resurrection, during which they are transformed into sons and daughters of God through the insorcism of the Spirit, that Spirit remains active throughout the remainder of believers' lives. It is, first, the means by which God and his salvific activity in the world through Jesus Christ is (and continues to be) understood. The cross puts on display a massive paradox. It shows the humiliating and mortal death of God's eternal son (see 1 Cor. 8:6; Phil. 2:6–11). As a result, it is a "scandal to Jews" (Ἰουδαίοις μὲν σκάνδαλον) and "folly to Gentiles" (ἔθνεσιν δὲ μωρίαν [1 Cor. 1:23]), groups who have tried and failed to understand God through human wisdom alone (see 1 Cor. 1:21a: "the world did not come to know God through wisdom [διὰ τῆς σοφίας]").[15] For Paul, however, it is precisely *in* folly that God's activity is perceived ("through the foolishness of the gospel proclamation [μωρίας τοῦ κηρύγματος], God thought it good to save those who believe" [1 Cor. 1:21b]). Proper comprehension of God's workings is therefore dependent upon some suprahuman force, namely the Holy Spirit: "For the Spirit searches into all things [τὸ γὰρ πνεῦμα πάντα ἐραυνᾷ], even the depths of God [τὰ βάθη τοῦ θεοῦ] ... no one knows the matters of God [τὰ τοῦ θεοῦ] except the Spirit of God [τὸ πνεῦμα τοῦ θεοῦ]." [1 Cor. 2:10–11). The ability to perceive and understand God's salvific activity in and through Jesus Christ is dependent upon the deity's direct intervention in the lives of believers through God's Spirit.[16]

Second, the baptismal Spirit is the means by which believers occupy different offices within the eschatological community. This is again apparent in 1 Corinthians, where a major point of contention is the diversity of spiritual gifts. The purpose of Paul's argument in 1 Corinthians 12, in which he employs the famous "body metaphor" of antiquity, is to establish distinct yet functionally equivalent positions for the various charisms within the church.[17] Paul claims that the confession the believers share—"Jesus is Lord" (Κύριος Ἰησοῦς [1 Cor. 12:3])— is born of the Holy Spirit, and the eschatological powers they manifest are the products of the same Spirit and work together for the common good of all (πρὸς τὸ συμφέρον [1 Cor. 12:7]).[18] Indeed, according to Paul, these various charisms represent the unity of the communal body that is established through faith and baptism "in" or "with" one Spirit (ἐν ἑνὶ πνεύματι [1 Cor. 12:13]).[19]

Thus, when one weaves together the baptismal teachings in Paul's letters to the Romans, Galatians, and Corinthians—all three of which the Markan community may have possessed[20]—one gains a panoramic sense of what baptism means and entails for the apostle. It is, first, a ritual performance of his gospel narrative. Through the (re)presentation of Christ's death and resurrection in the baptismal waters, believers simultaneously put themselves to death and synecdochically evoke the remainder of the gospel narrative through the proleptic anticipation of their future resurrections (Rom. 6:3–8). This mimetic and epiphanic experience effects the transformation of believers into sons (and daughters) of God (and members of the communal body of Christ) through the insorcism of the Spirit (Gal. 4:4–7; Rom. 8:14–17). This Spirit then remains with believers throughout their lives, gifting them with the necessary intellectual capacity to understand the paradox of the cross (1 Cor. 2:10–12) and distributing to them the spiritual abilities required to hold various spiritual offices within the church (1 Cor. 12).

Part II: Baptism for Mark

Because Mark's gospel is not an occasional epistle but an extended episodic narrative telling the story of Jesus' earthly mission, the evangelist communicates his understanding of baptism differently to Paul, who presumes the baptismal rite and unpacks its various significances according to the rhetorical needs of the moment. Though Mark teaches about the nature of Jesus and God, proper or necessary ritual praxis, discipleship, the limits of the mission, and so forth, his teachings are *shown* through the larger unfolding of his plot as often as (if not more often than) they are told. The significance of this fact should not be underestimated. Mark's narrative is logical, consistent, and complete, and that which opens the story stands in a concordant literary relationship to those episodes that follow. Understanding the full significance of Jesus' baptism in the River Jordan thus requires reading it in relation to the larger narrative of which it forms an integral part.

In what follows, I will argue that Mark tells a story that presumes that John's baptisms are proleptic enactments of the deaths of those who come to him and acknowledge their sins in the face of God's coming judgment (Mk. 1:4). For the evangelist, these are acts of self-abasement before the deity during which forgiveness is asked, but it is not (yet) granted. When Mark's Jesus is finally baptized by John, the epiphany that occurs there—Jesus' reception of the Spirit and acknowledgement as God's beloved child (Mk. 1:9–11)—is the proleptic manifestation both of Jesus' death and of the deity's assent. The mission of Jesus Christ, the Son of God who will "give his life as a ransom for many [λύτρον ἀντὶ πολλῶν]" (Mk. 10:45), has officially begun.[21] When Jesus later speaks of the baptism he *will* undergo (Mk. 10:38–39), his language is self-consciously intended to point back to his baptism in the River Jordan and forward to the cross. Just as Jesus underwent a symbolic death (physical baptism) at the beginning of the story as the inaugural act of his salvific mission, his physical death (symbolic baptism) must occur for his mission to be complete and forgiveness to be granted at the story's end (see Mk. 15:38–39).

At the opening of Mark's text, John the Baptist is introduced with the following words:

> 2. As it stands written in the book of Isaiah the Prophet, "Behold! I am sending my messenger before your face, who will prepare your way" [see Ex. 23:20; Mal. 3:1]; 3. the voice of one shouting in the wilderness, "Prepare the way

of the Lord! Make his paths straight!' [see Isa. 40.3], 4. John the Baptist was in the wilderness and proclaiming baptism of repentance for the forgiveness of sins (βάπτισμα μετανοίας εἰς ἄφεσιν ἁμαρτιῶν [Mk. 1:4]). 5. And all the land of Judea and all the people of Jerusalem [πᾶσα ἡ Ἰουδαία χώρα καὶ οἱ Ἱεροσολυμῖται πάντες] went out to him, and they were baptized by him in the Jordan river as they confessed their sins [ἐξομολογούμενοι τὰς ἁμαρτίας αὐτῶν] (Mk. 1:2–5).

The aggregated scriptural citation of Mk. 1:2–3, together with the description of John's dress (Mk. 1:6), is a clear signal to the evangelist's audience that John occupies the role of Elijah, the prophetic forerunner to the messiah (see Mk. 9:11–13; Mal. 3:22–24; 2 Kgs. 1:8). Yet, if "baptism of repentance for the forgiveness of sins" (βάπτισμα μετανοίας εἰς ἄφεσιν ἁμαρτιῶν [Mk. 1:4]) is taken to mean that John had an *actual* ability to forgive sin, contradictions quickly arise within the Markan narrative. At the level of Christology, Jesus' participation in a rite that washes sins away would seem to imply that the messiah is initially sinful and in need of repentance and forgiveness.[22] This is difficult to reconcile with the evangelist's statements elsewhere that forgiveness of sins is what Jesus has come to offer (see Mk 2:5–12; 10:45; 14:24), and with Mark's subtle but consistent way of presenting Jesus as a divine figure throughout the text, a literary feature of the Gospel of Mark that scholarship has increasingly come to recognize.[23]

More immediately, Mark's audience would see in the unfolding of Mark's plot that the acceptance of John's authority to forgive sins stands in direct conflict with the rejection of Jesus' authority to do the same. At Mark 1:5, the evangelist makes clear that the baptizer is respected by all, authority and subject alike. The whole Judean countryside (πᾶσα ἡ Ἰουδαία χώρα [Mk. 1:5]) and the entirety of the Jerusalem populace (οἱ Ἱεροσολυμῖται πάντες [Mk. 1:5])—a description that, while hyperbolic, should not be taken to exclude the Jerusalem intelligentsia[24]—has come out to the Jordan to be baptized by him. A little later in the narrative, it is learned that Herod also fears and protects John as a holy man (Mk. 6:14–16, 20). If Mark understands John's baptism to bring about actual forgiveness of sins, and he portrays him as a respected figure for doing so, there should be little problem with Jesus' ability to forgive sins less than a chapter later (Mk. 2:5–12), especially when that forgiveness is accompanied by a clear miraculous sign (the paralytic's restored ability to walk [Mk. 2:10–12]), something which does not occur, so far as the narrative relates, with John's baptisms (excluding, of course, the epiphany to Jesus himself [Mk. 1:9–11]). Yet, Christ's accruing this authority to himself is precisely what provokes the ire of certain members of the scribal class (τινες τῶν γραμματέων), who complain that such power is reserved for God alone (εἷς ὁ θεός [Mk. 2:7]).[25]

It is therefore unlikely that either Mark or his audience thought of John's "baptism of repentance for the forgiveness of sins" (βάπτισμα μετανοίας εἰς ἄφεσιν ἁμαρτιῶν [Mk. 1:4]) as entailing *actual* forgiveness. Rather, they perceived it as entirely symbolic, and this invites a different interpretation that neither undermines Mark's subtle high Christology nor disrupts the episodic concordance of his narrative. Some scholars, who have also noted the Christological and narrative contradictions associated with John's ritual, suggest that Jesus' undergoing a "baptism of repentance for the forgiveness of sins" is done "in solidarity with sinful humanity."[26] That is, in Jesus' case, no actual forgiveness is effected. Alternatively, others have proposed that, from the viewpoint of the evangelist and his community, "John's baptism was only a proleptic cleansing from sinfulness, since the true remission resulted from Jesus' death as a 'ransom for many' (10:45)."[27] In this case, the preposition εἰς in "baptism of repentance for [εἰς] the forgiveness of sins" (Mk. 1:4) does not imply purpose but, rather, something like a "goal."[28]

Both suggestions have merit, but neither is fully satisfying. One might ask, for example, on what exegetical grounds the case should be made for Mark's portraying a Jesus "in solidarity" with sinful humanity, or, alternatively, why it is necessarily the case that a proleptic "cleansing" is the only symbolic act that is in view. In the paragraphs that follow, I will attempt to supplement these good suggestions, and I will argue that, for the evangelist, it is not the case that persons undergoing John's baptism are undergoing a rite that necessarily washes away their sins. Rather, they are undergoing a rite that symbolically puts them to death in the hopes that that cleansing might eventually be effected.

In all of Mark's gospel, the noun βάπτισμα is found in a total of four verses (Mk. 1:4; 10:38, 39; 11:30) and forms of the verb βαπτίζω in a total of nine (Mk. 1:4, 5, 8, 9; 6:14, 24; 7:4; 10:38, 39). The majority of these occurrences carry little explanatory force for understanding the symbolism of John's baptism, as they are either used in titles for John (e.g., Mk. 6:14, 24), or the term's meaning is already assumed in the reference (e.g., Mk. 1:4, 8, 9; 11:30).[29] That said, a couple of Mark's usages warrant further investigation. The first is Mark 7:4, where, in an explanatory gloss to the Markan audience about Jewish purification practices, the evangelist uses the verb βαπτίζω to mean "wash": "and when they come from the agora, they do not eat if they do not wash themselves [βαπτίσωνται]." It is noteworthy that, in this same verse, Mark uses the accusative plural of the masculine noun βαπτισμός to describe the washing of various vessels, rather than the accusative plural of the neuter noun βάπτισμα, which he consistently uses for the baptismal rite. Though certainty is precluded, it is possible that, for Mark, there is a semantic difference between the two nouns.[30] If this is the case, the verb βαπτίζω has a broader range of meanings than does the noun, and one must be cautious about presuming that Mark 7:4 is a linguistic key to unlocking the meaning of John's "baptism of repentance for the forgiveness of sins" at Mark 1:4.

The second important case is Mark 10:38–39. There, both the noun βάπτισμα (twice) and verb βαπτίζω (four times) are placed on the lips of Jesus. When James and John come to the messiah to ask for positions of privilege in the eschatological kingdom, Jesus responds with his allusive question, "are you able to drink the cup which I drink [τὸ ποτήριον ὃ ἐγὼ πίνω] or to be baptized with the baptism with which I am baptized [τὸ βάπτισμα ὃ ἐγὼ βαπτίζομαι βαπτισθῆναι]?" (Mk. 10:38). When James and John respond that they are, Jesus repeats his words, this time as a prophecy: "The cup which I am drinking you will drink [τὸ ποτήριον ὃ ἐγὼ πίνω πίεσθε], and the baptism with which I am baptized you will be baptized [τὸ βάπτισμα ὃ ἐγὼ βαπτίζομαι βαπτισθήσεσθε]" (Mk. 10:39). Context necessitates that both the metaphors of cup and baptism refer to Christ's impending death. Consensus amongst biblical critics is that the "cup" to which Jesus alludes is the biblical "cup of wrath" (τὸ ποτήριον τοῦ θυμοῦ [Isa. 51:17]).[31] That is, Jesus has taken upon himself the vengeance of the deity in order to expiate the sins of the masses.[32] Alternatively, "baptism" (τὸ βάπτισμα) most probably alludes to the shared biblical and Graeco-Roman metaphor of "drowning" in overwhelming troubles.[33] As early as the 7th–6th century B.C.E., the verb βαπτίζω was already a common term used in descriptions of death at sea,[34] and, by the Second Temple period, the translator of Isaiah uses it to capture the sense of an overflowing torrent of lawlessness: "My heart is being led astray, and lawlessness drowns me [με βαπτίζει]. My soul has come into terror" (Isa. 21:4). Josephus similarly uses the term of Zion's acceptance of robbers into its indomitable walls, an act that would eventually "drown the city" (ἐβάπτισεν τὴν πόλιν [Josephus *B.J.* 4.135–7]) with destruction.[35] Like the cup (ποτήριον), then, baptism (βάπτισμα) in Mark 10:38–39 points forward to and functions as a metaphor for the death that Jesus will undergo for the sake of the people (see Mk. 10:45; 14:24).

At the same time, Jesus' metaphorical baptism must have equally evoked for Mark's audience John's physical baptism at the opening of the narrative. The rarity of the term "baptism" (βάπτισμα) in Mark's gospel (Mk. 1:4; 10:38, 39; 11:30), coupled with the fact that the baptismal rite was one in which all of the Markan community would have participated, invites this association.[36] John the Baptist's ostensible goal is, moreover, to help the masses attain forgiveness (Mk. 1:4), and this is precisely what Jesus' death—his impending "baptism"— accomplishes (Mk. 10:45; 14:24; see also Mk. 2:1–12). Thus, Mark 10:38–39 points both forwards and backwards. It looks towards the cross while simultaneously evoking Jesus' baptism in the River Jordan.

The connection I am suggesting Mark invites his audience to draw between Jesus' baptism in the River Jordan and his death upon the cross at Mark 10:38–39 is, in fact, confirmed by the language Mark uses to describe the two events. If one sets the description of Jesus' physical baptism (Mk. 10–11) side by side with Mark's description of the immediate aftermath of Jesus' death at the end of the gospel (Mk. 15:38–39), a linguistic mirroring appears (see Table 2.1).

Table 2.1 Comparison of Mark 1:10–11 and Mark 15:38–39

Mark 1:10–11	*Mark 15:38–39*
10. And, immediately, ascending from the waters, [Jesus] saw the heavens ripped apart [σχιζομένους] and *the Spirit* [τὸ πνεῦμα], as a dove descending into him [καταβαῖνον εἰς αὐτόν]. 11. And a voice came from the heavens: "You are my Son [ὁ υἱός μου], the beloved, in you I am well pleased."	38. And the veil of the temple was ripped [ἐσχίσθη] in two from top to bottom. 39. And the centurion who was standing there opposite [Jesus], once he saw that he had thus breathed out *his Spirit* [ἐξέπνευσεν], said, "Truly this man was a son of God [υἱὸς θεοῦ]."

The parallelism between these two episodes is clear. First, just as, at baptism, the heavens are ripped apart (σχιζομένους [Mk. 9:10]) and the inbreaking of the kingdom begins, so too is the temple veil ripped apart (ἐσχίσθη [Mk. 15:38]) at the cross, and God's presence loosed upon the world.[37] Second, as the Spirit (τὸ πνεῦμα [Mk. 9:10]) enters into Jesus at baptism, so too is it breathed out again (ἐξέπνευσεν [Mk. 15:39]) at his crucifixion. Third, as Christ is acknowledged as God's beloved child (ὁ υἱός μου [Mk. 1:11]) at the inauguration of his missionary career, so too is he (ironically?) acknowledged as such (υἱὸς θεοῦ [Mk. 15:39]) by the centurion at his death. Thus, the language and sequence of events Mark uses in the description of Jesus' death at Mark 15:38–39 mirrors the language and sequence of events of Christ's baptism at Mark 1:10–11. The two episodes are linked together, and the entire missionary activity of Christ is intercalated between them. Christ's baptism in the beginning and his "baptism" at the end are linguistically bound.

The binding of Mark 1:10–11 to Mark 15:38–39 has implications for how one should understand the purpose of John's baptism at Mark 1:4. If the linguistic connection between Mark 1:10–11 and Mark 15:38–39 makes it clear that Jesus' death is somehow associated with John's baptism, then Christ's metaphorical imagery of baptism-as-death at Mark 10:38–39 helps delineate the symbolic possibilities of the term "baptism" (βάπτισμα) itself within the gospel. Because Jesus' "baptism" at Mark 10:38–39 not only refers to the cross (as a metaphor for death), but also invites recollection of Jesus' physical baptism in the River Jordan (through word association and the fact that Jesus' death accomplishes that which John's baptism foretells), Mark's audience is encouraged to see death as operative in John's baptism, as well. On this point, Walter Klaiber's reading of Mark 1:4 is illustrative:

> To be submerged in water in the Old Testament means to be overwhelmed by the floods of judgment [Fluten des Gerichts] (compare Ps. 42:8; 88:8; Jonah 2:4). Jesus himself incorporates this image when, in Mk. 10:38f., he speaks about the baptism with which he will be baptized in light of his own death. To confess his sins and to allow himself to be baptized by John means allowing warranted judgment [verdiente Gericht] to be executed upon himself so as to be saved through judgment and to be freed to new life. In baptism, in being submerged by John, repentance [Umkehr] and forgiveness of sins [Vergebung der Sünden] occurs. The symbolism of baptism thus represents not only a 'cleansing' [reinwaschen] of sin (compare Ps. 51:4), but also the processing of guilt [die Verarbeitung der Schuld] through the symbolic anticipation of judgment [die zeichenhafte Vorwegnahme des Gerichts].[38]

In this citation, Klaiber is reconstructing the symbolic actions of what he believes to be the *historical* John the Baptist. He is thus comfortable hypothesizing both John's real claim to forgive sins and the historical Jesus' actual participation in the rite.[39] As discussed above, I judge it unlikely that either Mark or his community would have understood actual forgiveness of sins to occur in Mark 1:4–11. Nevertheless, Klaiber has rightly connected the symbolism of Mark 10:38–39 with John's ritual action. In the inaugural episode of his gospel narrative, Mark presumes that all who participate in John's baptisms symbolically die as they are "overwhelmed by the floods of judgment [Fluten des Gerichts]." At the level of the narrative, it is on one hand the means by which Mark's Judeans represent their sinfulness, and on the other they perform their readiness to accept any punishment the deity deems fit to impose. At the same time, their hope is that, through this demonstration, they might move God to pity and secure forgiveness for their sins.

The strengths of this interpretation for understanding Mark's larger literary project are multiple. Not only does it create symbolic parallelism between Jesus' baptism at the beginning of the gospel and his "baptism" at the end that couples with the already established linguistic parallelism between the two episodes, it also provides narrative reason for the prolepsis associated with John's baptism and for Jesus' participation in the rite at all. The implicit claim of Mark's gospel is that, when Jesus comes to John, he does so not only to demonstrate his solidarity with sinful humanity; he comes to *conclude* John's activity. By participating in John's rite, the knowing viewer recognizes that Jesus has anticipated his own crucifixion, and all that Judea has been seeking will shortly come to pass. Jesus' baptism is, in other words, the synecdochical manifestation of his salvific death for those with the eyes to perceive it. The self-abasement of the individual is no longer necessary, as the self-abasement of Christ will once and for all atone for the sins of the people.[40]

Final support for this reading can be found in the direct address of God at Jesus' baptism (Mk. 1:11). Upon arising from the waters of the Jordan, Jesus is infused with the Spirit ("he saw ... the Spirit [τὸ πνεῦμα], as a dove, descending into him [καταβαῖνον εἰς αὐτόν]" [Mk. 1:10]), the power by which he is able to perform his various miracles throughout the narrative.[41] Immediately afterwards, Jesus is recognized as God's beloved Son by a voice from heaven: "You are my Son [σὺ εἶ ὁ υἱός μου], the beloved [ὁ ἀγαπητός], in you I am well pleased [ἐν σοὶ εὐδόκησα]" (Mk. 1:11). Though these words are often taken to allude to Psalm 2:7 ("You are my son [υἱός μου εἶ σύ]. Today I have begotten you [σήμερον γεγέννηκά σε]"),[42] there is a growing consensus amongst biblical critics that an additional referent is Genesis 22:2: "Take your son [τὸν υἱόν σου], the beloved [τὸν ἀγαπητόν], whom you love [ὃν ἠγάπησας]."[43] For scholars who adopt this position, the use of the affectionate "beloved" (ἀγαπητός) invokes that other and most famous "beloved" son of the Jewish scriptures, Isaac, who is nearly immolated by his father at God's command.[44] Indeed, it is not just a single word, ἀγαπητός, but a word *cluster* that binds the texts together. Mark's divine disclosure follows the word order of Genesis 22:2 (see Table 2.2).

Table 2.2 Comparison of Genesis 22:2, Mark 1:11, and Psalm 2:7

Genesis 22:2 LXX	Mark 1:11	Psalm 2:7 LXX
Take your son, the beloved	You are my son, the beloved	You are my son... [lit. 'My son you are...]

In both Genesis 22:2 and Mark 1:11, "son" is the object that follows the verb governing its case (accusative and nominative, respectively), with the dependent adjective "beloved" then following the noun and connected by the definite article. Sandwiched in the middle of this noun phrase is a possessive genitive pronoun (σου/μου). The overlapping order does not preclude reference to Psalm 2:7, of course, but it does mean that there are stronger linguistic grounds than often recognized for seeing a double allusion in God's words to Jesus. In the divine epiphany that the messiah experiences at the River Jordan, Mark's audience hears an echo of the binding of Isaac—an echo that is heard again at the transfiguration (Mk. 9:7) and in the Parable of the Vineyard (Mk. 12:1–9), where the beloved son (υἱὸς ἀγαπητός [Mk. 12:6]) is killed by tenant farmers—and this, in turn, strengthens the associations between baptism and death that I have argued are contained within the actions of the baptizer and operative throughout Mark's gospel. Through one short phrase, Mark brings the whole of Isaac's binding before the mind's eye of his audience via the synecdochical poetics he shares with Paul.[45]

To conclude: I have tried to demonstrate that John's baptism in Mark's gospel does not function as a ritual cleansing of sin. Rather, John's baptisms are symbolic performances of drowning that signal to the deity the repentance of the masses. Associations between baptism and death are to be found within Jesus' baptism itself (the allusion to Gen. 22 at Mk. 1:11) and in episodes subsequent to it (Mk. 10:38–39; 12:6–9; 15:37–39). Jesus' baptism in the River Jordan is thus the proleptic enactment and synecdochical manifestation of his sacrificial death, and it signals the end of John's baptismal performances, as "baptisms of repentance" cease to be necessary once the messiah, who will die for the people's sins (Mk. 10:45), has come upon the stage. Mark's audience sees this confirmed in the disclosure of Jesus' messianic status: first, in his insorcism with the Spirit that will grant him his miraculous powers and, second, through his explicit designation as God's beloved Son by the voice from heaven. In the final section of this chapter, I will demonstrate how Mark has self-consciously constructed his narrative so as to anticipate Paul's baptismal ritual within his own story.

Part III: Anticipating the baptism of Paul

The parallelism between Paul and Mark on baptism-as-death can now be summarized. For both, baptism is a synecdochical ritual performance of dying (and rising) during which the baptizand is insorcized with Spirit and transformed into (or recognized as) a child of God. As the parentheses in the previous sentence make clear, this parallelism is not perfect. In Mark's gospel, Jesus is not baptized "into Christ" (εἰς Χριστόν), as Paul imagines Christ believers to be (Gal. 3:27; Rom. 6:3). Nor is there is any overt indication that, in rising from the waters, Jesus proleptically anticipates his resurrection, as Pauline baptizands do (Rom. 6:4–5, 8). Alternatively, Mark does not say anything about adoption, as Paul does (Gal. 4:4–6; Rom. 8:15). Indeed, Mark's changing Psalm 2:7 from "today I have begotten you [σήμερον γεγέννηκά σε]" to "in you I am well pleased [ἐν σοὶ εὐδόκησα]" (Mk. 1:11), speaks against seeing adoption in Jesus' baptism at all.[46] The result is that the symbolism of the Pauline and Markan baptismal rites seems to differ in some significant ways.

One can account for these apparent discrepancies, however, by presuming a Markan etiological hermeneutic vis-à-vis Paul and his mission. Baptism is, for Paul, the "lynchpin by which individual 'life-narratives' become grafted onto the meta-plot of Christ's death and resurrection."[47] Through the retrospective performance of Christ's death and resurrection, the baptizand dies to his or her past in order to be adopted by God and attain resurrection and eternal life (Rom. 6:3–11). Because the baptizand's fate is conformed to Christ's, an essential principle of the believer's new life in Christ is imitation—both of Paul (see 1 Cor. 4:16; Phil. 3:17) and of the messiah whom Paul imitates (see1 Cor. 11:1; 1 Thess. 1:6).[48] In this section, I will argue that Mark anticipates Paul's baptismal ritual, and reinforcing Pauline mimesis is an essential aspect of his etiological project. Like Paul's baptizand, Jesus' (narrated) life begins with baptism, and he is recognized as God's child therein. Like Paul's baptizand, Jesus is gifted with the Spirit that will allow him to perform his various spiritual abilities. Like Paul's baptizand, after participation in the rite, Jesus' existence is a liminal one in which his past is irrelevant, and his future is consistently and imminently before him. Finally, like Paul's baptizand, Jesus is baptized "into death." In each case, however, Mark anticipates and interconnects with Paul's significances rather than duplicating them. I will take a brief look at each of these correspondences in turn.

First, Mark's etiological approach elucidates why the gospel begins where it does. Pauline baptism, as the inaugural act of one's life "in Christ Jesus" (ἐν Χριστῷ Ἰησοῦ [Gal. 3:28]), finds itself anticipated by Jesus' baptism, the inaugural act of his missionary career. Mark's opening not only binds the beginning and end of his narrative together (see Mk. 1:9–11; 15:37–39); it binds the beginning of Jesus' mission with the beginning of believers' new lives in Christ. For Mark, those transformed in the (Pauline) baptismal waters and born to new life are to recognize that their messiah also underwent a similarly transformative experience at the outset of his career. Within the first episode of the narrative, Mark's audience would see that their lives *in* Christ mirror the beginning of Mark's life *of* Christ, thereby reinforcing Paul's insistence on the centrality of mimesis for all who put their faith in the messiah.[49]

Relatedly, Mark's etiological hermeneutic explains the language of adoption that occurs in Jesus' baptism. Though adoption is constitutive of the Pauline ritual (Rom. 8:15; Gal. 4:4–6), Paul also believes that Jesus is God's trueborn and preexistent Son (see Rom. 8:3; 32; Phil. 2:3–7) and the first of many brothers and sisters (Rom. 8:29; 1 Cor. 15:20). The tensive combination of these two assumptions—Christ as trueborn child and Christ as adoptive sibling—is operative in Mark's gospel, as well, and the evangelist is careful to construct the scene of Jesus' acknowledgment as God's beloved Son such that it is both evocative of and divergent from Pauline baptismal expectations. On one hand, the Pauline baptizand, once infused with the Spirit, is compelled *by* that Spirit to exclaim his or her transformation into God's child ("The Spirit [τὸ πνεῦμα] ... crying out [κρᾶζον], 'Abba! Father! [αββα ὁ πατήρ]'" [Gal. 4:6; see also Rom. 8:15]). On the other, during his baptism by John, the Markan Jesus is infused with the Spirit and recognized as the beloved Son *by* God ("You are my Son [σὺ εἶ ὁ υἱός μου], the beloved [ὁ ἀγαπητός]" [Mk. 1:11]). The direction of recognition is inverted: the Father first speaks to the Son (Mark), and then the Son, through the body of the baptizand, speaks (back) to the Father (Paul). Mark has thus made Jesus' divine filiation interlock with the adoption of Pauline baptism by creating a (literal) dialogue between the two. At the same time, by establishing Christ as the only baptizand to whom God speaks directly, he maintains an ontological distinction between messiah and believer.[50]

Second, on the subject of the Spirit, Mark informs his audience that Jesus, like Paul's believer, is suffused with divine energy in baptism. As a result, Jesus is able to manifest charismatic abilities throughout the gospel, and the charisms Jesus puts on display cohere in striking ways with what Paul imagines of himself or expects of his own baptizands. To take one example, in 1 Corinthians 12, after concluding his use of the body metaphor, Paul establishes the following hierarchy:

> And regarding those whom God appointed in the church, first are apostles [ἀποστόλους], second prophets [προφήτας], third teachers [διδασκάλους], then powers [δυνάμεις], then gifts of healing [χαρίσματα ἰαμάτων], helpful deeds [ἀντιλήμψεις], administrations [κυβερνήσεις], [and] the types of tongues [γένη γλωσσῶν] (1 Cor. 12:28).

To a greater of lesser degree, Paul embodies all of these categories. He proclaims the gospel (the essential function of an apostle [see Rom. 10:15; 1 Cor. 1:17; 15:1–8; 2 Cor. 11:7; Gal. 1:6–9, 11; 2:2; 1 Thess. 2:8; etc.]), he prophesies (e.g., 1 Cor. 13:9–10; Rom. 11:25–32), he provides pragmatic instruction (e.g., 1 Cor. 6–8), he performs deeds of power (e.g., 1 Cor. 2:4–5; 2 Cor. 12:12), he labors for and administers to his churches (1 Cor. 9:1–18; 16:1–12; 2 Cor. 8:16–24; 11:7–11; etc.),[51] and he is capable of speaking in tongues (1 Cor. 14:18). Only Paul's ability to heal is left unconfirmed (though later tradition would assign to him this charism [e.g., Acts 14:8–10; 19:11–12]).

Strikingly, in the Gospel of Mark, the opening five spiritual offices of Paul's hierarchy map precisely onto the actions Mark ascribes to Jesus immediately after his reception of the Spirit at baptism. First, Jesus is described as "proclaiming the gospel of God" (κηρύσσων τὸ εὐαγγέλιον τοῦ θεοῦ [Mk. 1:14]), just as an apostle would. Second, he *prophesies* the coming kingdom ("The time is fulfilled, and the kingdom of God has drawn near!" [Mk. 1:15]). Third, after having called Simon, Andrew, James, and John (Mk. 1:16–20), Jesus teaches [ἐδίδασκεν] in a synagogue at Capernaum (Mk. 1:21–22). Fourth, he performs a deed of power by driving an unclean spirit from a man (Mk. 1:23–26). Fifth and finally, he heals the mother-in-law of Simon, bedridden by fever (Mk. 1:29–31). At the first opportunity Mark has to introduce the spiritual abilities of Christ, Jesus embodies the very same and most important spiritual performances Paul has established—apostleship, prophecy, teaching, deeds of power, and healings—in the very same order that Paul presents them. Not only would Mark's audience perceive that their abilities imitate those of their messiah, but they would also see that the actions of Jesus narratively confirm the charismatic schema established and embodied by Paul.[52]

In addition, Paul and Mark not only agree on what one can do while "in the Spirit," they share similar opinions about what one *cannot* do, as well. In Mark's episode with the foreign exorcist, when John and the other disciples prevent an outsider from casting out demons in Jesus' name (Mk. 9:38), the messiah responds by saying, "Do not hinder him. For there is no one who will perform a powerful deed [δύναμιν] in my name [ἐπὶ τῷ ὀνόματί μου] and [then] swiftly be able to curse me [κακολογῆσαί με]" (Mk. 9:39). This statement presumes that the spiritual abilities a person manifests by invoking the "name" of Christ (ἐπὶ τῷ ὀνόματί μου) stem from a place of true and sincere conviction in Jesus' lordship. Were it otherwise, such a person would also be able to "curse" (κακολογέω) the messiah, but Jesus precludes this as a possibility.[53] Similarly, at 1 Corinthians 12:3, Paul opens his discussion of spiritual gifts with the following words: "I make known to you that no one speaking with the Spirit of God [οὐδεὶς ἐν πνεύματι θεοῦ λαλῶν] says, 'Jesus is accursed [Ἀνάθεμα Ἰησοῦς]!' And no one is able to say, 'Jesus is lord [Κύριος Ἰησοῦς]!' unless with the Holy Spirit [ἐν πνεύματι ἁγίῳ]." Both the Markan Jesus and Paul operate with a similar presupposition: a person who has the Spirit of God cannot deny the messiah. The infusion with the one makes the other impossible.

Indeed, not only are the suppositions the same, but the Markan Jesus' and Paul's apparent reasonings for this presupposition are similar. At 1 Corinthians 2:9–12, the apostle informs the Corinthians that a person can only comprehend the paradox of the cross via the reception of the Spirit. Without its infusion, God's salvific intervention in the world through the death of his child remains inscrutable (see 1 Cor. 1:19–24; 2:6–8, 13–15). Once one has come to recognize the truth through the reception of the Spirit, however, Paul presumes that that person is incapable of denying it (1 Cor. 12:3). The Markan Jesus' rationale is analogous, albeit exemplified in negative terms. Upon the messiah's return to Capernaum after naming the twelve (Mk. 3:16–20), Jesus' family tries to "seize him" (κρατῆσαι) because they believe he has "lost his mind" (ἔλεγον γὰρ ὅτι ἐξέστη [Mk. 3:21]). At the same time, scribes from Jerusalem descend upon the home where he is staying and claim that he drives out demons through the power of Beelzebul (Mk. 3:22). Jesus responds by speaking "in parables" (ἐν παραβολαῖς [Mk. 3:23]), first about divided motivations (Mk. 3:23–26), and then about robbing the house of a stronger man (Mk. 3:27), and he concludes with the following warning:

> Truly I say to you that all sins will be forgiven the sons of men [πάντα ἀφεθήσεται τοῖς υἱοῖς τῶν ἀνθρώπων τὰ ἁμαρτήματα] as well as their blasphemies, however often they blaspheme [καὶ αἱ βλασφημίαι ὅσα ἐὰν βλασφημήσωσιν]; but whoever blasphemes against the Holy Spirit [βλασφημήσῃ εἰς τὸ πνεῦμα τὸ ἅγιον], he does not attain forgiveness forever [οὐκ ἔχει ἄφεσιν εἰς τὸν αἰῶνα], as he is guilty [ἔνοχος] of an eternal sin [αἰωνίου ἁμαρτήματος] (Mk. 3:28–29).[54]

Commentators generally find satisfactory explanation for this declaration by linking it to Jesus' mission: to blaspheme against the Spirit is to reject the power with which Jesus is filled, thereby rejecting the legitimacy of the messiah's salvific activity on earth.[55] On this reading, the Spirit is both the means by which Christ casts out demons, and the source of the signs through which a person recognizes the activity of God in the world. If, for Paul, to receive the Spirit is to be granted the power to recognize the salvation God offers through Christ, the evangelist anticipates the apostle by taking his logic one step further at Mark 3:28–29. Mark's claim is that, because the Spirit is the means through which true knowledge is granted, to blaspheme it is to categorically reject the possibility of *ever* attaining that knowledge. Here again, a Markan etiological hermeneutic creates literary concordance between Paul's understanding of the purpose and function of the baptismal Spirit and Christ's use of and teachings about it within the Gospel of Mark. Not only do community members imitate the spiritual gifts of their messiah; they see a shared set of presuppositions about the nature of those gifts in Jesus and Paul.

Third, it has long been recognized that Pauline believers find themselves living in a liminal state. As they await the continued unfolding of the gospel narrative, the "now" and the "not yet" stand in tension with one another.[56] In the baptismal instruction of Romans 6, for example, the apostle speaks on one hand about what *has* happened to Christ: Christ has died (Rom. 6:3, 7; see also 1 Cor. 15:3), he has been buried (Rom. 6:4; see also 1 Cor. 15:4), and he has been raised (ἠγέρθη Χριστὸς [Rom. 6:4; see also 1 Cor. 15:4]). On the other, according to Paul, believers have died (ἀπεθάνομεν σὺν Χριστῷ [Rom. 6:8; see also 6:3, 5–6]), they have been buried (συνετάφημεν … αὐτῷ [Rom. 6:4]); but they *will* be raised (τῆς ἀναστάσεως ἐσόμεθα [Rom. 6:5]), and they *will* walk about in the newness of life (ἐν καινότητι ζωῆς περιπατήσωμεν [Rom. 6:4]).[57] Because believers die to the past but proleptically anticipate their resurrections, the time that intervenes is a liminal one in which the Spirit is active within the church.

The tensive now-but-not-yet quality of believers' baptisms and their subsequent lives "in Christ" finds itself once again anticipated in Mark's gospel. Jesus' baptism in the waters of the Jordan inaugurates his mission and signals the forgiveness for which John and his baptizands ask, but, at the same time, true forgiveness is only effected from the cross (Mk. 10:45), and the messiah's salvific work remains incomplete until that moment.[58] In the interim, Jesus is no longer the carpenter (ὁ τέκτων [Mk. 6:3]) but the earthly Christ, and his biological family is replaced with a new, social one (see Mk. 3:33–35). His impending death is ever before his eyes (Mk. 1:11; 2:18–20; 3:6; 8:31; 9:31; 10:32–33, 38–39, 45; 14:1–2; etc.), and he synecdochically manifests the future salvation he will offer through his miraculous healings and exorcisms.[59] In the pages of Mark's gospel, then, Jesus embodies liminality, and the liminality the Pauline baptizand experiences during his or her life after participation in the baptismal rite finds literary anticipation in Mark's gospel. Pauline mimesis is again affirmed, this time by believers recognizing that the liminal state into which they enter at their baptism (the transitional period before the End; a period of evangelical activity and hoped-for resurrection) is preceded by the liminal state into which Jesus entered at his own (the period of his mission, one that is concluded by his death and resurrection).

Fourth and finally, by having Jesus baptized into the "floods of judgment" (Mk. 1:4), Mark both roots Paul's ritual performance in the past and anticipates its associated blessings. If, for Paul, dying with Christ in baptism is to die to one's past sins and be born again to new life on the pattern of Christ (Rom. 6:3–11), Mark constructs his own baptismal story to explain why this is so. John's "baptism of repentance for the forgiveness of sins" signals to Mark's audience that Jesus has come to take upon himself a curse for the sake of the many (Mk. 10:38–39, 45; see also Gal. 3:13). In dying upon the cross (Mk. 15:37–39), Christ expiates the sins of the people, and that curse is transformed. As a result, believers can recognize that their own baptismal "deaths" are not only patterned upon Christ's death and resurrection; they are anticipated by his physical baptism in the River Jordan. Indeed, though the significance is different, Mark's audience could not have failed to recognize that, just as their baptisms were ritualized deaths, so too was Christ's. Christ "died" in the Jordan in solidarity with sinful human beings who metaphorically put themselves to death in order to acknowledge that sinfulness and embody their merited punishment (Mk. 1:4; 9–11). Jesus then dies at the end of the gospel (Mk. 15:37–39)—an event he refers to *as* baptism (Mk. 10:38–39)—in order to expiate those sins by taking the punishment human beings deserve upon himself. Mark's community is thus to see that the baptism of Jesus by John in the Jordan anticipates their own ritual performances, and the mimetic significances Paul has attached to the rite are reinforced once again.

To conclude: Mark has anticipated within his story the major elements of Pauline baptism (death, adoption, Spirit). Because mimesis is central to Paul's baptismal thinking—believers become sons and daughters as Christ is *the* Son (Gal. 3:27–4:6), and believers die and (proleptically) rise in baptism just as Christ died and rose from the dead (Rom. 6:3–9)—mimesis is also an essential element in Mark's etiological project vis-à-vis Pauline baptism. Indeed, it helps to bind together the Markan variations I have here presented. Mark's story begins with baptism because that is where believers' stories "in Christ" begin. Mark has Jesus receive the Spirit during the ritual because that is when believers receive the Spirit. The Markan narrative depicts Jesus living in a liminal state after the rite because liminality is an essential characteristic of Christ believers' existence after baptism. Finally, though the significances may differ, Mark depicts Jesus as metaphorically dying in his baptism because Pauline believers do. Yet Mark does not comprehensively incorporate Paul's ritual; instead, he takes those elements that are essential to it (death, adoption, Spirit), and he seeds them into his narrative, reinforcing Paul's emphasis on the patterning of believers' lives on the life of the messiah.

Conclusion

In this chapter, I have sought to demonstrate that Mark, through his etiological hermeneutic, works to anticipate the baptismal teachings of Paul. He and his community presume the whole sacred narrative of which the apostle and his mission form a part, and one of his purposes is to create clear and concordant literary progression between the life of Jesus and the teachings of the apostle. Thus, Mark has taken the epiphanic and transformative experience of Pauline baptism and seeded it into his story. All of the major significances Paul associates with the rite—death, sonship, Spirit—are found in Mark's narrative, but they are also deliberately crafted to appear anterior to Paul's teachings and reinforce his insistence on the patterning of believers' lives on that of the messiah. Because Jesus receives the Spirt and is acknowledged as God's beloved son at baptism (Mk. 1:10–11), Pauline believers receive the Spirit and acknowledge God as father at their own (Rom. 8:15–17; Gal. 3:27–4:6). Because the baptismal Spirit received by Jesus allows him to execute a variety of different charismatic offices (eg. Mk. 1:14–31), that same Spirit allows Pauline believers to do likewise (1 Cor. 12). (And, because the Markan Jesus makes a categorical prohibition against blaspheming the Holy Spirit [Mk. 3:28–29], Paul elucidates that prohibition by teaching that the Spirit is the vehicle by which God is able to be recognized [1 Cor. 2:9–12; see also 1 Cor. 12:3].) Because Jesus' life after baptism is a liminal period of earthly mission, the Pauline believer lives a liminal period of expectation before the second coming of the messiah.

Finally and most important, Mark anticipates Paul's baptism as a retrospective performance of the death and resurrection of Jesus Christ. John's "baptism of repentance for the forgiveness of sins" (Mk. 1:4) is not understood by either Mark or his community to entail actual forgiveness. Rather, John's baptism is the symbolic performance of death that petitions the deity *for* the remission of sin, and the epiphany that occurs at Jesus' baptism in Mark suggests to his audience that these petitions have been heard. John's ritualized executions come to an end as Jesus proleptically performs his own death and inaugurates his mission to "give his life as a ransom for the many" (Mk. 10:45). That act of ransom, which Jesus conceptualizes *as* baptism (Mk. 10:38–39), then transforms what the rite of baptism means and entails. What once was the embodiment of wrath and destruction has come to be the embodiment of hope and life through Jesus' salvific act. Mark has thus taken Paul's epiphanic ritual performance and crafted his story to show its evolution. That which was localized in Jesus at his actual baptism (sonship, Spirit [Mk. 1:9–11]), through his metaphorical "baptism" upon the cross (Mk. 15:37–39; 10:38–39), has become accessible to all believers through the retrospective performance of the messiah's death that occurs in their own performances of the rite (Rom. 6:3–9).

Notes

1 "Meta-plot" is the language of Mitchell, "Epiphanic Evolutions," 245 n. 27.
2 For a good discussion of the general context of Rom 6, see Hultgren, *Romans,* 197–9, 241–2.
3 Though Paul's question is a function of his dialectical style of argumentation, it is probable that this question echoes a real slogan Paul was thought to have affirmed (see Rom. 3:8: "And why not say—just as we are slandered [βλασφημούμεθα], and some say that we say—'Let us do evil [ποιήσωμεν τὰ κακά] in order that good might come [ἔλθη τὰ ἀγαθά]'?").

4 Hultgren, *Romans,* 243.

5 See, for example, Alain Gignac, *L'Épître aux Romains* (CBNT 6; Paris: Les Éditions du Cerf, 2014), 248; Hans Dieter Betz, "Transferring a Ritual: Paul's Interpretation of Baptism in Romans 6," in *Paul in His Hellenistic Context* (ed. Troels Engberg-Pedersen; Minneapolis: Fortress, 1995), 110; Leander E. Keck, *Romans* (ANTC; Nashville: Abingdon, 2005), 159; Brendan Byrne, *Romans* (SP 6; Collegeville: Liturgical Press, 1996) 189–90; Rudolf Schnackenburg, *Baptism in the Thought of Saint Paul* (trans. G. R. Beasely-Murray; New York: Herder and Herder, 1964), 33. For contrasting opinions, see Joseph A. Fitzmyer, *Romans* (AB 33; New York: Doubleday, 1993), 431; C. K. Barrett, *The Epistle to the Romans* (HNTC; New York: Harper and Row, 1957), 122; Ernst Käsemann, *Commentary on Romans* (trans. Geoffrey W. Bromiley; Grand Rapids: Eerdmans, 1980), 164–5; Hultgren, *Romans,* 242, 44. Walter Schmithals (*Der Römerbrief: ein Kommentar* [Gütersloh: Gerd Mohn, 1988], 189) takes a moderate position. On one hand, he allows that the vivid imagery of being "buried" (συνετάφημεν) and "co-crucified" (συνεσταυρώθη) with Christ may have been creative expansions by Paul. One the other, he believes the community would have already been aware of a "dying" and "rising with" pattern in baptism.

6 The necessity for the conformity of believers' fates to that of Christ is laid out in fullest detail in 1 Cor. 15. In this chapter, Paul seeks to bolster his community's faith in the coming resurrection that had come to be doubted, and, in a lengthy series of conditionals that highlight the absurdity of Christ believers' hopes if Jesus has not been raised, he excoriates the Corinthians for supposing that there might not be a general resurrection for all (see 1 Cor. 15:14–22; for good discussions of these verses, see Anthony Thiselton, *The First Epistle to the Corinthians* [NIGTC; Grand Rapids: Eerdmans, 2000], 1214–29; Roy E Ciampa and Brian S. Rosner, *The First Letter to the Corinthians* [PNTC; Grand Rapids: Eerdmans, 2010], 753–64; David E. Garland, *1 Corinthians* [BECNT; Grand Rapids: Baker Academic, 2003], 701–3).

7 This rupture is aptly summarized by Fitzmyer: "For Paul baptism tears a person from one's native condition ('in Adam'), from one's native proclivity ('in the flesh'), and from one's ethnic background ('under the law'). It thus incorporates the person of faith 'into Christ' so that one lives 'in Christ' and 'for God' in order that one may be one day 'with the lord' (1 Thess 4:17)" (*Romans,* 430). See also Schnackenburg, *Baptism,* 8–39; Keck, *Romans,* 160; Byrne, *Romans,* 189; Robert Jewett, *Romans* (Hermeneia; Minneapolis: Fortress, 2007), 383; Gignac, *Romains,* 248.

8 On the connection of these verses to baptism, see Hultgren, *Romans,* 310–17.

9 For a good general introduction to the structure and purpose of Paul's letter to the Galatians, see Bruce Longenecker, "Galatians," in Dunn, *Cambridge Companion to Saint Paul,* 64–73.

10 There is, famously, debate about what Paul means when he says, "Abraham believed in God, and it was reckoned to him as righteousness" (Ἀβραὰμ ἐπίστευσεν τῷ θεῷ, καὶ ἐλογίσθη αὐτῷ εἰς δικαιοσύνην [Gal. 3:6]). The debate is encapsulated in the skirmish between Richard B. Hays and James D. G. Dunn (see Richard Hays, "πίστις and Pauline Christology: What is at Stake?" and James D. G. Dunn, "Once More, πίστις Χριστοῦ," in *Pauline Theology Volume IV: Looking Back, Pressing On* [eds. E. Elizabeth Johnson and David M. Hay; Atlanta: Scholars Press, 1997], 35–60 and 61–81). Hays has provocatively suggested that, for Paul, Abraham's faithfulness is primarily a type of Christ's, and, "just as Abraham trusted in God" (καθὼς Ἀβραὰμ ἐπίστευσεν τῷ θεῷ [Gal 3:6a]), so too did the messiah, with the result that justification was reckoned to both (ἐλογίσθη ... εἰς δικαιοσύνην [Gal. 3:6b]). For Hays, Abraham is "a typological foreshadowing of Christ himself" and he functions in Galatians as a "subversive counterreading" to the Abraham story as deployed by Paul's adversaries (Hays, "πίστις and Pauline Christology," 47). Dunn on the other hand counters that, if Abraham functions synonymously in Romans and Galatians, one runs into an insoluble problem: in Romans 4, Paul is *attacking* the traditional

Jewish understanding of Abraham as the archetypal model of faithfulness. As such, Gen. 15:6 has to be understood as prior to and independent of later exemplary representations of Abraham's obedience to God (see Gen. 17, 22). Thus, πίστις does not refer to Abraham's faithfulness in Paul's thinking. Rather, it refers to his *faith*; that is, his naked trust in God's promise (Dunn, "Once More, πίστις Χριστοῦ," 75–6). This monograph does not seek to determine whether it is more accurate to speak of the "faith" or "faithfulness" of Abraham. Neither choice will negatively affect my conclusions, so I present both here as equal interpretive possibilities.

11 There is broad agreement amongst commentators that these verses hearken back to and expand upon the shared baptismal experience of the Galatians communities. See, for example, Hans Dieter Betz, *Galatians* [Hermeneia; Philadelphia: Fortress, 1979], 181–5; J. Louis Martyn, *Galatians* (AB 33; New York: Doubleday, 1997), 378–83; Frank J. Matera, *Galatians* (SP 9; Collegeville: Liturgical Press, 1992), 145–7; Hans Lietzmann, *An die Galater* (HNT 10; Tubingen: J.C.B. Mohr [Paul Siebeck], 1932), 23; Martinus C. de Boer, *Galatians: A Commentary* (Louisville: Westminster John Knox, 2011) 243–4; Robin Scroggs and Kent I. Groff, "Baptism in Mark: Dying and Rising with Christ," *JBL* 92 (1973) 538–9; cf. James D.G. Dunn, *A Commentary on the Epistle to the Galatians* (BNTC; London: A&C Black, 1993), 203–4.

12 At a metaphysical level, "putting on Christ" (Χριστὸν ἐνεδύσασθε [Gal. 3:27]) signifies the believer's incorporation into Christ's body and transformation into a new being (Betz, *Galatians,* 187; Martyn, *Galatians,* 382–3; Matera, *Galatians,* 146; Lietzmann, *Galater,* 23–4). It is the "action by means of which [believers'] lives and destinies and very identities become bound up with Christ" (Dunn, *Galatians,* 203). At a practical level, "putting on" may also evoke the baptizand's clothing himself in fresh white garments after submersion in water (Scroggs and Groff, "Baptism," 537–40), though this suggestion is more speculative.

13 For Paul, Christ is Abraham's true heir: "The promises have been spoken to Abraham and to his seed [τῷ σπέρματι αὐτοῦ]. It does not say, to his seeds [τοῖς σπέρμασιν], as if to many, but as if to one [ὡς ἐφ᾽ ἑνός]: 'and to your seed' [τῷ σπέρματί σου], who is Christ [ὅς ἐστιν Χριστός]" (Gal. 3:16). For a good discussion of this verse and its context, see Hays, *The Faith of Jesus Christ,* 135–8.

14 To be sure, there is debate as to when, precisely, a Christ-believer receives the Spirit. Martyn, for example, does not link spiritual infusion with baptism; instead, he suggests that the Spirit of God invades the hearts of believers when Paul first *preached* to them, long before baptism would have occurred (Martyn, *Galatians,* 284; see also Martinus C. de Boer, *Galatians: A Commentary* [NTL; Louisville: Westminster John Knox, 2011], 265–6). Other scholars, however, argue that the Spirit is received *through* the baptismal rite (Lietzmann, *Galater,* 23; Peter Stuhlmacher, *Paul's Letter to the Romans: A Commentary* [trans. Scott J. Hafemann. Louisville: Westminster John Knox, 1994], 98–9; Matera *Galatians,* 143–7). While I incline towards the latter position, it must be admitted that the precise moment of spiritual infusion cannot be determined with certainty. It is clear, however, that for Paul the power of the Holy Spirit is activated and displayed in baptism. Regardless of whether or not it is received prior to the rite, Paul designates baptism as the moment at which one's possession of the Spirit is witnessed and ratified by both the baptizand and a community of his or her fellow believers.

15 For discussion, see Joseph Fitzmyer, *First Corinthians* (AB 32; New Haven: Yale University Press, 2008), 157–8.

16 So Hans-Josef Klauck, *1 Korintherbrief* (NEB 7; Würzburg: Echter Verlag GmbH, 1984), 30; Thiselton, *Corinthians,* 259–60. On the rhetorical context of Paul's extended discussion of wisdom and Spirit (1 Cor. 2:6–16), see Margaret M. Mitchell, *Paul, the Corinthians, and the Birth of Christian Hermeneutics* (Cambridge: Cambridge University Press, 2010), 41–3.

17 See Margaret M. Mitchell, *Paul and the Rhetoric of Reconciliation: An Exegetical Investigation of the Language and Composition of 1 Corinthians* (Louisville: Westminster John Knox, 1991), 157–75, 267–80.

18 In his list of spiritual offices at 1 Cor. 12:7–10, Paul is careful underscore that all charisms serve to build up the community, and, though distinct from one another, no one of them can claim superiority (for discussion, see Mitchell, *Rhetoric of Reconciliation,* 267–8; Fitzmyer, *Corinthians,* 466–71; Thiselton, *Corinthians,* 936–89).

19 "For, with one Spirit [ἐν ἑνὶ πνεύματι], we all [ἡμεῖς πάντες] have been baptized into one body [εἰς ἓν σῶμα ἐβαπτίσθημεν]—whether Jew or Greek; whether slave or free—and we all [πάντες] have been given to drink one Spirit [ἓν πνεῦμα ἐποτίσθημεν]." I have chosen to translate the prepositional phrase as instrumental rather than locative, but this is a contested point. Thiselton (*Corinthians,* 997–8) rightly argues that linguistic specificity here is less important than Paul's deep concern that, by virtue of being baptized by (or in) one Spirit, there can no longer be any "categorization or elitism" within the church.

20 See Chapter 1, Part II(A) for my argument.

21 "For the Son of Man did not come to be served but to serve [διακονηθῆναι ἀλλὰ διακονῆσαι] and to give his life as a ransom for many [λύτρον ἀντὶ πολλῶν]." On the centrality of this verse for Mark, see Marcus, *Mark 8–16,* 757: "The ransom saying, with which [Mk. 10:35–45] concludes (10:45b), is of central importance in Mark's narrative because it is the clearest Markan reflection on the saving purpose of Jesus' death (cf. 14:24). That death is to be a 'ransom,' a payment of the price that the 'many' are unable to pay themselves."

22 It is clear that, as early as Matthew, Mark could be read in this way. Aside from containing a separate birth narrative that makes Jesus' exalted status unambiguously clear (Matt. 1:18–21), Matthew redacts Jesus' baptism as follows: "Then Jesus, from Galilee, was present at the Jordan with John in order to be baptized by him [τοῦ βαπτισθῆναι ὑπ' αὐτοῦ]. But John was preventing him [διεκώλυεν αὐτὸν], saying, 'I have need of being baptized by you [ὑπὸ σοῦ βαπτισθῆναι], and you come to me?' And, answering, Jesus said to him, 'Let it be for now [ἄφες ἄρτι]. For it is thus fitting for us to fulfill all righteousness [πληρῶσαι πᾶσαν δικαιοσύνην]'" (Matt. 3:13–15). Regardless of what one makes of the phrase "to fulfill all righteousness" (πληρῶσαι πᾶσαν δικαιοσύνην), it is clear that Matthew has expanded the Markan narrative so as to exclude any implication that Jesus might require some form of personal repentance (for discussion, see Ulrich Luz, *Matthew* [trans. James E. Crouch; 3 vols.; Hermeneia; Minneapolis: Fortress, 2001–7], 1.140–3).

23 For a recent and nuanced treatment of Markan high Christology, see Richard B. Hays, *Echoes of Scripture in the Gospels* (Waco: Baylor University Press, 2016), 61–78.

24 See Collins, *Mark,* 142; Marcus, *Mark 1–8,* 156.

25 There is a potential objection to my claim that John is a figure respected by the Jerusalem authorities. In an argument with the chief priests, scribes, and elders during Jesus' final kerygmatic activity in Jerusalem, the baptism of John becomes the subject of debate (Mk. 11:27–33). It is demanded of Jesus that he explain on what authority he does what he does (Mk. 11:28), and Jesus responds by saying that, should the authorities tell him whence comes the baptism of John, he will give them the information they seek (Mk. 11:29–30). Jesus' interlocutors now find themselves caught in a rhetorical snare. On one hand, should they say, "from heaven," Jesus will attack them as hypocrites for not believing the baptizer (Mk. 11:31). On the other, should they attribute his baptism strictly to a human source, the crowds, who believe John to be a prophet, would themselves attack: "they were afraid of the crowd, for they all held John was truly a prophet [τὸν Ἰωάννην ὄντως ὅτι προφήτης ἦν]" (Mk. 11:32). The implication seems to be, then, that the Jerusalem authorities did not accept the baptizer's authority, or they would admit its heavenly source without fear of reprisal.

In my judgment, however, Mark is not saying that the authorities reject John's message *per se*. Rather, they reject the idea that the "stronger one" (ὁ ἰσχυρότερος [Mk. 1:7]) points to Jesus. Though Mark typologically identifies John the Baptist with Elijah (see Mk. 1:6 [comp. 2 Kgs. 1:8]; Mk. 9:13), and he makes it clear that Jesus is superior to this figure (see Mk. 9:4–7), at the level of the *characters* within Mark's story, there is confusion about the person with whom the eschatological Elijah (see Mal. 3:22-4) is to be identified: some equate him with John the Baptist (see Mk. 6:15), others with Jesus (see Mk. 8:28), and still others imagine an entirely separate celestial entity (see Mk. 15:35–36, see also Mk. 9:4–5). If the Jerusalem authorities imagine that it is Elijah who heralds the end times (Mk. 9:11), then the "stronger one" to whom John refers must, for them, point either to God (presuming they identify John with Elijah) or a distinct and still anticipated heavenly figure. Because they reject the possibility that Jesus' power has a heavenly origin (Mk. 3:22; see also Mk. 2:7; Mk. 14:64; etc.), they exclude the possibility that Jesus is himself to be equated with Elijah (something that Jesus also rejects [see Mk. 8:28–30; Mk. 9:11–13]). Thus, in Mk. 11:27–33, the authorities are unable to answer Jesus' question because they are unwilling to provide Jesus opportunity to claim that he is the "stronger one" of whom John spoke (for similar readings, see Marcus, *Mark 8–16*, 797, 799–800; Ludger Schenke, *Das Markusevangelium: literarische Eigenwart—Text und Kommentarung* [Stuttgart: Kohlhammer, 2005], 271; cf. Francis J. Moloney, *The Gospel of Mark* [Grand Rapids: Baker Academic, 2002], 231).

26 This language comes from M. Eugene Boring (*Mark: A Commentary* [NTL; Louisville: Westminster John Knox, 2006], 44): "Without a word of explanation, Jesus takes his place in the line of repentant humanity preparing for the eschatological act of God. Jesus' initial appearance in Mark is *in solidarity with sinful humanity*. The one we readers have heard of addressed in 1:2 as belonging to the transcendent world appears in this world as one of us" (emphasis added). See also John R. Donahue and Daniel J. Harrington, *The Gospel of Mark* (SP 2; Collegeville: Liturgical Press, 2002), 64–5; Ulrich W. Mauser, *Christ in the Wilderness: The Wilderness Theme in the Second Gospel and its Basis in the Biblical Tradition* (London: SCM Press, 1963) 94–5; R. T. France, *The Gospel of Mark* (NIGTC; Grand Rapids: Eerdmans, 2002), 76.

27 Marcus, *Mark 1–8*, 156; see also Schenke, *Markusevangelium*, 51–2; Robert A. Guelich, *Mark 1–8:26* [WBC 34a; Dallas: Word Books, 1989], 20.

28 See Herbert Weir Smyth, *Greek Grammar* (Harvard University Press, 1984), 376, §1686d.

29 Mk. 1:8, where John predicts that the stronger one will come and "baptize you with Holy Spirit [βαπτίσει ὑμᾶς ἐν πνεύματι ἁγίῳ]" is, however, noteworthy. On one hand, what it means to "baptize with the Holy Spirit" is assumed rather than explained. On the other, there is here striking overlap with Paul's own formulation, "with one spirit [ἐν ἑνὶ πνεύματι] we have all been baptized into one body [ἡμεῖς πάντες εἰς ἓν σῶμα ἐβαπτίσθημεν]" (1 Cor. 12:13). It may be that Mark quite directly evokes Pauline baptismal experience in this verse.

30 Contrast Mark's usage, for example, with the author of Colossians, who does use the masculine noun for the ritual at Col. 2:11–12: "In [him] you were also circumcised with a circumcision not made by hands, in the stripping of the body of the flesh through the circumcision of Christ, buried together with him in baptism [συνταφέντες αὐτῷ ἐν τῷ βαπτισμῷ], in which you were also raised up with him [συνηγέρθητε] through faith in the power of God who raised him from the dead [διὰ τῆς πίστεως τῆς ἐνεργείας τοῦ θεοῦ τοῦ ἐγείραντος αὐτὸν ἐκ νεκρῶν]." Interestingly, given how closely this passage echoes Rom. 6:4–8, it is noteworthy that Paul there uses the neuter noun βάπτισμα rather than the masculine noun βαπτισμός.

31 E.g., Marcus, *Mark 8–16*, 747; 752; Collins, *Mark*, 496; Moloney, *Mark*, 205; Sherman E. Johnson, *A Commentary on the Gospel According to Saint Mark* (HNTC 2; New York: Harper & Brothers, 1960), 179; France, *Mark*, 416; C. E. B. Cranfield, *The*

Gospel According to Saint Mark (CGTC; Cambridge: Cambridge University Press, 1959), 337–8; William L. Lane, *The Gospel According to Mark* (NICNT 2; Grand Rapids: Eerdmans, 1974), 380; Walter Klaiber, *Das Markusevanglium* (BNT; Neukirchen-Vluyn: Neukirchener Verlag, 2010), 201; Wilfried Eckey, *Das Markusevangelium: Orientierung am Weg Jesu* (Neukirchen-Vluyn: Neukirchener Verlag, 1998), 343; Joachim Gnilka, *Das Evangelium nach Markus* (EKK; 2 vols.; Solothurn und Düsseldorf: Benziger Verlag, 1994), 1.101–2. I will discuss the cup metaphor in more detail in Chapter 3, Part III.

32 Because Jesus prophesies that both James and John will also drink from "the cup" (τὸ ποτήριον), a word here should be said about the significance of their own deaths. Collins plausibly suggests that, while James' and John's deaths are not "for the many" (Mk. 10:45), they are, nevertheless, "for the sake of the Gospel" and the continued mission of the church (Collins, *Mark,* 497; see also Col. 1:24). Thus, though similar in form, their deaths have an ecclesiological rather than universal significance.

33 See, for example, Marcus, *Mark 8–16,* 747–8, who provides an important list of metaphorical *comparanda*: "In nonbiblical Greek, words of the *bapt-* group are used figuratively for the immersion of people in various sorts of evils (see e.g., Josephus, *War* 4.137, Libanius, *Orations* 18.286 …) and in the OT and Jewish texts water and flood imagery are deployed in a similar way (see, e.g., Ps. 42:7; Isa. 43:2; 1QH 11[3]:28–36). Sometimes, as in 1QH 11(3):28–36, the overflowing evil is eschatological in nature, and this eschatological sense carries over to the figurative uses of *baptisma* and *baptisthēnai* in Luke 12:50, as the highly apocalyptic context of that saying shows." For a fuller list of comparisons that takes into account variant readings in both the Aquila and Symmachus versions of the Septuagint, see Hans F. Bayer, *Das Evangelium des Markus* (HTA 5; Witten: SCM R. Brockhaus, 2008), 376. The idea of "drowning" in troubles without either using "baptism" or "baptize" is also not uncommon. See, for example, Psalm 41:8 (LXX), which reads, "Abyss [ἄβυσσος] calls upon abyss at the sound of your cataracts [εἰς φωνὴν τῶν καταρρακτῶν σου]. All of your upswells and your waves [πάντες οἱ μετεωρισμοί σου καὶ τὰ κύματά σου] have passed over me [ἐπ᾽ ἐμὲ διῆλθον]."

34 A farcical example occurs in Aesop's Fable 75. There, a monkey survives a shipwreck and is carried upon a dolphin's back to Athens. When the two near Piraeus, the dolphin asks the monkey if he knows the port, but the monkey, mistaking the dolphin to be referring to a man, claims Piraeus to be an old friend. In response to the deception, the dolphin chokes the monkey "by drowning him" (βαπτίζων αὐτόν [*fab. Aes.* 75.14–15]; the Greek text is taken from Augustus Hausrath and Herbert Hunger, *Corpus Fabularum Aesopicarum* [vol 1.1; 2nd edn; Leipzig: Teubner, 1970]).

35 "But the guards of the cities, partly by hesitation to suffer evil and partly by hatred for the nation, were aiding little or not at all those who were suffering [τοῖς κακουμένοις] until the robber-chiefs of the troop contingents everywhere [οἱ τῶν πανταχοῦ συνταγμάτων ἀρχιλῃσταί], having been gathered together by the chorus of despoliations throughout the land [μέχρι κόρῳ τῶν κατὰ τὴν χώραν ἁρπαγῶν ἀθροισθέντες], and having become a mass of wickedness [πονηρίας στῖφος], stole into the heart of Jerusalem, a city lacking a general, and which, by ancient custom, receives all fellow tribesmen without precaution. And [it did so] because, at that time, everyone was imagining that all those allies streaming in came with good will [ἀπ᾽ εὐνοίας ἥκειν]. It was this which [ὃ δή], even apart from sedition, later *drowned the city* [ἐβάπτισεν τὴν πόλιν] in destruction." The Greek text is taken from Josephus, *The Jewish War: Books III–IV* (trans. H. ST. John Thackeray; Cambridge: Harvard University Press, 1927). The emphasis in the quotation is my own.

36 The invitation for the Markan audience to perceive their own baptisms in Mk. 10:38–9 is noted by, amongst others, Marcus, *Mark 8–16,* 752–4; Donahue and Harrington, *Mark,* 311; France, *Mark,* 416–17; Collins, *Mark,* 496–7; and Moloney, *Mark,* 205.

37 A connection rightly noted by Donahue and Harrington, *Mark,* 65; France, *Mark,* 77; Boring, *Mark,* 45.

38 Klaiber, *Markusevangelium,* 22; see also p. 201 for his discussion of Mk. 10:38–39.

39 See Klaiber, *Markusevangelium,* 26.

40 Jesus is here analogous to the biblical scapegoat, and Mark's audience may have been invited to associate Jesus' baptism with the scapegoat ritual, as well. Compare Lev. 16:21–22: "And Aaron will set his hands upon the head of the living he-goat, and he will recite over him all the lawless actions of the sons of Israel [πάσας τὰς ἀνομίας τῶν υἱῶν Ἰσραηλ] and all their injustices [πάσας τὰς ἀδικίας αὐτῶν] and all their sins [πάσας τὰς ἁμαρτίας αὐτῶν], and he will set them upon the head of the living he-goat, and he will send it forth through a prepared man into the wilderness [εἰς τὴν ἔρημον (see Mk. 1:12)]. And the he-goat will take upon itself their injustices [τὰς ἀδικίας αὐτῶν] into an inaccessible land, and he will send the he-goat into the wilderness."

41 There is broad consensus amongst commentators that Jesus' ability to perform miracles in the narrative comes from his insorcism with the Holy Spirit at baptism. Collins' words are representative: "As Aesop was given gifts of wise speech by Isis and the Muses, Jesus is endowed with the divine Spirit on this occasion, the power *that enables him* to teach with authority, to heal and to cast out demons" (*Mark,* 147 [emphasis added]). See also Marcus, *Mark 1–8,* 165; Guelich, *Mark,* 35; France, *Mark,* 77; Boring, *Mark,* 45; Moloney, *Mark,* 36–7; Schenke, *Markusevangelium,* 54.

42 See, amongst others, Marcus, *Mark,* 163; Collins, *Mark,* 150; France, *Mark,* 79–83; Donahue and Harrington, *Mark,* 66–9; and Ernst Haenchen, *Der Weg Jesu* (Berlin: Töpelmann, 1966), 54–5. On the interpretation of the Psalm itself, see Mitchell Dahood, *Psalms 1–50* (AB 16; New York: Doubleday, 1965), 7–14; Gnilka, *Markus,* 1.52–3.

43 See Boring, *Mark,* 45–6; Marcus, *Mark 1–8,* 162; Jon Levenson, *The Death and Resurrection of the Beloved Son: The Transformation of Child Sacrifice in Judaism and Christianity* (New Haven: Yale University Press, 1993) 202; Camille Focant, *L'Évangile selon Marc* (CBNT 2; Paris: Les Éditions du Cerf, 2010), 69–70; Klaiber, *Markusevanglium,* 27–8; Eckey, *Markusevangelium,* 76–7. For a good general discussion of "beloved" in these verses, see Simon Légasse, *Naissance du Baptême* (LD 153; Paris: Les Éditions du Cerf, 1993), 59–63.

44 As Simon Légasse (*L'Évangile de Marc* [2 vols.; LDC 5; Paris: Les Éditions du Cerf, 1997], 1.91) rightly notes, "… *agapètos,* quand il traduit l'hébreu *yahîd* in l'Ancien Testament, est toujours en rapport avec la mort d'un fils ou d'une fille unique, la permier en liste étant Isaac (emphasis original)."

45 I will discuss the Aqedah in more detail in Chapter 4.

46 It is possible that Mark has altered the words based upon the larger context of the psalm itself. The Greek version of Ps. 2 does not make clear when the "begetting" takes place. Ps. 2:6–7 reads, "But I *have been* established by him as king upon Zion [ἐγὼ δὲ κατεστάθην βασιλεὺς ὑπ' αὐτοῦ ἐπὶ Σιων], his holy mountain, proclaiming the commandment of the Lord. The Lord *said* to me [εἶπεν πρός με], "You are my son [υἱός μου εἶ σύ]; today I have begotten you [σήμερον γεγέννηκά σε] (emphasis added)." Through the use of aorist verbs, the Psalm speaks of events that have either already occurred in the past, or, if understood as gnomic, have not occurred in historical time at all. One suspects that Mark has used this passage as a proof text for Jesus' messianism because of its wider context (it speaks of God's "anointed one" [ὁ Χριστός] against whom the rulers of the earth have aligned themselves [Ps. 2:2] but for whom the nations [ἔθνη] *will* inevitably become an inheritance [Ps. 2:8–9, future tense]), and he excises the line about begetting because, if placed within his narrative, its implications would run counter to those of the Psalm itself, which speaks of the begotteness of the son in the past or outside of historical time entirely. Thus, the judgment of France (*Mark,* 82–3) on Mk. 1:11 is most probably correct: "The divine declaration

and the whole experience of which it forms a part is not phrased in such a way as to suggest that Jesus at this point becomes something which he was not before … Jesus does not have to wait until the resurrection to become God's son; he is so already, and there is no hint that even at his baptism this is a new factor. What is new here is launching into the public exercise of the role for which he, as Son of God, is thus prepared."

47 Mitchell, "Epiphanic Evolutions," 245 n. 27.

48 In addition to explicit calls for imitation, Paul calls for believers to model their actions on Christ implicitly. At Rom. 12:1, for example, Paul writes, "I exhort you, brothers and sisters, through the mercies of God, present your bodies as a living sacrifice [θυσίαν ζῶσαν], holy, pleasing to God, your rational service [τὴν λογικὴν λατρείαν ὑμῶν]." The language of sacrifice here evokes the sacrificial language the apostle regularly uses to describe Jesus' own death (e.g., Rom. 3:25; 1 Cor. 5:7; 11:24–25).

49 Indeed, Mark subtly emphasizes the necessity of imitation throughout his gospel. This is done via his consistent use of the verb "to follow" (ἀκολουθέω) as a metaphor for discipleship (Mk. 1:18; 2:14; 8:34; 10:21, 28, 52; etc.). Mk. 8:34, in which Jesus says, "if someone wishes to follow [ἀκολουθεῖν] me, let him deny himself [ἀπαρνησάσθω ἑαυτόν] and take up his cross [ἀράτω τὸν σταυρὸν αὐτοῦ] and follow me [ἀκολουθείτω μοι]," is particularly evocative, as Christ, too, has denied himself (see Mk. 3:32–35) and dies upon a cross (Mk. 15:37–39). For a good discussion of the metaphorical nature of Mk. 8:34 and the verses that follow, see Troels Engberg-Pedersen, "Paul in Mark 8:34–9:1: Mark on what it is to be a Christian," in Becker et al., *Mark and Paul,* 189–209. On "following" as a metaphor for discipleship, see Elizabeth Struthers Malbon, "Disciples/Crowds/Whoever: Markan Characters and Readers," in eadem, *In the Company of Jesus,* 72–8 (repr. from *NovT* 28 [1986], 104–30).

50 The dialogue between father and son that I am suggesting occurs in baptism may find some additional support in an unexpected place: Gethsemane. While Paul's baptismal cry of "Abba! Father!" does not occur within Mk. 1:9–11, the evangelist employs the same language at Mk. 14:36. During his vulnerable moment in the garden, Jesus' prayer that he be spared his impending death is written as follows: "Abba, Father [αββα ὁ πατήρ], all things are possible for you; take this cup [τὸ ποτήριον τοῦτο] from me. But not what I wish, but what you [wish]." It is surprising that so few exegetes read this language as reminiscent of baptism, despite its being combined with a reference to cup, thereby forming a close parallel with Mk. 10:38. (Commentators generally read αββα ὁ πατήρ at Mk. 14:36 as underscoring Jesus' unique and intimate connection to God. See, for example, Boring, *Mark,* 399; France, *Mark,* 584, Schenke, *Markusevangelium,* 326; Marcus, *Mark 8–16,* 978. Gnilka, *Markus,* 2.260.) Both verses occur within pericopes framing the final and ill-fated proselytizing activity of Jesus in Jerusalem, and both evoke the language of rituals patterned on the death of Christ in order to foreshadow that death. Mk. 10:38 does so by means of metonymy, making the ritual titles sobriquets for the cross. Mk. 14:36 follows this same pattern vis-à-vis "cup," but, with baptism, the evangelist surprisingly elects to evoke a *moment* of the baptismal experience. The result is that the baptismal dialogue is already present in full in the Markan narrative, but its ultimate significance is not. At this literary moment, because Christ has not died and been raised, an expression of despair stands in for an expression of joyful ecstasy. Only when Christ's salvific activity on earth is concluded and God's love vindicated will it be appropriate for the baptizand, conjoined with the Spirit, to cry out to his or her adoptive Father with joy.

51 Mitchell, drawing upon the work of Earle Hilgert (*The Ship and Related Symbols in the New Testament* [Assen: van Gorcum, 1962]), suggests that Paul's selection of the term κυβέρνησις is intentional. Its more literal meaning of "steersmanship" underscores for the Corinthian community their need to be "steered wisely" and act as "concordant

passengers" (*Rhetoric of Reconciliation*, 163–4; see also Thiselton, *Corinthians*, 1021–2). If true, Paul, as the author of a letter comprehensively designed to level factionalist behavior in Corinth, is the ultimate embodiment of the κυβέρνησις. He is the one keeping the ship afloat by guiding it clear of factionalist rocks.

52 There is one item in the apostle's list does not find home in the Gospel of Mark: glossolalia, the speaking in tongues. Its omission is likely due to the fact that glossolalia was a contentious spiritual ability in the early church (for discussion, see Fitzmyer, *Corinthians*, 508–9; Hans Conzelmann, *1 Corinthians* [trans. James W. Leitch; Hermeneia; Philadelphia: Fortress, 1974], 233–4), and Paul both thoroughly challenges its benefits (1 Cor. 14, esp. vv. 1–6, 14–17, 21–25) and relegates it to a subordinate position in his own charismatic hierarchy (Klauck, *1 Korintherbrief*, 91–2. See also Fitzmyer, *Corinthians*, 483–4). By not mentioning it, Mark allows Paul to claim the ability to speak in tongues for himself ("I give thanks to God [that] I speak in tongues [γλώσσαις λαλῶ] more than all of you [ὑμῶν μᾶλλον]" [1 Cor. 14:18]) without risk of his doing so contradicting the teachings of the messiah, who neither confirms nor denies its validity.

53 On κακολογέω, see Focant, *Marc*, 362: "Employé seulement ici et dans une citation en 7,10 … le verbe κακολογέω a pour substrat le plus frequent le verbe hébreu *qll* lorsqu'il est employé dans la LXX, ce qui invite à lui donner le sens de blasphémer ou de maudire … Donc l'enjeu n'est sans doute pas une simple atteinte à la reputation de Jésus, mais le rejet de sa personne et de son message." On the passage more generally, see Moloney, *Mark*, 189; France, *Mark*, 377.

54 For a fuller discussion of the context of this passage, see Collins, *Mark*, 226–35.

55 So Marcus, *Mark 1–8*, 284: "In the Markan context, blasphemy against the Spirit means the sort of total, malignant opposition to Jesus that twists all the evidence of his life-giving power into evidence that his is demonically possessed (see 3:22, 30) … in Mark's view, the true source of Jesus' exorcistic and miracle working power is not an unclean spirit but the Holy Spirit, the power of God's new age." See also Collins, *Mark*, 234–5; Boring, *Mark*, 175; Focant, *Marc*, 150; Moloney, *Mark*, 83; Morna D. Hooker, *The Gospel According to Saint Mark* (BNTC; Peabody: Hendrickson, 1991) 117.

56 This process is articulated well by James R. Edwards, *Romans* (NIBCNT 6; Peabody: Hendrickson, 1992) 162: "Authentic Christian existence always stands with one foot in the old life and one in the new. The Christian life is one of tension between Adam and Christ, sin and Grace, flesh and Spirit, death and life. Fallen human nature, which is with us from birth to death, pulls in one direction, and the regenerated life in Christ, which extends from conversion to eternity, pulls even more powerfully in the other."

57 For select commentators who recognize the liminal nature of Rom. 6, see Fitzmyer, *Romans*, 434; Keck, *Romans*, 161–2; Jewett, *Romans*, 402; Hultgren, *Romans*, 247–8, Schmithals, *Römerbrief*, 188. Gignac, *Romains*, 247.

58 The decisiveness of Jesus' break with his past may be evoked in the language Mark uses to describe the baptismal event itself. The verb "tear" (σχίζειν: "he saw the heavens being torn apart [σχιζομένους]" [Mk. 1:10]), is unusual imagery to describe an epiphany in biblical narrative, a fact well recognized by commentators (e.g., Marcus, *Mark 1–8*, 166; Collins, *Mark*, 148; France, *Mark*, 77; Boring, *Mark*, 45; Klaiber, *Markusevangelium*, 26; Guelich, *Mark*, 32; Moloney, *Mark*, 36; Gnilka, *Markus*, 1.51–2). The revelation of the divine from the heavens is more often described using the verb "open" (ἀνοίγω). This is the case, for example, with Ezek. 1:1: "I was in the midst of a host of captives at the river Chorab and the heavens were opened [ἠνοίχθησαν οἱ οὐρανοί], and I saw visions of God [ὁράσεις θεοῦ]" (see also Gen. 7:11; Isa. 24:18; 63:19; Matt. 3:16; Lk. 3:21; Rev. 4:1). Because Mark's choice of this verb demonstrates that "heaven itself has drawn near, the barrier between it and earth has been ripped apart, [and] the power of the new age has begun to flood the earth" (Marcus, *Mark 1–8*, 166), it may well be that Mark envisions a horizontal dimension associated with this vertical inbreaking. Everything prior to this moment in Jesus' life ceases to have any significance as he enters into the period of his mission.

59 For a fuller discussion, see Chapter 1, Part VII.

3 The body and the blood

In the last chapter, I sought to demonstrate that Mark anticipates Pauline baptism within his story and bolsters its associated significances, namely Paul's insistence on the patterning of believers' lives on the life of Christ. In this chapter, I will demonstrate that the epiphanic performance of Christ's death (re)-presented in the Pauline Eucharistic meal also finds itself anticipated in Mark's story of the Last Supper, and, once again, Pauline significances are anticipated. This time, however, Mark does not focus on Christomorphic mimesis; rather, he picks up the theme of unity that Paul underscores in his rhetorical engagements with the rite.

As before, this chapter falls into three parts, and I begin with Paul. First, as an *episode* of Paul's gospel narrative (the meal "on the night on which he was handed over" [1 Cor. 11:23]), I will demonstrate the Eucharist is prospective. It looks towards the cross as an event that is subsequent to the historical meal, and it proleptically performs it through the breaking of the bread (Christ's body) and the pouring of the wine (Christ's blood). Second, as a *rite* celebrated within the Paul's church, it is on one hand a retrospective performance of Jesus' final meal and his death that follows it, and on the other a prospective anticipation of the second coming of the messiah (see 1 Cor. 11:26). Finally, I will show that, for Paul, it is through the consumption of the Eucharistic bread that believers acknowledge their membership in one body (into which they were incorporated through baptism [see Gal. 3:27–28]) and their subsequent equality in the eyes of the Lord (see 1 Cor. 10:16–17; 12:12–27).

Following my analysis of Paul, I turn to the Gospel of Mark. For the evangelist, the Lord's Supper is also a rite (Paschal dinner) that looks forward to and proleptically performs Jesus' death. Insofar as it alludes to Jesus' exalted status (see Mk. 14:25: "… until that day when I drink it anew in the kingdom of God"), it also evokes, by way of synecdoche, the whole gospel plot. At the same time, Mark employs the elements of the meal to underscore a broader argument for unity. Through his miraculous feeding narratives that take place within both Jewish (Mk. 6:30–44) and Gentile (Mk. 8:1–9) territory, Mark demonstrates that the body given up "for the many" (Mk. 10:45; see also Mk. 14:24) is distributed *to* the many, both Jew and Gentile alike. For Mark, then, bread-as-body functions as a symbol for the unification of the Jewish and Gentile missions.

Finally, I will argue that Mark deploys the Last Supper self-consciously to anticipate Paul. First, because the Eucharist is a timeless memorial rite for the death of Jesus Christ to which Paul attaches substantial ecclesiological significances, Mark threads references to the Eucharist into his text in order to anticipate and bolster those significances. Mark composes his story such that the bread that is given to the thousands (both Jews and Gentiles) evokes the language of the Last Supper—an episode that, for both Mark and Paul, performs Christ's death—and this, in turn, confirms for Mark's community that, when they consume Christ's body during their own celebrations of the Eucharist, they are acknowledging and affirming Paul's universal and unified community into which they have entered through Jesus' death upon the cross. In other words, I will demonstrate that, within his narrative of the earthly mission of Jesus, Mark seeks to draw out and underscore the universal significance of the Eucharist implicit in Paul's localized argument against factionalism in Corinth.

Second, I will compare the language of Mark's and Paul's Last Supper scenes. Throughout this monograph, in order to circumvent any inference that Mark anachronistically lifts Paul from his letters and throws him back into the past, I have avoided the term "incorporation" when describing Mark's etiological project. There is, however, a condition under which such language is appropriate: if an event occurring during the life of Christ is already, *for Paul*, an episode of the gospel narrative, Mark is free to incorporate it into his story. Because the Eucharist contains an *episode* of the gospel—the meal "on the night on which [Jesus] was handed over" (1 Cor. 11:23), which serves as the inaugural event of Paul's timelessly performed ritual—Mark includes that episode within his story. At the same time, I will suggest that Mark recognizes Paul's story of the Last Supper to be rhetorically and ritually contingent, and, as a result, he composes an idealized account that appears anterior to, and anticipatory of, the Eucharist that Paul presents.

Part I: The Eucharist in Paul

Paul's sustained engagement with the Eucharist occurs in his first letter to the Corinthians. At some point in the mid '50s C.E., the apostle learns by various reports (both oral and written) that his Corinthian community is plagued by factionalism and beginning to fracture. There is debate over apostolic allegiance (1 Cor. 1:12–17), disagreement about proper sexual activity and gender roles (1 Cor. 5:1–13; 7:1–16; 11:2–17), disregard for the weak and less educated (1 Cor. 8:7–13; 10:19–33), abuses of wealth (1 Cor. 11:17–22), hierarchization born from diversity in charismatic gifts (1 Cor. 12–14), and doubts about the nature of the resurrection (1 Cor. 15).[1] In the latter half of the letter, where issues of the community's "coming together" predominate (1 Cor. 11:2–14:4), Paul discusses the Eucharist, with the tradition he (re)produces functioning as a corrective to those celebrating the Lord's Supper (κυριακὸν δεῖπνον [1 Cor. 11:20]) without the remainder (and perhaps majority) of their brothers and sisters (see 1 Cor. 11:21–22).[2] At 1 Cor. 11:23–26, Paul tells the divided community the following story:

23. For I have received from the Lord that which I have handed on to you [Εγὼ γὰρ παρέλαβον ἀπὸ τοῦ κυρίου, ὃ καὶ παρέδωκα ὑμῖν]: that the Lord Jesus, on the night on which he was handed over [ἐν τῇ νυκτὶ ᾗ παρεδίδετο], took bread [ἔλαβεν ἄρτον] 24. and, once he had given thanks [εὐχαριστήσας], he broke it [ἔκλασεν] and said, "This is my body [Τοῦτό μού ἐστιν τὸ σῶμα], the one for you [τὸ ὑπὲρ ὑμῶν]. Do this in my memory [τοῦτο ποιεῖτε εἰς τὴν ἐμὴν ἀνάμνησιν]. 25. In the same way also [he did with] the cup [ὡσαύτως καὶ τὸ ποτήριον] after the dinner [μετὰ τὸ δειπνῆσαι], saying, "This cup is the new covenant in my blood [Τοῦτο τὸ ποτήριον ἡ καινὴ διαθήκη ἐστὶν ἐν τῷ ἐμῷ αἵματι]. Do this, as often as you drink, in my memory [τοῦτο ποιεῖτε, ὁσάκις ἐὰν πίνητε, εἰς τὴν ἐμὴν ἀνάμνησιν]. 26. For as often as you eat this bread and drink this cup, you proclaim the death of the Lord until he comes [τὸν θάνατον τοῦ κυρίου καταγγέλλετε, ἄχρις οὗ ἔλθῃ]."

The story Paul summarizes here is an episode of the gospel narrative he claims to have received "from the Lord" (ἀπὸ τοῦ κυρίου [1 Cor. 11:23]), and he maintains that it is a reproduction of the tradition with which the Corinthian community is already familiar ("I handed it over to you" [ὃ καὶ παρέδωκα ὑμῖν]). It is also a complex layering of perspectival orientations to the cross. On one hand, the story is retrospective. During the celebration of the Eucharist, Paul's community looks back, to "the night on which [Jesus] was handed over [ἐν τῇ νυκτὶ ᾗ παρεδίδετο]" (1 Cor. 11:23)—words which, when coupled with Paul's "on behalf of you" (τὸ ὑπὲρ ὑμῶν [1 Cor. 11:24]), echo Isaiah 53:12's suffering servant[3]—and, in its ritualized performance, the community (re)presents both Jesus' final meal and the cross, as it is there that the metaphorical "brokenness" of Jesus' body for the community is summoned, and the blood of the new covenant is shed (1 Cor. 11:24–25; see also Ex. 24:5–8; Jer. 38:31–32 LXX).[4]

On the other hand, this event is prospective and synecdochical. As an *episode* of the gospel narrative ("the night on which [Jesus] was handed over [ἐν τῇ νυκτὶ ᾗ παρεδίδετο]"), it proleptically performs the messiah's death ("This is my body, the one for you [τὸ ὑπὲρ ὑμῶν]" [1 Cor. 11:24]; "This cup is the new covenant *in my blood* [ἐν τῷ ἐμῷ αἵματι]" [1 Cor. 11:25]), and it looks forward to a future liturgical context in which the Last Supper is celebrated by a community of believers ("Do this in my memory [τοῦτο ποιεῖτε εἰς τὴν ἐμὴν ἀνάμνησιν]" [1 Cor. 11:24, 25]). At the same time, as a timeless *rite* celebrated by the Corinthian community, it looks forward to Christ's second coming ("For as often as you eat this bread and drink this cup, you proclaim the death of the Lord until he comes [ἄχρις οὗ ἔλθῃ]"). Thus, the *episode* proleptically performs Jesus' death through the breaking of his body and pouring out of his blood, and, via the memorialization of that death through the performance of the *rite*, the end of the gospel is synecdochically proclaimed. In the context of Paul's post-resurrection communities, the Last

Supper *qua* episode coalesces with the Eucharist *qua* rite, and Paul's synecdochical hermeneutic is operative at both the level of gospel story and the level of liturgical praxis.

In light of the complex perspectival orientations summarized above, and in anticipation of arguments to follow in this chapter, Paul's claim to reproduce a rite that the Corinthians already know ("that which I handed on to you [ὃ καὶ παρέδωκα ὑμῖν]" [1 Cor. 11:23]) must be investigated. There is reason to doubt the veracity of this declaration. It appears, for example, that Paul has separated the elements of the Eucharist. It is unlikely that the wine that is drunk "after the dinner" (μετὰ τὸ δειπνῆσαι [1 Cor. 11:25]) is a part of the tradition he or the Corinthians know. Rather, Paul separates the elements in order to force the community to gather and share the Eucharist together. As Mitchell has suggested, "Possibly to counter the π-ρολαμβάνειν of 11:21, Paul urges the order of the bread, meal, and cup with μετὰ τὸ δειπνῆσαι in the tradition (11:25) to end the separatism by the preliminary (not so) common meal."[5]

Similarly, there is reason to doubt the traditional nature of Paul's famous *anamnesis* formula, "Do this in my memory [τοῦτο ποιεῖτε εἰς τὴν ἐμὴν ἀνάμνησιν]" (1 Cor. 11:24, 25). Paul's key to solving the problem of the Corinthians' factionalism vis-à-vis communal meals *is* the call to remembrance. As David E. Garland explains,

> What is to be remembered, as far as Paul is concerned, is that the "crucified one" gave his body and sacrificed his blood in an expiatory death that brings the offer of salvation to all persons ... By partaking of the bread and the cup, [the Corinthians] recall that sacrifice and symbolically share in its benefits. This conscious imitation of the Last Supper expressed in this liturgical formula allows [Paul] to make his point forcefully; they are to imitate Christ's example of self-giving. Everything they do in their meal should accord with his self-sacrifice for others. They should be prepared to give of themselves and their resources for others.[6]

Garland emphasizes that the meal is the solemn commemoration of and identification with the death of Christ, and Paul's call to recollection reorients believers to a state of service and selflessness precisely in a setting in which these qualities are not being displayed (1 Cor. 11:21–22). To be sure, Garland takes the *anamnesis* formula to be a part of the tradition that Paul has received. Yet, given the rhetorical aptness of the call to remembrance as it occurs in 1 Corinthians, one suspects that Paul may here have expanded the tradition to fit the particular rhetorical needs of the moment.[7]

Finally and most controversially, there is reason to question the historicity of "new" in Paul's covenant (ἡ καινὴ διαθήκη [1 Cor. 11:25]). It is rhetorically expedient for Paul to underscore the "newness" of the covenant for his Corinthian believers, as the factionalist behavior within the church seems to be undermined by Jeremiah's prophecy itself. A few verses after the prophet's famous, "'Behold! Days are coming,' says the Lord, 'and I will establish [διαθήσομαι] in the house of

Israel and in the House of Judah a new covenant [διαθήκην καινήν]'" (Jer. 38:31 LXX [31:31 MT]), to which 1 Corinthians 11:25 alludes, Jeremiah prophesies what that new covenant will entail.[8] He says,

> Each one shall not teach his fellow citizen [οὐ μὴ διδάξωσιν ἕκαστος τὸν πολίτην αὐτοῦ], and each one [shall not teach] his brother [τὸν ἀδελφὸν αὐτοῦ], saying, 'Know the Lord [γνῶθι τὸν κύριον]' because all will know me [πάντες εἰδήσουσίν με], from their little to their big [ἀπὸ μικροῦ αὐτῶν καὶ ἕως μεγάλου αὐτῶν], because I will be merciful towards their injustices [ἵλεως ἔσομαι ταῖς ἀδικίαις αὐτῶν], and I shall remember their sins no more [ἁμαρτιῶν αὐτῶν οὐ μὴ μνησθῶ ἔτι] (Jer. 38:34 LXX).

It is possible that, through the synecdochical utilization of the καινή, Paul musters Jeremiah to aide in the battle against Corinthian factionalism, as the prophet's words could be taken as an indirect chastisement of the community's actions. At the end of 1 Corinthians 11, Paul diagnoses physical ailments within the community as being the result of a failure to "discern the body" (διακρίνων τὸ σῶμα) during the celebration of the Eucharist (see 1 Cor. 11:28–33). For Paul, the community's unequal participation in the rite is symptomatic of a failure to recognize who the Lord is and for what he stands, as the "body" of which Paul speaks refers both to the body of the Lord that is (re)presented in the Eucharist *and* to the community that has become Christ's "body" as a result of their individual baptisms (1 Cor. 12:12–13).[9] This failure has resulted in certain community members growing sick, and some have even died (1 Cor. 11:30, more on this below). Paul may therefore have added "new" to "covenant" (καινὴ διαθήκη) at 1 Corinthians 11:25 in order to evoke Jeremiah's larger prophecy and remind the community that they are all supposed to "know the Lord" (γνῶθι τὸν κύριον), something which their divisions during the Eucharist demonstrably controvert. They thus run the risk of invalidating Jeremiah's words and proving themselves unworthy of the new covenant to which the prophet bears witness, and, through the synecdochical utilization of the καινή, Paul warns them of this danger.

Importantly, none of the changes I have suggested are intrinsically unlikely. On one hand, "after supper" (μετὰ τὸ δειπνῆσαι [1 Cor. 11:25]) is so subtle that Paul could profess its presence in the tradition while simultaneously claiming its suspension during his missionary activity in the city of Corinth. The *anamnesis* formulae and reference to "new" covenant, on the other hand, draw out that which is already implied in the performance of the rite: the Eucharist is a memorial that makes present for the community the crucified messiah, and the covenant established through Christ's death is definitionally "new," as any covenant made between God and humanity posterior to Sinai would be. Thus, though certainty remains elusive, exegetes must be cautious about presuming that the tradition Paul "has received" (1 Cor. 11:23) is necessarily fixed in the apostle's mind.

Regardless of what one makes of the traditional nature of Paul's words, it is the case that, as with baptism, Paul presumes the performance of the Eucharist is epiphanic. An encounter with the deity is thought to occur via the consumption of Jesus' body and blood. Paul's shocking warning that immediately follows his narration of the Lord's Supper story attests to this:

> But let each man examine himself [δοκιμαζέτω δὲ ἄνθρωπος ἑαυτὸν], and then let him eat from the bread and drink from the cup. For the one eating and drinking eats and drinks judgment [κρίμα ἑαυτῷ] upon himself if he does not discern the body correctly [μὴ διακρίνων τὸ σῶμα]. For this reason, many amongst you are weak [ἀσθενεῖς] and with fever [ἄρρωστοι], and some number sleep [κοιμῶνται ἱκανοί] (1 Cor. 11:28–30).

Whatever Paul imagines occurring at the moment of its consumption, it is clear that partaking of the Eucharist unworthily results in spiritual reproach. If the community is not properly disposed, the bread and cup are not only able to make believers physically ill, but they also have the power to kill ("some number sleep [κοιμῶνται ἱκανοί]" [1 Cor. 11:30]). The rite that (re)presents Jesus' final meal, his death upon the cross, and proleptically looks toward and proclaims his second coming is infused with spiritual power. Because the Corinthians are acting in a fashion that is undeserving of the bread and wine, Paul claims that the spiritual energies contained within the elements are inflicting sickness and death upon them.[10]

Finally, I note that Paul's Eucharist is not limited to 1 Corinthians 11:17–34. Echoes of the rite are heard throughout the letter. For example, by evoking the oneness of the community created through the consumption of its elements (1 Cor. 10:16–17), Paul corrects community members who disregard the significance of meats sacrificed to idols (1 Cor. 10:19–33).[11] Similarly, he uses the Eucharist to bring low those spiritualists who have elevated themselves above their peers (1 Cor. 12–14), recalling for them their shared baptismal experience and the cup from which they drink, binding them all together as equals in the Lord (1 Cor. 12:12–13).[12]

For Paul, then, the Eucharist is the means by which believers affirm their bondedness: "Since there is one bread [εἷς ἄρτος], we, the many, are one body [ἓν σῶμα], because we have all partaken of that one bread [ἐκ τοῦ ἑνὸς ἄρτου μετέχομεν]" (1 Cor. 10:17). The one bread (ἄρτος [see 1 Cor. 11:23]) of which believers partake allows Paul to claim that there is one body in which all participate: "For just as the body is one [τὸ σῶμα ἕν ἐστιν] and has many members [μέλη πολλὰ ἔχει], and all the members of the body, though they are many, are one body [ἕν ἐστιν σῶμα], so too is Christ [οὕτως καὶ ὁ Χριστός]" (1 Cor. 12:12). Paul thus uses the Eucharist and its shared bread to uphold both variation and interconnectedness within the eschatological community. It is through the consumption of the bread and wine that believers acknowledge their incorporation into the one body of Jesus Christ. The specific role each plays within the body is (in theory) irrelevant for the purposes of status. Rather, all are essential to the proper functioning and identification of the body of the messiah (see 1 Cor. 12:14–27).[13]

To conclude: for Paul, the Eucharist is a flexible rite that is, first, a complex of perspectival orientations to the cross. As an *episode* of the gospel narrative, it is prospective: it proleptically performs Jesus' death and synecdochically evokes the remainder of the gospel narrative. As a timeless *rite* celebrated by the community, however, it is the retrospective performance of both the Last Supper and Jesus' death, and, through its performance, the gospel narrative, as a whole, is recalled and proclaimed (1 Cor. 11:26). Second, the Eucharist is the means by which believers the world over continuously affirm their incorporation into the body of Christ and the communal unity that exists (or should exist) as a result. Though the body may contain many members, because those members make up one body they are all equal in the eyes of the Lord (1 Cor. 10:17).

Part II: The Eucharist in Mark

The narrative context for the Last Supper in the Gospel of Mark is as follows: two days before Passover (Mk. 14:1), Jesus is anointed by an anonymous woman (Mk. 14:3–9), whose episode, together with that of the poor woman at the well (Mk. 12:41–44), frames Jesus' long eschatological discourse (Mk. 13). The anointing woman's actions are so exemplary that Jesus announces to his disciples, "Truly I say to you, wherever the gospel is proclaimed in the whole world [ὅπου ἐὰν κηρυχθῇ τὸ εὐαγγέλιον εἰς ὅλον τὸν κόσμον], what she has done will also be told in memory of her [εἰς μνημόσυνον αὐτῆς]" (Mk. 14:9).[14] The anointing woman's story is itself then framed by two narratives of wicked men: the plot by the chief priests and scribes to kill Jesus (Mk. 14:1–2), and Judas' agreement to "hand [Jesus] over to them" (αὐτὸν παραδοῖ αὐτοῖς [Mk. 14:10]) in exchange for silver (Mk. 14:10–11).[15] Mark then presents the events that occur on the eve of Passover itself (Mk. 14:12).[16] Jesus first predicts the location of his meal (Mk. 14:12–16), and later, as the disciples recline and eat the Passover supper (ἀνακειμένων αὐτῶν καὶ ἐσθιόντων [Mk. 14:18]), he prophesies the betrayal that must occur in accordance with the scriptures: "One of you will hand me over [εἷς ἐξ ὑμῶν παραδώσει με] … because the Son of Man departs just as it is written about him [καθὼς γέγραπται περὶ αὐτοῦ]" [Mk. 14:18, 21]).[17] After this troubling prediction, Mark presents his version of the Lord's Supper:

> 22. And while they were eating, [Jesus], after taking bread [λαβὼν ἄρτον], once he had blessed it [εὐλογήσας], he broke it [ἔκλασεν], and he gave it to them [ἔδωκεν αὐτοῖς], and he said [καὶ εἶπεν], "Take, this is my body [τοῦτό ἐστιν τὸ σῶμά μου]." 23. And after taking the cup [λαβὼν ποτήριον], once he had given thanks [εὐχαριστήσας], he gave it to them, and they all drank from it. 24. And he said to them, "This is my blood of the covenant [Τοῦτό ἐστιν τὸ αἷμά μου τῆς διαθήκης], that which is poured out on behalf of many [ὑπὲρ πολλῶν]. 25. Truly I say to you that I shall not ever drink from the fruit of the vine until that day when I drink it anew in the Kingdom of God [ἕως τῆς ἡμέρας ἐκείνης ὅταν αὐτὸ πίνω καινὸν ἐν τῇ βασιλείᾳ τοῦ θεοῦ] (Mk 14:22–25).

Mark's story of the Last Supper is a prospective one; it points forward to and performs Jesus' death, and it synecdochically evokes the gospel episodes that follow. The broken bread (Mk. 14:22) (re)presents Jesus' broken body. The wine (Mk. 14:24) (re)presents his shed blood that establishes a new covenant upon the model of the old (see Ex. 24:5–8, esp. 24:8: "Behold! The blood of the covenant" [ἰδοὺ τὸ αἷμα τῆς διαθήκης]). "On behalf of the many" (ὑπὲρ πολλῶν [Mk. 14:24]), when coupled with the language of Mark 14:18 and 21 ("will hand over [παραδώσει] … as it is written [καθὼς γέγραπται]"), proleptically fulfills the prophecy of Isaiah 53:12, where the suffering servant is said to be handed over (παρεδόθη) for the sake of the people's sins (διὰ τὰς ἁμαρτίας).[18] Finally, the "Kingdom of God" evokes the gospel's end and the final consummation of the world.[19] Though scripture serves as the typological backdrop for the majority of Mark's words, it witnesses authoritatively to that which has *yet* to occur, and it forces Mark's audience to look ahead to the cross and beyond.

The Last Supper is also utilized by the evangelist for missionary purposes. Within the first few chapters, Mark introduces the idea of a universal mission (Mk. 3:7–8),[20] and, before the narrative's end, the audience is informed that the global proclamation of the gospel is an essential part of the unfolding salvation-historical story (Mk. 13:10; see also 7:24–30). Indeed, the borderless mission of Jesus is consistently (and paradoxically) represented *within* the borders of Palestine in Mark's narrative. *Pace* Papias (apud Eusebius, *H.E.* 3.39.15), Jesus' disparate travels are not the result of disordered traditions about the messiah;[21] rather, they are the consistent and self-conscious literary (re)presentation of Christ's global undertaking, and Mark signals this by means of subtle, but extremely important, internal narrative clues.[22] The phrase "to the other side" (εἰς τὸ πέραν [Mk. 4:35; 5:21; 6:45; 8:13]), for example, serves as a boundary marker, delineating Jesus' activity in Jewish and then Gentile territory on the western and eastern sides of the sea of Galilee. During his activity on one "side" or the other, contextual elements within the setting signal for Mark's audience the ethnicity of the recipients of the proclamation. For example, after traveling from Capernaum (for this location, comp. Mk. 2:1, 13 with Mk. 4:1) "to the other side" (εἰς τὸ πέραν [Mk. 4:35]), Mark twice makes it clear that the exorcism of the Gerasene demoniac occurs in Gentile territory. First, the healing takes place in, and the demoniac subsequently proclaims what Jesus has done to, the Decapolis (Mk. 5:1, 20), a center of Greek culture in Palestine.[23] Second, he tells his audience that "there was a great herd of pigs [ἀγέλη χοίρων μεγάλη] feeding next to the mountain" (Mk. 5:11), which one would not expect to find in Jewish territory. Despite the subtlety of Mark's clues, however, the universality of Jesus' mission is methodically (re)presented.[24] If a Jewish demoniac is exercised (Mk. 1:23–28), so too is one on "the other side" (Mk. 5:1–13); if a healing occurs amongst the Jews (Mk. 1:29–30), it will not be long until such occurs amongst Gentiles (Mk. 7:31–37); if a daughter is restored to her Jewish father (Mk. 5:35–43), a daughter will be restored to her Gentile mother (Mk. 7:24–30); and, if thousands are fed on one shore (Mk. 6:35–44), thousands will be sated on its opposite (Mk 8:1–9). Importantly, these types of messianic demonstrations are always witnessed by the Jew *first* (πρῶτον [see Mk. 7:27]).

Thus, by the time Mark's audience hears Jesus' proclamation at Mark 13:10—"And it is necessary [δεῖ] that the gospel be proclaimed first amongst all the nations [εἰς πάντα τὰ ἔθνη]"—they are well prepared for it. The eschatological work of Christ is not confined within a geographical territory or delineated along particular ethnic lines. The inclusion of the nations is a fundamental and thoroughgoing element in the salvation-historical narrative.[25] It is enacted in Christ's ministry, written upon his lips, and, ultimately, effected from the cross.

In the service of this mission, Mark employs the language of the Last Supper. After the episode with the Gerasene demoniac (Mk. 5:1–20), Jesus goes back "to the other side" (εἰς τὸ πέραν [Mk. 5:21]), back to Jewish territory. The change in ethnic focus is signaled for Mark's audience by the synagogue leader who immediately solicits Jesus for aid (Mk. 5:21–23, 35–43) and then by Jesus' return to his "homeland" (εἰς τὴν πατρίδα [Mk. 6:1], presumably Nazareth [see Mk. 1:9]). After Jesus' unsuccessful missionary activity there (Mk. 6:2–6), and the sending of the twelve in which is intercalated the death of John the Baptist (6:7–13, 14–29, 30–32), Jesus and his disciples take a boat "to a deserted place" (εἰς ἔρημον τόπον [Mk. 6:32]. Importantly, Jesus and his disciples do not travel "to the other side" [εἰς τὸ πέραν] at this moment). This is the context for Jesus' first feeding narrative, a story replete with Jewish themes.[26] The crowds that follow Jesus are made to sit down, and the messiah, "after taking the five loaves [λαβὼν τοὺς πέντε ἄρτους] and two fish, and having looked up into heaven, blessed [εὐλόγησεν] and broke the loaves [κατέκλασεν τοὺς ἄρτους], and he gave them to his disciples [ἐδίδου τοῖς μαθηταῖς] to set before them [ἵνα παρατιθῶσιν αὐτοῖς]" (Mk. 6:41). This language closely parallels Mark's description of Jesus' action vis-à-vis the bread in the Last Supper: "After taking bread [λαβὼν ἄρτον], once he had blessed it [εὐλογήσας], he broke it [ἔκλασεν], and he gave it to them [ἔδωκεν αὐτοῖς]" (Mk. 14:22). In both the Last Supper and the first feeding miracle, Jesus "takes" bread (λαβὼν τοὺς πέντε ἄρτους/λαβὼν ἄρτον), "blesses" it (εὐλόγησεν/εὐλογήσας), "breaks" it (κατέκλασεν/ἔκλασεν), and he distributes it to his disciples (ἐδίδου τοῖς μαθηταῖς/ἔδωκεν αὐτοῖς). The one scene clearly intends to recall the other.

The second miraculous feeding occurs at Mark 8:1–8, this time in Gentile territory. Immediately prior to the episode, Jesus encounters the Syro-Phoenician woman in Tyre (Mk. 7:24–30). From there, in perhaps his most convoluted geographical expedition, Jesus heads north, passing through Sidon (διὰ Σιδῶνος), to get to the sea of Galilee among the districts of the Decapolis (εἰς τὴν θάλασσαν τῆς Γαλιλαίας ἀνὰ μέσον τῶν ὁρίων Δεκαπόλεως [Mk. 7:31]). Jesus has, in other words, gone straight north, then east, and then south in order to go south east. As a historical journey, this itinerary makes no sense. That said, Mark's concern is not historical but literary. His goal is to make it clear that the second feeding occurs in Gentile territory by piling up geographical references to Gentile locations.[27] Seeing the crowd's hunger (Mk. 8:2–3), Jesus asks them to recline, "and after taking the seven loaves [λαβὼν τοὺς ἑπτὰ ἄρτους], once he had given thanks [εὐχαριστήσας], he broke them [ἔκλασεν] and gave them to his disciples [ἐδίδου τοῖς μαθηταῖς] to set them out [ἵνα παρατιθῶσιν]"

(Mk. 8:6). Again, the resonances with Mark's Last Supper are obvious: Jesus "takes" bread (λαβὼν τοὺς ἑπτὰ ἄρτους/λαβὼν ἄρτον), "gives thanks" (εὐχαρι-στήσας [see Mk. 14:23]), "breaks" it (ἔκλασεν), and he distributes it to his disciples (ἐδίδου τοῖς μαθηταῖς/ἔδωκεν αὐτοῖς). The one notable variation is Jesus' "giving thanks" (εὐχαριστήσας) over the bread, which is the action he performs over the cup during his final meal with the disciples (Mk. 14:23). It is possible that Mark is self-consciously evoking the second element of the Eucharist via his poetics of synecdoche here. By combining the first element of the Last Supper with the thanksgiving over the second, he simultaneously brings to his audience's mind both. That said, one should be cautious about reading too much significance into this divergence, as "blessing" and "giving thanks" are interchangeable ritualized actions in an ancient meal context,[28] and the logic of Mark's theological poetics does not require that the cup come into view explicitly. If Mark's lexical variation is deliberate, it is likely because he seeks to emphasize the connection, but this assumption is not necessary. By evoking the Eucharistic bread, the cup is brought along with it.

Mark's Last Supper thus demonstrates narratively the universality of Jesus' mission. When Jesus speaks of his death as a "ransom for the many" (λύτρον ἀντὶ πολλῶν [Mk. 10:45]), the feeding miracles help to show that the "many" includes both Jews and Gentiles. This is precisely what the disciples do not understand at Mark 8:14–21.[29] Jesus' notice about the leaven of the Pharisees and the leaven of Herod (βλέπετε ἀπὸ τῆς ζύμης τῶν Φαρισαίων καὶ τῆς ζύμης Ἡρῴδου [Mk. 8:15]) serves as a warning against misconceptions about the messiah's authority, in this case his authority vis-à-vis matters of halakhic exclusivity. Jesus' words, together with his questioning of the hardness of the disciples' hearts ("do you have a hardened heart [πεπωρωμένην … τὴν καρδίαν]?" [Mk. 8:17]), evoke the words of Mark 3:1–6 (see also Mk. 6:52), where the Pharisees keep watch over Jesus to see if he will heal a man with a withered hand on the Sabbath (Mk. 3:1–2). There, when Jesus asks, "is it permitted to do good or ill on the Sabbath?" (ἔξεστιν τοῖς σάββασιν ἀγαθὸν ποιῆσαι ἢ κακοποιῆσαι [Mk. 3:4]), he receives no answer, and, "grieving at the hardness of their hearts [ἐπὶ τῇ πωρώσει τῆς καρδίας αὐτῶν]" (Mk. 3:5), Jesus proceeds to effect the healing. The Markan audience is then informed that "the Pharisees [οἱ Φαρισαῖοι] immediately begin taking counsel with the Herodians [μετὰ τῶν Ἡρῳδιανῶν] as to how they could destroy him [ὅπως αὐτὸν ἀπολέσωσιν]" (Mk. 3:6). Mark 3:1–6 thus anticipates Mark 8:14–21. The attenuation of rigid halakhic observation creates space for Gentile inclusion, and Jesus' warning to the disciples at Mark 8:15 is a call to reject the sort of obstinate adherence of which the Pharisees are exemplary and the Herodians enforcers.[30] The bread that the disciples have brought with them (singular, like the bread of the Last Supper [see Mk. 14:22]) is sufficient for all. This is what the multiplication of the loaves and the leftover fragments demonstrate.

To conclude: the Markan account of the Last Supper is a prospective performance of the death of Jesus Christ occurring in a ritual context (the Passover meal) that synecdochically evokes the remainder of the whole gospel story (it looks ahead to the full realization of the Kingdom of God [Mk. 14:25]). At the same time, Mark deploys the elements of the Eucharist as symbols for unity. The language of Jesus' final meal is utilized by Mark in his miraculous feedings to embody narratively the mission to the Gentiles that Jesus says must (δεῖ) occur before the final consummation of the world (Mk. 13:10). In the next section, I will argue that Mark has found precedent for deploying the elements of the Eucharist in the way that he has in Paul, and he does so not only to reinforce Paul's argument against factionalism, but to underscore the equality of the Jewish and Gentile missions that Paul so adamantly maintains.

Part III: Anticipating the Eucharist of Paul

In this section, I will suggest that Mark has crafted his narrative in order to anticipate Paul. On one hand, Mark deploys the elements of the Eucharist in the service of an argument for unity. Building upon Paul's reasoning in 1 Corinthians, Mark underscores the universality implicit in Paul's context-specific argument against factionalism and reinforces Paul's claims for the equality of a mission to both Jews and Gentiles.

On the other hand, Mark crafts his account of the institution of the rite itself to appear both concordant with, and anterior to, Paul's. Because Mark assumes Paul's words to be as much a summary of the tradition as they are a (re)presentation of it, he attempts to compose an idealized version of the story from which that summary might seem to derive. In other words, Mark perceives that Paul's Eucharist is rhetorically contingent, and he deliberately presents a Last Supper that appears to be older and more stable, as a result.

First, Mark's story, as a whole, is the literary anticipation of Paul's vision: "the gospel [τὸ εὐαγγέλιον] … is the power of God for salvation to all those who believe [παντὶ τῷ πιστεύοντι], to the Jew first and also to the Greek [Ἰουδαίῳ τε πρῶτον καὶ Ἕλληνι]" (Rom. 1:16; see also Rom. 2:9–10).[31] Throughout the narrative, Jesus performs miracles, preaches, and symbolically (re)presents his sacrificial death to the Jew first and then to the Gentile. Mark thus agrees with Paul that there is one universal mission with two coequal branches (Jew and Gentile), and he seeds both into his narrative through the missionary activity of the earthly Christ. Mark's using the "oneness" of the Eucharistic bread (Mk. 14:22: ἄρτος [sg.]; Mk. 8:14: εἷς ἄρτος) as the primary metaphor for justifying this mission not only creates a historical precedent for Paul's universalism, it does so in thoroughly Pauline fashion. For Paul, through the consumption of the Eucharist, believers acknowledge and reaffirm their unity within the one body of Jesus Christ into which they have all been baptized: "Since there is one bread [εἷς ἄρτος], we, the many, are one body [ἓν σῶμα], because we have all partaken of that one bread [ἐκ τοῦ ἑνὸς ἄρτου μετέχομεν] (1 Cor. 10:17; see also 1 Cor. 12:12–13). Though Paul only mentions the bread of the Eucharist in 1 Corinthians, the unifying significance of the rite most probably extends beyond the factionalist situation in Corinth (compare, for example, the language of 1 Cor. 10:17 with Rom. 12:5). Recognizing this, Mark attempts to draw out the broader significance embedded within Paul's rhetorically contingent argument, and, by narrativizing Pauline Eucharistic unity within a story about the earthly mission of Christ, the evangelist anticipates and reinforces Paul's position vis-à-vis the memorial rite. The (universal) unity that comes through the consumption of Christ's body for Paul now finds historical precedent in Jesus' miraculous feeding miracles during his earthly life.

Second, Mark has crafted his Last Supper to appear anterior to the Last Supper tradition as represented in Paul. Scholars regularly presume that the New Testament presents two streams of Eucharistic tradition: Mark's (and Matthew's [Mk. 14:22–25; Matt. 26:26–29]) on one hand, and Paul's (and Luke's [1 Cor. 11:23–26; Lk. 22:17–20]) on the other.[32] This division is based upon observed linguistic, theological, and ritualistic differences between the two accounts, though there is continued scholarly debate as to which of the two streams is to be considered the older or more "authentic" representation of the final meal of Jesus Christ.[33] If one starts from a presupposition that Mark knows Paul and is familiar with the contextual nature of Paul's argument in 1 Corinthians, however, a new possible reconstruction opens up, one in which there is a single Last Supper tradition reflected and adapted within the New Testament: the tradition that is presented by Paul at 1 Corinthians 11:23–26.

That Mark might be aware of the context-specific nature of Paul's argument in 1 Corinthians is not as improbable as it may, at first, appear. At the turn of the second century C.E., Clement of Rome already recognizes 1 Corinthians as a contextual argument against factionalism, and he appeals to it in his own letter to undermine the infighting he sees occurring within the Corinthian church of his day. He writes:

> 1. Take up the epistle of the blessed Paul the apostle [τὴν ἐπιστολὴν τοῦ μακαρίου Παύλου τοῦ ἀποστόλου]! 2. What did he first write (πρῶτον ... ἔγραψεν] to you in the beginning of the gospel? 3. Truly, he instructed [ἐπέστειλεν] you spiritually about himself and Cephas and Apollo [περὶ ἑαυτοῦ τε καὶ Κηφᾶ τε καὶ Ἀπολλώ], because even then [καὶ τότε] you had become factional [προσκλίσεις ὑμᾶς πεποιῆσθαι]. 4. But that factionalism [ἡ πρόσκλισις ἐκείνη] had brought upon you less sin, for you had become factionalized [προσεκλίθητε] over esteemed apostles and a man who was approved by them [ἀποστόλοις μεμαρτυρημένοις καὶ ἀνδρὶ δεδοκιμασμένῳ παρ' αὐτοῖς]. But now think about who has disturbed you and tarnished the reputation of your renowned love for others![34]

Clement's words here show familiarity with the contents of 1 Corinthians (comp. 1 Cor. 1:12–13; 3:4–9), which suggests that he possesses a copy of the letter, and his invitation to his addressees to pick up the epistle presumes the Corinthians' possession of it, as well. More important, Clement's use of aorist verbs ("he wrote" [ἔγραψεν]; "he instructed [by letter]"; [ἐπέστειλεν]; "you became factionalized" [προσεκλίθητε]; etc.), coupled with the adverbial phrase "even then" (καὶ τότε) and the far demonstrative adjective "that" (ἐκείνη) in "that factionalism" (ἡ πρόσκλισις ἐκείνη), demonstrates that the bishop was aware of earlier problems that had plagued the Corinthian community. Though, for Clement, Paul's status as "blessed" (μακάριος) confers upon his instruction a universal and transtemporal significance, it is nevertheless clear that the bishop is also cognizant of that instruction's rootedness in a particular historical moment. Indeed, Clement leverages that rootedness in order to magnify the shame of the Corinthians: however misguided it may have been, at least the factionalism of the Corinthians "back then" stemmed from a pious devotion to apostolic founders; now, however, they are in full-scale revolt against church authority "on account of one or two persons" (δι᾽ ἓν ἢ δύο πρόσωπα [1 Clem. 47.6; see also 1 Clem. 44.1–6]).

If Clement, at the end of the first or beginning of the second century, had a sense of the ecclesiological problems in Corinth in the mid '50's C.E., there is no reason to suppose that Mark (who was writing some decades earlier) did not, as well. This recognition has important implications for how one understands Mark's treatment of Paul's Lord's Supper "tradition," especially when it is remembered that Eucharistic celebrations were not fixed in the first or early second centuries. The Didache, for example, a handbook of early Christian teaching generally thought to have been compiled in the late decades of the first or early decades of the of the second century C.E., presents a very different version of the Eucharistic meal—one that begins with the cup and contains virtually no emphasis on Christ's death—than does Paul or the synoptic gospels.[35] More important, the later synoptic gospels themselves, which are literarily *dependent* upon Mark, present different versions of the same event. Luke, for example, combines Mark's text with Paul's Eucharist to create a literary hybrid between the two.[36] The changes wrought by Matthew, a "tradition-oriented author" who reproduces all but four pericopes of Mark and follows his narrative sequence from chapter 12 onwards,[37] are even more telling. In his account, Matthew adds an additional imperatival command to Jesus' words over the bread: "Take, *eat*" (λάβετε φάγετε [Matt. 26:26]; comp. Mk. 14:22), and he turns Mark's description of the disciples' action vis-à-vis the cup—"and they all drank from it" (καὶ ἔπιον ἐξ αὐτοῦ πάντες [Mk. 14:23])—into a command on the lips of Jesus: "Drink from it, all of you" (πίετε ἐξ αὐτοῦ πάντες [Matt. 26:27]). He inserts "for the many" (περὶ πολλῶν) between the definite article and participle "poured out" (τὸ περὶ πολλῶν ἐκχυννόμενον) rather than after it (comp. Mk. 14:24: τὸ ἐκχυννόμενον ὑπὲρ πολλῶν). He adds the explanatory "for the forgiveness of sins" [εἰς ἄφεσιν ἁμαρτιῶν [Matt. 26:28]) after Jesus' words over the cup, and, finally, he adds "with you" (μεθ᾽ ὑμῶν [Matt. 26:29]) to Jesus' prophecy of the eschatological banquet. Though minor, these changes indicate that even a staunch traditionalist like Matthew does not consider Jesus' actions and words over the bread and cup to be linguistically fixed, and, if a "tradition-oriented author" can make such adaptations, there is no reason to suppose that Mark is not capable of doing the same with the material from which he works. Thus, if it can be demonstrated that divergences in Mark's Eucharist from the Pauline account are not changes that undermine but support Paul's positions, the possible dependence

Table 3.1   1 Corinthians 11:23–26 and Mark 14:22–25

1 Corinthians 11:23–26	*Mark 14:22–25*
23. For I have received from the Lord that which I have handed on to you: that the Lord Jesus, on the night in which he was handed over, **took bread** [ἔλαβεν ἄρτον] 24. **and,** *once he had given thanks* [εὐχαρι στήσας], **he broke it and said** [ἔκλασεν καὶ εἶπεν] "This is my body [Τοῦτό μού ἐστιν τὸ σῶμα], the one for you [τὸ ὑπὲρ ὑμῶν]. Do this in my memory." 25. *In the same way also [he did with] the cup* [ὡσαύτως καὶ τὸ ποτήριον] after the dinner, saying, "This cup is the new covenant in my blood [Τοῦτο τὸ ποτήριον ἡ καινὴ διαθήκη ἐστὶν ἐν τῷ ἐμῷ αἵματι]. Do this, as often as you drink, in my memory. 26. For as often as you eat this bread and drink this cup, you proclaim the death of the Lord until he comes."	22. And while they were eating, [Jesus], **after taking bread** [λαβὼν ἄρτον], **once he had blessed it** [εὐλογήσας], **he broke it** [ἔκλασεν], and he gave it to them, **and he said** [καὶ εἶπεν], "Take, this is my body [τοῦτό ἐστιν τὸ σῶμά μου]." 23. And *after taking the cup* [λαβὼν ποτήριον], *once he had given thanks* [εὐχαριστήσας], he gave it to them, and they all drank from it. 24. And he said to them, "This is my blood of the covenant [Τοῦτό ἐστιν τὸ αἷμά μου τῆς διαθήκης], that which is poured out on behalf of the many [ὑπὲρ πολλῶν]. 25. Truly I say to you that I shall not ever drink from the fruit of the vine until that day when I drink it anew in the Kingdom of God."
23. Ἐγὼ γὰρ παρέλαβον ἀπὸ τοῦ κυρίου, ὃ καὶ παρέδωκα ὑμῖν, ὅτι ὁ κύριος Ἰησοῦς ἐν τῇ νυκτὶ ᾗ παρεδίδετο **ἔλαβεν ἄρτον** 24. καὶ *εὐχαριστήσας* **ἔκλασεν καὶ εἶπεν,** Τοῦτό μού ἐστιν τὸ σῶμα τὸ ὑπὲρ ὑμῶν· τοῦτο ποιεῖτε εἰς τὴν ἐμὴν ἀνάμνησιν. 25. ὡσαύτως καὶ τὸ ποτήριον μετὰ τὸ δειπνῆσαι, λέγων, Τοῦτο τὸ ποτήριον ἡ καινὴ διαθήκη ἐστὶν ἐν τῷ ἐμῷ αἵματι· τοῦτο ποιεῖτε, ὁσάκις ἐὰν πίνητε, εἰς τὴν ἐμὴν ἀνάμνησιν. 26. ὁσάκις γὰρ ἐὰν ἐσθίητε τὸν ἄρτον τοῦτον καὶ τὸ ποτήριον πίνητε, τὸν θάνατον τοῦ κυρίου καταγγέλλετε, ἄχρις οὗ ἔλθῃ.	22. Καὶ ἐσθιόντων αὐτῶν **λαβὼν ἄρτον εὐλογήσας ἔκλασεν** καὶ ἔδωκεν αὐτοῖς **καὶ εἶπεν,** Λάβετε, τοῦτό ἐστιν τὸ σῶμά μου. 23. καὶ λαβὼν ποτήριον εὐχαριστήσας ἔδωκεν αὐτοῖς, καὶ ἔπιον ἐξ αὐτοῦ πάντες. 24. καὶ εἶπεν αὐτοῖς, Τοῦτό ἐστιν τὸ αἷμά μου τῆς διαθήκης τὸ ἐκ χυννόμενον ὑπὲρ πολλῶν· 25. ἀμὴν λέγω ὑμῖν ὅτι οὐκέτι οὐ μὴ πίω ἐκ τοῦ γενήματος τῆς ἀμπέλου ἕως τῆς ἡμέρας ἐκείνης ὅταν αὐτὸ πίνω καινὸν ἐν τῇ βασιλείᾳ τοῦ θεοῦ.

of the one author upon the other should not be dismissed on the grounds of linguistic deviation.

In order to demonstrate my thesis, a sustained linguistic investigation into the Lord's Suppers of Mark and Paul is necessary. By way of introduction to my comparative analysis, then, I here set the accounts side by side and highlight their relevant overlaps through typographical emphases (Table 3.1).

In terms of lexical and syntactical parallelism, there are striking points of contact between the two Lord's Suppers. First is the boldfaced type: "He took bread and, once he had given thanks, he broke it and said …" (ἔλαβεν ἄρτον καὶ εὐχ αριστήσας ἔκλασεν καὶ εἶπεν [1 Cor. 11:23]), and "after taking bread, once he had blessed it, he broke it … and said …" (λαβὼν ἄρτον εὐλογήσας ἔκλασεν … καὶ εἶπεν [Mk. 14:22]). The phrases use the same verb (λαμβάνω), placed in the aorist tense, with the same accusative object, ἄρτον, which comes after the verb in both instances. There is then an interchangeable aorist participle of prayer (offered before meals [εὐχαριστήσας/εὐλογήσας]) modifying the ἄρτον, ἔκλασεν with the object ἄρτον ellipsed, and finally an introduction to direct speech with καὶ εἶπεν. The only significant difference between the phrases is Mark's insertion of "and he gave it to them ..." (καὶ ἔδωκεν αὐτοῖς) and Paul's use of καὶ linking ἄρτον with the thanksgiving.

Second, the bold underlined "This is my body" (Τοῦτό μού ἐστιν τὸ σῶμα [1 Cor. 11:24]) and "this is my body" (τοῦτό ἐστιν τὸ σῶμά μου [Mk. 14:22]) mirror each other almost exactly. The only variation is the placement of the μού. Whereas it comes at the beginning of Jesus' quoted speech in Paul, it comes at the end of Jesus' words in Mark. Nevertheless, the object upon which both depend (τὸ σῶμα) is the same.

Third, the italicized words read as follows: "Once he had given thanks ... In the same way also [he did with] the cup ..." (εὐχαριστήσας... ὡσαύτως καὶ τὸ ποτήριον [1 Cor. 11:25]) and "after taking the cup, once he had given thanks ..." (λαβὼν ποτήριον εὐχαριστήσας [Mk. 14:23]). If the ὡσαύτως ("in like manner") of 1 Corinthians 11:25 is understood to have its logical meaning of "in the same way," then Paul imagines a close parallelism in Jesus' *actions* over bread and cup, just as Mark narrates.[38] Mark writes at Mark 14:22: "after taking the bread, once he had blessed it, he broke it and gave it to them," (λαβὼν ἄρτον εὐλογήσας ἔκλασεν καὶ ἔδωκεν αὐτοῖς). At Mark 14:23, he writes, "After taking the cup, once he had given thanks, he gave it to them" (λαβὼν ποτήριον εὐχαριστήσας ἔδωκεν αὐτοῖς). With the exception of a single καὶ and ἔκλασεν (which one cannot do with a cup) the syntax used of Jesus' actions is exactly the same (aorist participle of λαμβάνω, accusative object, interchangeable aorist participles of mealtime prayers, aorist indicative of δίδωμι, and the dative plural, αὐτοῖς).[39] What Paul describes as happening in shorthand form by means of the correlative ὡσαύτως, Mark tells in full. For the sake of visual clarity, I have written out the (hypothetical) words of Paul's ὡσαύτως and I set them side by side with Mark (Table 3.2).

The apostle uses a single adverb, ὡσαύτως, to evoke a complete recitation of actions he has just narrated, and Mark, perceiving this rhetorical maneuver, reads the ὡσαύτως literally. Thus, with only minimal modifications to Paul's bread formulation, Mark narrates in full Paul's assumed actions over the cup.

Fourth, one finds the double underlined, "This cup is the new covenant in my blood" (Τοῦτο τὸ ποτήριον ἡ καινὴ διαθήκη ἐστὶν ἐν τῷ ἐμῷ αἵματι [1 Cor. 11:25]), and "This is my blood of the covenant" (Τοῦτό ἐστιν τὸ αἷμά μου τῆς διαθήκης [Mk. 14:24]). For the moment, it is enough to note that these

Table 3.2 1 Corinthians 11:23–24 and Mark 14:22–23

1 Corinthians 11:23–24	Mark 14:22–23
ἔλαβεν ἄρτον καὶ εὐχαριστήσας ἔκλασεν καὶ εἶπεν ...	λαβὼν ἄρτον εὐλογήσας ἔκλασεν καὶ ἔδωκεν αὐτοῖς καὶ εἶπεν ...
ἔλαβεν τὸ ποτήριον [μετὰ τὸ δειπνῆσαι] καὶ εὐχαριστήσας εἶπεν ...	λαβὼν ποτήριον εὐχαριστήσας ἔδωκεν αὐτοῖς ... καὶ εἶπεν αὐτοῖς ...

phrases contain many of the same lexemes (Τοῦτο, διαθήκη, εἰμί, ἐγώ, αἷμά). Though the verses also present substantial verbal and syntactical variation, I will argue below that these variations can similarly be explained by Paul's use of ὡσαύτως and Mark's literal reading of it.

Fifth and finally, both 1 Corinthians 11:24 and Mark 14:24 utilize "on behalf of" (ὑπέρ) plus a genitive plural to describe the salvific nature of Christ's death. Jesus has given his life "on behalf of" others. For both Mark and Paul, the climactic effects of the entire salvation-historical drama are condensed within and synecdochically evoked through a single prepositional phrase.

To be sure, for all the linguistic similarities between Mark's and Paul's Lord's Suppers, there are also some notable discrepancies. The most important divergences are the following: Paul's using a second person plural, ὑμῶν ("you" [1 Cor. 11:24]), instead of Mark's πολλῶν ("the many" [Mk. 14:24]) and his affixing "on behalf of you" (τὸ ὑπὲρ ὑμῶν) to the bread instead of the cup (1 Cor. 11:24); Paul's *anamnesis* formulae (1 Cor. 11:24, 25); his cup being drunk *after* the meal (μετὰ τὸ δειπνῆσαι [1 Cor. 11:25]); the lexical variation between Mk. 14:24 and 1 Cor. 11:25, particularly Paul's cup being that of the *new* covenant (ἡ καινὴ διαθήκη [1 Cor. 11:25]); and, finally, Paul's "proclaiming the death of the Lord until he comes" (τὸν θάνατον τοῦ κυρίου καταγγέλλετε, ἄχρις οὗ ἔλθῃ [1 Cor. 11:26]), which is nowhere found in Mark.[40] I will analyze each of these divergences in turn.

First, there is no significant conceptual difference between Paul's "on behalf of you" (ὑπὲρ ὑμῶν [1 Cor. 11:24]) and Mark's "on behalf of the many" (ὑπὲρ πολλῶν [Mk. 14:24]). Though the objects differ, the lack of a second person plural personal pronoun is not unexpected in the context of the Markan narrative. Whereas Paul is speaking explicitly to individuals circumscribed within a geographically delineated community (albeit with universal significance still in view), Mark's language at Mark 14:24 is self-consciously formulated to embrace more than those disciples present at the Last Supper in Jerusalem, and it therefore evokes Christ's words at Mark 10:45 and the broadly redemptive significance contained therein: "For the Son of Man did not come to be served but to serve and to give his life as a ransom *for many* [ἀντὶ πολλῶν]."[41] Moreover, both Mark and Paul are referentially equivalent. As noted in Part I of this chapter, there is good reason to believe that 1 Corinthians 11:23–24 ("handed over ... 'for you'" [παρεδίδετο ... ὑπὲρ ὑμῶν]) evokes Isaiah 53:12's "he was handed over for the sake of their sins" (διὰ τὰς ἁμαρτίας αὐτῶν παρεδόθη). Paul's Eucharist thus calls to mind the same prophetic text as Mark 14:24.[42] Through the synecdochical evocation Isaiah's suffering servant, both Mark and Paul express the universal significance of Christ's death in the Last Supper.

Second, there is the transposition of Mark's ὑπὲρ πολλῶν, placed after the cup (Mk. 14:24) instead of after the bread (1 Cor. 11:24). Mark here makes a simple correction. For both the evangelist and apostle, Christ's *blood* is the covenant sacrifice ("the new covenant [ἡ καινὴ διαθήκη] in my blood [ἐν τῷ ἐμῷ αἵματι]" [1 Cor. 11:25]; "my blood [τὸ αἷμά μου] of the covenant [τῆς διαθήκης]" [Mk. 14:24]), and each uses language evocative of Exodus 24:8 to express this.[43] In placing "for the many" (ὑπὲρ πολλῶν [Mk. 14:24]) after the cup, Mark accomplishes two things: first, "for the many" is now associated with that element of the Eucharist that establishes a covenant "for the many" in the biblical narrative. It is not the body of the sacrificial animals that seals God's covenant with the Israelite people (ὁ λαός [Ex. 24:7]); it is the blood.[44] Second, the change allows Mark to expand the parallelism of action over bread and cup that he perceives in Paul's ὡσαύτως. It now includes the words, as well. It is only after Jesus blesses, distributes, and says "this is my body/blood" (τοῦτό ἐστιν τὸ αἷμά/τὸ σῶμά μου [Mk. 14:22, 24]) that Mark expands the words of institution with additional explication (more on this below).[45]

Paul's *anamnesis* formula, "do this in remembrance of me (τοῦτο ποιεῖτε εἰς τὴν ἐμὴν ἀνάμνησιν [1 Cor. 11:24, 25]), is not found in Mark because the evangelist does not take it to be narratively appropriate to the story that he tells. He presumes (rightly, in my judgment) that Paul has inserted the calls to remembrance into his Eucharist for the purposes of his argument. Paul's *anamnesis* formulae contain the critically important τοῦτο ποιεῖτε ("do this" [1 Cor. 11:24, 25]), words signaling a timeless institution, directed to celebrants presuming the repeated consumption of Christ's body and blood with full retrospective knowledge of its salvific significance.[46] As I argued above, the historical event that is "the night on which he was handed over" (ἐν τῇ νυκτὶ ᾗ παρεδίδετο [1 Cor. 11:23])—an *episode* of the gospel narrative that, for Paul, looks towards the cross—is simultaneously a timeless *rite* celebrated by the community that looks back to and recalls Jesus' death. Paul's retrospective and prospective perspectives on the Eucharist thus overlap and blend together, and Paul capitalizes on this temporal fusion by inserting the call to remembrance to underscore for the Corinthian community that the factionalism they manifest contrasts starkly with the humility and self-sacrifice of Jesus. Because Mark's text is synecdochical, and it anticipates and evokes later Pauline rituals rather than repeats them, he is unwilling to collapse the distance between the historical and liturgical events. Mark's inserting an *anamnesis* formula into his story of the Last Supper would be anachronistic and unnecessary. At the level of Mark's audience, the memorial quality of the Lord's Supper—indeed, of the gospel as a whole[47]—is recognized irrespective of an appeal to treat it as such. Mark's narrative thus assumes the eventual memorialization of the Last Supper, but the evangelist leaves it to the apostle to make the connection explicit.

Relatedly, Mark interprets Paul's sharing of the cup "after dinner" (μετὰ τὸ δειπνῆσαι [1 Cor. 11:25]), which results in the elements of the Eucharist being split over the course of the meal, as another apostolic innovation resulting from the factionalist situation at Corinth. Because he does not take the Pauline structure to be normative, Mark includes the breaking of bread and the sharing of the cup *during* Passover supper ("and *while* they were eating [καὶ ἐσθιόντων αὐτῶν] ..." [Mk. 14:22]). As one might expect, in a story presenting the rite's inauguration, Mark shows events unfolding in their idealized form: the original Lord's Supper was not divided; it took place amongst equals at a shared meal (indeed, even Judas is included in the sharing [Mk. 14:18–21; cf. Matt. 26:25, where Judas is singled out for ironic identification [σὺ εἶπας]).

On the problem of linguistic and syntactical deviation between Mark 14:24 and 1 Corinthians 11:25, Paul's ὡσαύτως is again explanatory. As noted, Mark finds warrant for creating parallel *actions* over the elements of the Eucharist through Paul's use of the adverb. Seeing as it is demonstrably not the case that Paul's Jesus does anything "ὡσαύτως" vis-à-vis his *words* over cup and bread, however,[48] Mark corrects and composes the perfectly balanced "this is my body" (τοῦτό ἐστιν τὸ σῶμά μου [Mk. 14:22]) and "this is my blood" (τοῦτό ἐστιν τὸ αἷμά μου [Mk. 14:24]). Instead of drawing explicit attention to the timeless rite *as such* ("do this in remembrance of me") within a historical narrative that purports to provide its etiology, Mark cues the reader to its future legacy by using balanced and (possibly) liturgical language.[49] This change has the added benefit of clarifying Paul's account. What the apostle means by marking "cup" (τὸ ποτήριον) as the new covenant "in my blood" ("This cup is [ἐστιν] the new covenant [ἡ καινὴ διαθήκη] in my blood [ἐν τῷ ἐμῷ αἵματι]" [1 Cor. 11:25]) is now clear: it is not the cup itself that symbolizes the covenant; it is the blood which rests inside ("This is my blood of the covenant [τὸ αἷμά μου τῆς διαθήκης]" [Mk. 14:24]).[50]

Regarding Paul's "new" covenant (ἡ καινὴ διαθήκη [1 Cor. 11:25]), I have already suggested that there is reason to believe it to be another Pauline modification of the tradition. Should it belong to the tradition Paul knows, however, it is nevertheless the case that any covenant established between humanity and God via the medium of Christ assumes newness and need not be stated. Mark 14:24's "my blood of the covenant" (τὸ αἷμά μου τῆς διαθήκης) may lack the word, but, as R. T. France points out,

> It is impossible to draw out that symbolism implied by the echo of Ex. 24:8 without using such language [as καινή] and thus bringing to mind the prophecy of a new covenant in Jer. 31:31–34 [Jer. 38:31–34 LXX], and it seems likely that both Jesus and Mark would have understood Jesus' conventional language in that light.[51]

Thus, Mark's Last Supper looks towards the cross, and he presumes his audience will recognize the newness of the covenant established through the blood that is shed there. Explicit designation of it as such is unnecessary.

Finally, Paul's statement at 1 Corinthians 11:26—"For as often as you eat this bread and drink this cup, you proclaim the death of the Lord [τὸν θάνατον τοῦ κυρίου καταγγέλλετε] until he comes [ἄχρι οὗ ἔλθη]"—requires comment. The explanatory γάρ and the movement from Christ speaking in the first person (1 Cor. 11:24–25) to his being spoken about in the third (1 Cor. 11:26) signals a change in speaker.[52] Paul here resumes his teaching, unpacking the significance of the Eucharist and evoking, by way of synecdoche ("you proclaim the *death* of the lord [τὸν θάνατον τοῦ κυρίου]"), the gospel narrative in which all Corinthians have come to hope and believe.

Because the voice of the epistolary Paul is resumed at 1 Corinthians 11:26, its omission in Mark is unsurprising. That said, Paul's "until he comes" (ἄχρις οὗ ἔλθη) is noteworthy. The language is plainly eschatological, as many commentators have noted.[53] It can be compared fruitfully with the eschatological prediction Jesus makes at the end of the Markan Last Supper: "Truly I say to you that I shall not ever drink from the fruit of the vine until that day [ἕως τῆς ἡμέρας ἐκείνης] when I drink it anew in the Kingdom of God [ἐν τῇ βασιλείᾳ τοῦ θεοῦ]" (Mk. 14:25). This phrase imagines the full inbreaking of the messianic kingdom. "Kingdom of God" (ἡ βασιλεία τοῦ θεοῦ) is a Markan synecdochical designator: it looks towards the conclusion of the gospel narrative, and it is a shorthand form for the final intervention of God in human history (see, for example, Mk. 1:15; 9:1).[54] Only *after* the second coming and the establishment of divine sovereignty will Jesus taste the fruit of the vine once more. Jesus' words are thus conceptually similar to Paul's.[55] Both the evangelist and apostle close their Lord's Suppers with a clear look to the end, synecdochically evoking not only the death of Christ, but the very last episodes of the gospel narrative: the second coming of the messiah and the final consummation of the world.[56]

My argument for the linguistic differences in Mark's and Paul's Lord's Suppers may now be summarized. I suggest, first, that Mark presumes that Paul has presented a Eucharist to his Corinthian community that is flexible and rhetorically contingent. The evangelist thus incorporates into his own story the tradition Paul references (the night "on which [Jesus] was handed over" [1 Cor. 11:23]), but he feels free to adapt it, presenting an idealized version of the story from which the Pauline tradition might seem to derive. There is, therefore, significant overlap in the two accounts: both contain parallel actions over bread and cup, both take the Eucharistic elements to be (re)presentations the sacrifice of Christ "for the many," both pattern the establishment of the (new) covenant on Exodus 24:3–11, and both presume that, through the performance of the rite, the end of the gospel is synecdochically recalled. At the same time, however, anything that Mark takes to be a secondary modification by Paul in the service of his argument against factionalism is either excised or adapted: The *anamnesis* formulae and Paul's explicit designation of the covenant as "new" are cut, the bread and cup are brought together instead of being split, Jesus' words—like his actions—over the elements are balanced, and the significance of the blood as that which establishes the new covenant on the pattern of the old is brought forth. The cumulative effect of these changes is the transformation of the "tradition" Paul hands on to the Corinthians into a paraphrase.[57] Mark wants his audience to recognize that the original Last Supper differed from Paul's presentation of it, but Paul's account nevertheless remains fully concordant with that original scene. I suggested in Part I of this chapter that Paul adds to the tradition "after dinner" (μετὰ τὸ δειπνῆσαι [1 Cor. 11:25]), the *anamnesis* formulae (1 Cor. 11:24, 25), and "new" (καινή [1 Cor. 11:25]), all of which are inserted to bolster the apostle's argument for concord. One might now add to this list Paul's "on behalf of you" (ὑπὲρ ὑμῶν [1 Cor. 11:24]), placed after the bread instead of the cup. Mark may have understood this to be another means by which Paul accentuates his argument for unity. Just as the *anamnesis* formulae underscore Jesus' self-abasement and serve as a foil to the Corinthians' factionalist behavior, so too does attaching "on behalf of you" to the Eucharist's first element. The body of which all partake, and in which all participate, is the same body that is humbly given up for the sake of all.[58]

To conclude: I have argued, first, that Mark has drawn out the universality implicit within Paul's argument. The consumption of Christ's body and blood within the Corinthian church signifies, for Paul, the community's affirmation that they have been baptized into and are now members of one body, that of Jesus Christ. Mark takes the cup and bread and uses it in an argument for universal unity, the unity of the missions to Jews and Gentiles. By making this change, Paul's Gentile mission is anticipated and justified within Mark's gospel, and Paul's rhetorical tactic of using the Eucharist as a symbol for unity now has historical precedent.

Second, I have sought to show that the Last Supper scenes presented in Paul and Mark are, despite linguistic and syntactical variation, concordant. By the end of the first century, 1 Corinthians was already recognized as a highly context-specific argument against factionalism (Clement of Rome), and verbal discrepancies between Eucharist accounts cannot be taken as *a priori* evidence for different traditions, as there are discrepancies amongst Eucharists even when the texts are dependent upon one another (Matthew and Luke on Mark). Mark could thus be fully aware of Paul's Eucharist "tradition" in 1 Corinthians 11:23–26 and still adapt it for reasons of his own. In the service of presenting a Last Supper that appears to be idealized and from which Paul's might seem to derive, I suggest that Mark has modified Paul's story. That which he takes to be essential he keeps, and that which is unnecessary or anachronistic he excises. The cumulative effect of these changes is to create the impression that Paul's words at 1 Corinthians 11:23–26 are not to be read as a (re)presentation of the Last Supper; instead, they are to be taken as a rhetorically determined paraphrase of it.

Excursus: the cup of blessing and the cup of wrath

I have shown in the analysis that Mark and Paul employ the bread of the Eucharist as a symbol for unity. The cup functions similarly for both authors, but it is never given the same attention as is Christ's body-as-bread, particularly in the Gospel of Mark. The reason for Mark's omission is likely due to his interest in telling the story of how Paul's "cup of blessing" (τὸ ποτήριον τῆς εὐλογίας [1 Cor. 10:16]) was once the biblical "cup of wrath" (ποτήριον τοῦ θυμοῦ [see Isa. 51:17]) that has been transformed through Jesus' death upon the cross. Because Mark's primary goal in presenting this transformation is not to bolster Paul's argument for (universal) unity (though it does not contradict it), I present my reading of the materials here.

At 1 Corinthians 10:16a, Paul asks, "the cup of blessing [τὸ ποτήριον τῆς εὐλογίας] that we bless, is it not fellowship [κοινωνία] with the blood of Christ?" Though Paul does not explain what "fellowship" (κοινωνία) means (contrast with 1 Cor. 10:16b–17, where Paul first speaks of the fellowship [κοινωνία] that occurs through the breaking of the bread, and then he explains that that fellowship is rooted in the oneness of the bread), it is probable that Paul has in mind a biblical passage like Psalm 115:3–4 LXX (Ps. 116:12–13 MT): "What can I give back [ἀνταποδώσω] to the Lord for all those things [περὶ πάντων ὧν] he has given back to me [ἀνταπέδωκέν μοι]? I shall take the cup of salvation [ποτήριον σωτηρίου], and I shall call upon the name of the Lord!"[59] The cup, for Paul, underscores the shared means by which believers remember Christ's death and affirm the salvation that has come to them through it.

A little later in the same letter, Paul says, "For with one Spirit [ἐν ἑνὶ πνεύματι] we all [ἡμεῖς πάντες] have been baptized [ἐβαπτίσθημεν] into one body [εἰς ἓν σῶμα], whether Jew or Greek, slave or free, and we all have been given to drink [ἐποτίσθημεν] one Spirit [ἓν πνεῦμα]" (1 Cor. 12:13). I previously suggested that Paul evokes the Eucharistic cup through the language of "drinking" the Spirit (πάντες ἓν πνεῦμα ἐποτίσθημεν [see also 1 Cor. 10:2–4]).[60] This creates an association between Eucharist and baptism, where the Spirit also features prominently (ἐν ἑνὶ πνεύματι ἡμεῖς πάντες … ἐβαπτίσθημεν). Within Paul's larger argument for concord, then, the cup points forward to the salvation that all believers will attain as a result of Christ's death, and it points back to the baptismal ritual that (re)presents that death and incorporates believers into the body of their messiah.

In the Gospel of Mark, the evangelist also uses the cup to evoke baptism. He makes an overt connection between the two at Mark 10:38 ("Are you able to drink the cup [τὸ ποτήριον] which I drink, or [are you able] to be baptized [βαπτισθῆ-ναι] with the baptism [τὸ βάπτισμα] with which I am baptized [βαπτίζομαι]?"), and he makes an implicit one at Mark 14:36 ("Abba [αββα], Father, all things are possible for you. Take this cup [τὸ ποτήριον τοῦτο] from me").[61] For Mark, cup and baptism point forward to Jesus' impending suffering and death. In the same way that Jesus' baptism proleptically enacts God's judgment,[62] the cup is the proleptic enactment of God's wrath.[63] It recalls a biblical passage like Isaiah 51:17: "Wake up! Wake up! Arise, Jerusalem, you who drinks the cup of wrath [ποτήριον τοῦ θυμοῦ] from the hand of the Lord. For you drink from the cup of calamity [τὸ ποτήριον … τῆς πτώσεως], the goblet of wrath [κόνδυ τοῦ θυμοῦ], and you emptied [it] out [ἐξεκένωσας]." Jesus' death upon the cross is here represented by Mark as the outpouring of God's anger and judgment upon the messiah who has willingly elected to suffer vicariously for the many.

But how does one get from the image of a "cup of wrath" in Mark to the "cup of blessing" (τὸ ποτήριον τῆς εὐλογίας) in Paul? I suggest that Mark is familiar with both cups, and he attempts to show how the one has been transformed into the other. Just as Jesus' baptism (Mk 1:9–11) proleptically anticipates Jesus' taking upon himself the floods of judgment, and, through his death upon the cross, the significance of the rite is transformed, so too does Jesus drink the cup of wrath at his death, and its contents are changed thereby. Through Jesus' self-sacrifice, that which once represented a curse has become its opposite, and, in partaking of the cup, believers acknowledge their blessed state through the (re)performance of the event that created it. To the degree that recognizing the roots of Paul's "cup of blessing" bolsters arguments for concord, Mark's story about the cup could be taken to be in the service of them. That said, I suspect Mark's primary goal is not in bolstering Pauline arguments for unity *per se*. Rather, he seeks to create historical precedent for a reference with obscure origins.

Conclusion

In this chapter, I have explored the Eucharists of Mark and Paul, both their perspectival orientations to the cross and the language they use in their Last Supper scenes and beyond. I have sought to show that Paul's Eucharist is, on one hand, a ritual (re)performance of the cross that is a complex blending of perspectives. As an *episode* of the gospel narrative (the night "on which [Jesus] was handed over"), the scene prospectively performs Jesus' impending crucifixion. As a *rite* that is a timeless memorial and (re)presentation of Jesus' death that looks towards his second coming (1 Cor. 11:26), the Eucharist is primarily retrospective—it looks back to and performs Jesus' final meal and the cross. Regardless of the perspective, however, the Eucharist remains synecdochical: through the performance of one episode, the rest of the narrative is recalled within the mind of the reader, and an epiphanic encounter with the deity is thought to occur as a result.

On the other hand, Mark's Last Supper is, by virtue of being a narrative set during the earthly life of Christ, prospective. It is the proleptic performance of the cross that synecdochically evokes the conclusion of the gospel narrative through Jesus' prophecy of the eschatological banquet (Mk. 14:25). Once again, the performance of the scene would invite Mark's audience to recall the entirety of the gospel narrative, one that extends well beyond Mark's 16 chapters and, as is the thesis of this monograph, numbers Paul and his mission amongst its essential episodes.

Thus, Mark has once again taken one of Paul's performances of the death of Christ and seeded it into his narrative. For Paul, the Eucharist ritually affirms the incorporation of all believers into the body of Jesus Christ. Mark recognizes this significance, and he employs the Last Supper to underscore Paul's larger theological and ecclesiological project: the inclusion of the Gentile nations within salvation history as a result of the death of Christ. Regarding the language of the Eucharist, Mark has, rightly to my mind, recognized that Paul does not present at 1 Corinthians 11:23–26 a word-for-word recitation of the rite he first presented to the Corinthians. Instead, Paul has rhetorically adapted the ritual. This allows Mark significant freedom in his incorporation of it, and he composes an idealized account from which Paul's language can be thought to derive.

Notes

1 For a concise introduction to 1 Corinthians and the various challenges Paul finds himself facing in this letter, see Jerome Murphy-O'Connor, "1 and 2 Corinthians," in Dunn, *Cambridge Companion*, 75–83. For longer introductions, see Thiselton, *Corinthians*, 1–52 and Fitzmyer, *Corinthians*, 19–91. For a discussion of the compositional unity of 1 Corinthians and the rhetorical tactics Paul employs against the Corinthians' various forms of factionalist behavior, see Mitchell, *Rhetoric of Reconciliation*, 184–295.

2 On 1 Cor. 11:2–14:4 as a rhetorical unit, see Mitchell, *Rhetoric of Reconciliation*, 258–60. For discussion of the causes of division at the celebration of the Eucharist, see Jerome Murphy-O'Connor, *St. Paul's Corinth: Texts and Archaeology* (GNS

6; Wilmington: Glazier, 1983), 153–61; Gerd Theissen, *The Social Setting of Pauline Christianity: Essays on Corinth* (trans. J.H. Schütz; Philadelphia: Fortress, 1982), 145–74; Wayne A. Meeks, *The First Urban Christians: The Social World of the Apostle Paul* (2nd edn.; New Haven: Yale University Press, 2003), 67–8; Ben Witherington III, *Conflict & Community in Corinth: A Socio-Rhetorical Commentary on 1 and 2 Corinthians* (Grand Rapids: Eerdmans, 1995), 247–9. For a more recent analysis and comprehensive survey of the available evidence and exegetical arguments, see Barry D. Smith, "The Problem with the Observance of the Lord's Supper in the Corinthian Church," *BBR* 20.4 (2010), 517–44.

3 Isa. 53:12 reads as follows: "For this reason he will inherit many and he will divide the spoils of the strong because [ἀνθ' ὧν] his life [ἡ ψυχὴ αὐτοῦ] was handed over [παρεδόθη] unto death, and he was reckoned amongst the lawless [ἐν τοῖς ἀνόμοις ἐλογίσθη]. And he himself took up [ἀνήνεγκεν] the sins of many [ἁμαρτίας πολλῶν], and, for the sake of their sins [διὰ τὰς ἁμαρτίας], he was handed over [παρεδόθη]." I will discuss Paul's use of the suffering servant in more detail in Chapter 4, Part I(A). For now, however, it is sufficient to note that the apostle's use of "handed over" (παρεδίδετο) with agent unexpressed (a divine passive?) at 1 Cor. 11:23 echoes the servant's being handed over (παρεδόθη), and Paul's description of Jesus' death "for you" (ὑπὲρ ὑμῶν) at 1 Cor. 11:24 is likely a conceptual parallel to the servant's taking up "the sins of the many" (ἁμαρτίας πολλῶν). For discussion, see Witherington III, *Conflict & Community*, 250; Thiselton, *Corinthians*, 877; Fitzmyer, *Corinthians*, 436, 440; Richard B. Hays, *First Corinthians* (Interpretation; Louisville: John Knox, 1997), 198.

4 Regardless of the normality of a thanksgiving for and breaking of the bread before the Jewish Passover meal (see Fitzmyer, *Corinthians*, 436–7), I am in agreement with the assessment of Hays, *Corinthians*, 199–200: "The proclamation of the Lord's death occurs not just in preaching that accompanies the meal; rather, the community's sharing in the broken bread and the outpoured wine is itself an act of proclamation, an enacted parable that figures forth the death of Jesus 'for us' and the community's common participation in the benefits of that death". For Paul, the actions of breaking bread and pouring wine have additional significances. They (re)present the crucifixion of Jesus Christ for the community.

5 Mitchell, *Rhetoric of Reconciliation*, 265; see also Smith ("Lord's Supper," 528–32), who makes a sustained and largely convincing argument for this position.

6 Garland, *1 Corinthians*, 548; see also Fitzmyer, *Corinthians*, 440–1; Thiselton, *Corinthians*, 880–2.

7 This is the conclusion of William Whallon, "The Pascha in the Eucharist," *NTS* 40 (1994), 130–1. Fitzmyer adopts a moderate position. He believes that Paul's initial call to remembrance (1 Cor. 11:24) likely predates the apostle (though it still "may represent a secondary feature in the early tradition" [*Corinthians*, 440]), but he also suggests that, when one gets to the *anamnesis* formula in 1 Cor. 11:25, "More than likely, Paul is responsible for the repetition of the memento directive in this verse, and the sense in which he understands it is expressed in v. 26" (*Corinthians*, 444).

8 On Jeremiah's prophecy standing in the background of Paul's Eucharist, see Fitzmyer, *Corinthians*, 442–4.

9 See Klauck, *1 Korintherbrief*, 84.

10 A reading supported by numerous commentators. See, for example, Fitzmyer, *Corinthians*, 446–8; Raymond F. Collins, *First Corinthians* (SP 7; Collegeville: Liturgical Press, 1999) 435–41; Hans-Josef Klauck, *Herrenmahl und hellenistischer Kult: Eine religionsgeschichtliche Untersuchung zum ersten Korintherbrief* (Münster: Aschendorff, 1982), 323–9, esp. 327; Bruce J. Malina and John J. Pilch, *Social Science Commentary on the Letters of Paul* (Minneapolis: Fortress, 2006), 111; Witherington III, *Conflict & Community*, 252; Richard A. Horsley, *1 Corinthians* (ANTC; Nashville: Abingdon, 1991), 162–3.

11 For more detailed discussion, see Mitchell, *Rhetoric of Reconciliation*, 142, 254–6; Witheringon III, *Conflict and Community*, 224–6; Collins, *Corinthians*, 379–80; Ciampa and Rosner, *Corinthians*, 476; Craig S. Keener, *1–2 Corinthians* (NCBC; New York: Cambridge University Press, 2005), 87–8; Lietzmann, *An die Korinther* (HNT 9; Tubingen: J.C.B. Mohr [Paul Siebeck], 1969), 48; Fitzmyer, *Corinthians*, 391–2.

12 "For in one spirit [ἐν ἑνὶ πνεύματι] we all have been baptized into one body [εἰς ἓν σῶμα], whether Jew or Greek, slave or free, and we all have been given to drink [ἐποτίσθημεν] one Spirit [ἓν πνεῦμα]" (1 Cor. 12:13). Admittedly, there is debate regarding the relationship of these words to the Eucharist. Collins (*Corinthians*, 458), makes a connection explicit: "A twofold reference to the 'one Spirit' links baptism and eucharist to the charisms about which he had written in 12:4–11." More often, however, commentators see an implicit linkage. See, for example, Keener, *1–2 Corinthians*, 103; Lietzmann, *Korinther*, 63; Conzelmann, *1 Corinthians*, 212 n. 17; Klauck, *1 Korintherbrief*, 89; Horsley, *Corinthians*, 171; cf. Ciampa and Rosner, *Corinthians*, 591–2. The connection is generally drawn through Paul's negative analogy at 1 Cor. 10:1–4, where the Israelites are all "baptized into Moses," (εἰς τὸν Μωϋσῆν ἐβαπτί-σθησαν [1 Cor. 10:2]), consume the same spiritual bread (τὸ αὐτὸ πνευματικὸν βρῶμα [1 Cor. 10:3]), and drink the same spiritual drink (τὸ αὐτὸ πνευματικὸν … πόμα [1 Cor. 10:4]). In these verses, one sees baptism, spiritual food, and spiritual drink all linked, and this binds them thematically to 1 Cor. 12:13 (for further discussion of 1 Cor. 10:1–4, see Mitchell, *Rhetoric of Reconciliation*, 138 and 252–4; Fitzmyer, *Corinthians*, 379–80; Conzelmann, *1 Corinthians*, 165–7; Klauck, *1 Korintherbrief*, 70–1). That "spiritual food" and "spiritual drink" should be connected to the Eucharist is confirmed by the Didache, where "spiritual food" and "spiritual drink" are synonymous with its elements: "You, almighty Lord, have established all things for the sake of your name [ἕνεκεν τοῦ ὀνόματός σου], and you gave food and drink for the sons of men for enjoyment, in order that they might give thanks to you [σοι εὐχαριστήσωσιν]. And you gifted us [ἡμῖν ἐχαρίσω] spiritual food and drink [πνευματικὴν τροφὴν καὶ ποτόν] for eternal life through Jesus, your Son [εἰς ζωὴν αἰώνιον διὰ Ἰησοῦ τοῦ παιδός σου]" ([Didache 10:3]). Thus, it is probable that Paul's "we all have been given to drink [ἐποτίσθημεν] one Spirit [ἓν πνεῦμα]" (1 Cor. 12:13) evokes the Eucharistic cup, as "drinking the Spirit" is here combined with baptism, which evokes 1 Cor. 10:1–4, and 1 Cor. 10:1–4 serves as a negative analogy to the baptisms and Eucharists celebrated in Corinth.

13 For discussion of these verses and their importance in Paul's argument against factionalism, see Mitchell, *Rhetoric of Reconciliation*, 157–64.

14 These words are, of course, famously ironic, as a person who is afforded no name in Mark's gospel is also the person whose actions will be remembered eternally.

15 See Elizabeth Struthers Malbon, "The Major Importance of the Minor Characters in Mark," in eadem, *In the Company of Jesus*, 215–21 (repr. from *The New Literary Criticism and the New Testament* [eds. Elizabeth Struthers Malbon and Edgar V. McKnight; Sheffield: Sheffield University Press, 1994], 58–86) for a concise and helpful summary of this pericope.

16 Literally: "on the first day of unleavened bread [τῇ πρώτῃ ἡμέρᾳ τῶν ἀζύμων], when they sacrifice the Passover [ὅτε τὸ πάσχα ἔθυον]." There is a calendrical difficulty here that I will discuss in more detail in Chapter 4, Part II(C).

17 See Moloney, *Mark*, 282: "There is a paradoxical connection between Judas' action and God's design; the passion predictions have already said that Jesus *must* (δεῖ, 8:31) be handed over (παραδίδοται, 9:31; παραδοθήσεται, 10:33)."

18 For scholars who note an allusion to Isa. 53 in Mk 14:24, see Collins, *Mark*, 657; Standaert, *Marc*, 3.1010; France, *Mark*, 570; Moloney, *Mark*, 286 n. 52; Lane, *Mark*, 507; Eckey, *Markusevangelium*, 453; Marcus, *Mark 8–16*, 958; Gnilka, *Markus*, 2.245–6; Stein, *Mark*, 652. It is also often pointed out that Mk 14:24 recalls Mark's mission statement at 10:45: "For the Son of Man did not come to be served but to serve and

to give his life [δοῦναι τὴν ψυχὴν] as a ransom for the many [ἀντὶ πολλῶν]" (see e.g., Collins, *Mark*, 656–7; Donahue and Harrington, *Mark*, 396; C. S. Mann, *Mark* [AB 27; New York: Doubleday, 1986], 416–20; France, *Mark*, 570–1; Moloney, *Mark*, 285–6; Lane, *Mark*, 507; Eckey, *Markusevangelium*, 453; Dom Benoît Standaert, *Évangelie selon Marc: Commentaire* [3 vols.; ÉBib 61; Pendé: J. Gabalda, 2010], 3.1010–11; Robert H. Stein, *Mark* [BECNT; Grand Rapids: Baker Academic, 2008], 652; Focant, *Marc*, 527; Schenke, *Markusevangelium*, 320; Gnilka, *Markus*, 2.245–6). I will discuss the overlap in more detail in Chapter 4, Part II(A), but it is worth noting here that Mk 10:45 bears a remarkable conceptual similarity to Isaiah 53:12's "because [ἀνθ᾽ ὧν] his life [ἡ ψυχὴ αὐτοῦ] was handed over [παρεδόθη] unto death … and he took up the sins of the many [ἁμαρτίας πολλῶν]." This overlap strengthens, albeit indirectly, the connection between Mk. 14:24 and Isa. 53.

19 On the eschatology of the phrase ἡ βασιλεία τοῦ θεοῦ, see Collins, *Mark*, 154-5.

20 "A great crowd from Galilee [ἀπὸ τῆς Γαλιλαίας] and from Judea [ἀπὸ τῆς Ἰουδαίας] [followed], and from Jerusalem [ἀπὸ Ἱεροσολύμων] and from Idumea [ἀπὸ τῆς Ἰδουμαίας], and from across the Jordan [πέραν τοῦ Ἰορδάνου] and [from] around Tyre and Sidon [περὶ Τύρον καὶ Σιδῶνα] a great multitude, having heard all that he was doing [ἀκούοντες ὅσα ἐποίει] came to him." On the universality of these various locations, see Moloney, *Mark*, 75, France, *Mark*, 154.

21 Papias famously attempts to justify Mark's apparent disorder as follows: "Because Mark had become an interpreter of Peter [ἑρμηνευτὴς Πέτρου], as many things as he remembered, he recorded accurately [ἀκριβῶς], yet the things said or done by the Lord are not in order [οὐ … τάξει]. For [Mark] neither heard the Lord nor followed him, but later, as I said, he [followed] Peter, who composed his teachings [ἐποιεῖτο τὰς διδασκαλίας] for particular needs [πρὸς τὰς χρείας] but who did not compose them as an ordered account of the Lord's discourses [σύνταξιν τῶν κυριακῶν … λογίων], with the result that Mark has not erred at all [οὐδὲν ἥμαρτεν] in so writing some things as he remembered them. For he had forethought for one thing only: that he not leave off any of the things which he heard or falsify anything in them."

22 On Jesus' various journeys to both Jews and Gentiles, see Rhoads et al., *Mark as Story*, 66–9; Malbon, "How does the Story Mean?" 42–54. Moloney, *Mark*, 13; James R. Edwards, *The Gospel According to Mark* (PNTC; Leicester: Apollos, 2002), 18; Marcus, *Mark 1-8*, 21, 260–1, 335.

23 See Malbon, "Narrative Criticism," 25–6. On the Decapolis, see Donahue and Harrington, *Mark*, 168; Guelich, *Mark*, 286.

24 Some contextual clues are less subtle than others. For example, in the regions of Tyre and Sidon at Mk. 7:26, Mark explicitly narrates a Gentile healing: "The woman was Greek [ἡ δὲ γυνὴ ἦν Ἑλληνίς], a Syro-Phoenician by birth [Συροφοινίκισσα τῷ γένει]."

25 The articulation of Klaiber, *Markusevangelium*, 250 is apt: "Bevor [das Ende und die Zeichen] hereinbrechen werden, muss *zuerst* das Evangelium allen Völkern verkündigt werden. Dieses *muss* steht parallel zu der Aussage von v. 7. Nicht nur die Krise der menschlichen Gemeinschaft, sondern auch die Verkündigung des Evangeliums an alle Menschen gehört zu den Dingen, die nach Gottes Plan geschehen müssen und geschehen werden" (emphasis original). See also, Eckey, *Markusevangelium*, 421–2; Focant, *Marc*, 489–90; Marcus, *Mark 8–16*, 883, 886; Collins; *Mark*, 606–7.

26 Moloney, *Mark*, 146 notes the following: "the desert location (vv. 31, 35), the shepherd [Ps. 23:1] (v. 34), the sitting in companies (vv. 39–40 [reflecting the companies on the march in the desert at Ex. 18:21–5; Num. 31:14; Deut. 1:15]), connections with Ps. 23 (vv. 34, 39, 42), bread in the desert (v. 41), and the collection of the fragments into twelve baskets (v. 43)" (See also, Guelich, *Mark*, 343–4).

27 Additionally, though there is no obvious scriptural allusion that introduces this feeding miracle as there was in the previous feeding episode (see Mk. 6:34: "And [Jesus] took pity on them, because they were as sheep without a shepherd

[ὡς πρόβατα μὴ ἔχοντα ποιμένα]" [comp. Nu. 27:17: ὡσεὶ πρόβατα οἷς οὐκ
ἔστιν ποιμήν; see also Jdth. 11:19]), some commentators have suggested that, in
Jesus' statement, "Some of them have come from far away [ἀπὸ μακρόθεν ἥκασιν]"
(Mk. 8:3), Mark evokes a passage like Isa. 60:3–4: "And kings [βασιλεῖς] will go to
your light [τῷ φωτί σου] and nations [ἔθνη] to your brilliance [τῇ λαμπρότητί
σου]. Lift your eyes round about [ἆρον κύκλῳ τοὺς ὀφθαλμούς] and behold
your children having been gathered together [συνηγμένα τὰ τέκνα σου]! Behold,
all your sons have come from far away [ἥκασιν πάντες οἱ υἱοί σου μακρόθεν],
and your daughters will be lifted on [their] shoulders!" This prophecy could have
been read by early Christ believers as referring to the Gentile nations, and Mark
may have sought to echo it. For a good discussion of the interpretive possibilities,
see Moloney, *Mark*, 152–6 (and 115–16); see also Guelich, *Mark*, 390–9; Marcus,
Mark 1–8, 492; France, *Mark*, 305–9. Collins, *Mark*, 369 incorrectly assumes that
the healing of the deaf mute in Mark 7:31–37 takes place in Jewish territory, thereby
suggesting (378, 383) that the second feeding story takes place in Jewish territory,
as well.

28   Collins discusses the difference between these verbs throughout her commentary
(*Mark*, 325, 379 n. 18, 655–6), but her ultimate conclusion is that their variation is
"compatible with the practice of prayers before and after meals among Jews in the
late Second Temple period" (379), and that the terms are relatively interchangeable
(see also Guelich, *Mark*, 405–6; Johnson, *Mark*, 231). Importantly, neither Mark
nor Paul is consistent in his usage. Mark, as noted, uses εὐχαριστέω in reference
to the bread in the second feeding miracle (Mk. 8:6) and in reference to the wine in
the Eucharist (Mk. 14:23), while he uses εὐλογέω vis-à-vis the bread in the first miracle (Mk. 6:41) and over the bread in the Last Supper (Mk. 14:22). Alternatively, Paul
uses εὐχαριστέω over the bread in the Eucharist at 1 Cor. 11:24 and εὐλογέω over
the cup at 1 Cor. 10:17, but his use of ὡσαύτως ("in the same way") at 1 Cor. 11:25
suggests that he imagines εὐχαριστέω being used over the cup instead of εὐλογέω
there. For an alternative opinion, see Paul F. Bradshaw, *Eucharistic Origins* (Oxford:
Oxford University Press, 2004), 8–9.

29   See Werner H. Kelber, *Mark's Story of Jesus* (Philadelphia, Fortress, 1979), 30–42, esp.
40–1. See also Jeffrey B. Gibson, "The Rebuke of the Disciples in Mark 8:14–21," *JSNT*
27 (1986), 31–47. Though I agree with the thrust of the latter's thesis, he does misread some of the evidence. For example, he claims that that the first feeding miracle
(Mk. 6:32–44) takes place in Gentile territory ("Rebuke," 33), which is difficult to
justify exegetically.

30   On the Herodians, their connection to Herod (presumably Herod Antipas, who ruled
over Galilee during this period), and Mark's historical perception of them, see Martin
Meier, *A Marginal Jew: Rethinking the Historical Jesus* (5 vols.; New York: Doubleday,
1991–2016), 3.560–5; see also Marcus, *Mark 1–8*, 249–50; idem, *Mark 8–16*, 815–16.
For an example of the Herodians taking on the role of political enforcer, see the controversy surrounding paying taxes to Caesar (Mk. 12:13–17). Ultimately, it is probable that Mark understands Herod's partisans to be political rather than religious
opponents. They align with the Pharisees insofar as doing so helps them to keep the
peace amongst the people. This does not nullify the Herodians' opposition to Jesus'
crossing of Halakhic boundaries, of course, but it does suggest that their reason for
doing so is motivated by the potential unrest it might cause, rather than because Jesus
has somehow transgressed the sacred. As Marcus rightly notes, since "Jesus came
from a realm ruled by Herod Antipas, spoke of the coming kingdom of God, and was
commonly believed to be descended from David," he was perceived as political threat
(Marcus, *Mark 8–16*, 822).

31   It should be noted that the "Jew first" pattern is not only found in Romans. It also
occurs in 1 Corinthians (1:22–24; 10:32; 12:13) and Galatians (Gal. 3:28), two other
letters to which it is plausible that Mark had access.

32 See, for example, Joachim Jeremias, *The Eucharistic Words of Jesus* (trans. Norman Perrin; London: SCM Press, 1966), 138–203; Enrico Mazza, *The Celebration of the Eucharist: The Origin of the Rite and the Development of Its Interpretation* (trans. Matthew J. O'Connell; Collegeville: Liturgical Press, 1999), 22–4. In more recent discussions of the Eucharistic liturgy, the primacy of Mark's or Paul's tradition is less the focus than the broader question of how and where the bread and wine (or water) of the Graeco-Roman meal came to be connected with Jesus' body and blood and the common meal transformed into a sacred rite (see Andrew McGowan, "Rethinking Eucharistic Origins," *Pacifica* 23 [2010], 173–191; Paul F. Bradshaw and Maxwell E. Johnson, *The Eucharistic Liturgies: Their Evolution and Interpretation* [Collegeville: Liturgical Press, 2012], 1–24; Stephen R. Shaver, "A Eucharistic Origins Story: Part 1: The Breaking of the Loaf," *Worship* 92 [2018], 204–21; idem, "A Eucharistic Origins Story: Part 2: The Body and Blood of Christ," *Worship* 92 [2018], 298–317). For good surveys of the discussion, see Robert J. Daly, S.J., "Eucharistic Origins: From the New Testament to the Liturgies of the Golden Age," *TS* 66 (2005), 6–9; Bradshaw, *Eucharistic Origins*, 1–15.

33 According to Jeremias (*Eucharistic Words*, 186–9), Paul's is the oldest *written* account, but it is also the most thoroughly Hellenized and likely reflects an early Antiochene formula. Linguistic considerations therefore lead him to judge Luke's account to be older than Paul's and Mark's account older to be older than both (see also Rudolph Pesch, *Das Abendmahl und Jesu Todesverständnis* [Breisgau: Herder, 1978], 21–53, who argues that the formula Paul uses is based on a "Kultätiologie" that predates the apostle but is posterior to the formula as found in Mark). Alternatively, Mazza (*Celebration of the Eucharist*, 24–34) argues that Luke's account presents the earliest redaction of the Last Supper story on the basis of its ritual proximity to the structure of Jewish festive meals. For those scholars who take Paul's version to be oldest, their judgments are made on the grounds of its temporal proximity to the historical Last Supper, its imbalanced phrasing over the elements, and/or its superimposition of a (perceived) secondary memorial rite onto a meal originally devoid of such significance (see e.g., Hyam Jaccoby, "Paul and the Eucharist," *NTS* 37 [1991], 261–5; Bradshaw and Johnson, *Eucharistic Liturgies*, 23–4; Shaver, "Eucharistic Origins: Part 2," 300–1, 311–12; Cranfield, *Mark*, 426–7).

34 For more information on Clement, see Chapter 1, note 18.

35 For the Didachist, the eating of the bread and drinking of the wine do not symbolize the consumption of Jesus' body and blood (see Didache 9.1–3), and, though he, like Mark and Paul, presents a Eucharist that symbolizes unity on a universal scale, he does not root that unification in the death of Jesus Christ. Instead, he writes, "Just as this bread fragment [τοῦτο <τὸ> κλάσμα] was scattered upon the mountains [διεσκορπισμένον ἐπάνω τῶν ὀρέων] and became one [ἐγένετο ἕν] once it had been gathered together [συναχθέν], so too let your church [σου ἡ ἐκκλησία] be gathered together [συναχθήτω] from the ends of the earth into your kingdom [εἰς τὴν σὴν βασιλείαν], because yours is the glory and the power forever [εἰς τοὺς αἰῶνας]" (Didache 9.4 [the Greek text has been taken from Holmes, *Apostolic Fathers*, 334–69]). The Didachist avoids any implication that it is in the consumption of Jesus' flesh or blood that universality is affirmed, and, as a result, metaphysical participation or existence "in Christ"—in striking contrast to Paul and Mark—is here nowhere in view. For a concise introduction to the Didache, see Michael W. Holmes, *The Apostolic Fathers* (Grand Rapids: Baker Academic, 2007), 334–43. For a more thoroughgoing discussion, see Huub van de Sandt and David Flusser, *The Didache: Its Jewish Sources and its Place in Early Judaism and Christianity* (CRINT III.5; Minneapolis: Fortress, 2002), 1–52, esp. 49–52; Kurt Niederwimmer, *The Didache* (Hermeneia; Minneapolis: Fortress, 1998). 1–54, esp. 42–54. On the Eucharist specifically, see Huub van de Sandt, "Why does the Didache Conceive of the Eucharist as a Holy Meal?" *VC* 65 (2011) 1–20.

36 See Pervo, *Dating Acts,* 64–7.

37 Ulrich Luz, "Matthew the Evangelist: A Jewish Christian at the Crossroads," in idem, *Studies in Matthew* (Grand Rapids: Eerdmans, 2005), 5.

38 This correlative adverb could have a variety of nuances, ranging from a simple and relatively casual "likewise" to the denotation of exact patterning. Ultimately, Paul's intended meaning is less important than what Mark thought Paul meant by using it, and there is some significant biblical precedent for his taking the position that Paul had in mind exact repetition. In perhaps the most famous articulation of lex talionis in all of scripture, Lev. 24:19–21 states, "And if someone should inflict a blemish [δῷ μῶμον] upon his neighbor, *in the same manner* [ὡσαύτως] as he did to the other [ὡς ἐποίησεν αὐτῷ], it will be done in return to him [ἀντιποιηθήσεται αὐτῷ]: fracture [σύντριμμα] for fracture, eye [ὀφθαλμὸν] for eye, tooth [ὀδόντα] for tooth. In whatever manner [καθότι ἂν] he inflicts a blemish upon a person, thus it will be inflicted upon him [δοθήσεται αὐτῷ]. Whoever strikes a person and he dies, let that person be put to death [θανάτῳ θανατούσθω]!"

39 See Marcus, *Mark 8–16,* 966 (figure 45) for a similar schematization of actions (and words) over bread and cup.

40 For a similar listing, see Collins, *Corinthians,* 426.

41 On the universal significance of Paul's words of institution, see Klauck, *1 Korintherbrief,* 83: "'Für euch' beim pln/lk Brotwort, das ein älteres 'für die vielen' an gleicher Stelle (anders mk/mt) ersetzt, hat eminent soteriologische Bedeutung. Es bezieht die Mitfeiernden in die Selbsthingabe Jesu als Heilserreignis ein." For further discussion, see Garland, *1 Corinthians,* 546–8; Ciampa and Rosner, *Corinthians,* 552–3; Fitzmyer, *Corinthians,* 439–40; Conzelmann, *1 Corinthians,* 198; Thiselton, *Corinthians,* 878. For bibliography on the connection between Mk. 14:24 and Mk. 10:45, see this chapter, note 18.

42 For additional discussion and bibliography see Part II, note 18 of this chapter. On Mark's adaptation of Isa. 53 more broadly, see Chapter 4, Part II(A) of this monograph.

43 Exodus 24:8 LXX reads as follows: "And Moses, having taken the blood [λαβὼν … τὸ αἷμα], poured [κατεσκέδασεν] it upon the people, and he said, 'Behold! The blood of the covenant [τὸ αἷμα τῆς διαθήκης] which the Lord has established for you.'" The list of scholars who suggest that Mark or Paul (or both) draw on Ex. 24:6–8 could be expanded indefinitely. I note only the following: Moloney, *Mark,* 286; Collins, *Mark,* 656–7; France, *Mark,* 570; Marcus, *Mark 8–16,* 958, 966; Cranfield, *Mark,* 427; Lane, *Mark,* 507; Klaiber, *Markusevangelium,* 273; Eckey, *Markusevangelium,* 453; Gnilka, *Markus,* 2.245; Standaert, *Marc,* 3.1009; Ciampa and Rosner, *Corinthians,* 552; Keener, *1–2 Corinthians,* 98; Garland, *1 Corinthians,* 547; Lietzmann, *Korinther,* 57; Fitzmyer, *Corinthians,* 443; Conzelmann, *1 Corinthians,* 199 n. 73. On the narrative warrant Mark may derive from Ex. 24:3–11 for the consumption of blood, see Jeffrey Stackert, "'This is the Blood of My Covenant': The Markan Last Supper and the Elohistic Horeb Narrative," *BR* 62 (2017), 48–60.

44 Incidentally, this correction also explains Mark's use of τὸ ἐκχυννόμενον ("poured out" [Mk. 14:24], not found in 1 Cor. 11:23–26). For both Mark and Paul, Christ's blood not only evokes the covenant sacrifice; it evokes the suffering servant of Isaiah who dies for the sake of the people's sins (διὰ τὰς ἁμαρτίας αὐτῶν [Isa. 53:12]). The association between the two is facilitated by the fact that the suffering servant is himself likened to a sacrificial animal: "as a sheep [πρόβατον] he was led to slaughter [ἐπὶ σφαγήν]" (Isa. 53:7, discussed in more detail in Chapter 4). Unlike Paul, however, whose conflation of covenant sacrifice and suffering servant is presumed rather than articulated, Mark utilizes the language of Christ's blood "pouring out" (τὸ ἐκχυννόμενον [Mk. 14:24]) to make this linkage clear. At Gen. 9:6, where God establishes his first covenant with Noah, murder is prohibited with the following words, "The one who pours out the blood of a human being [ὁ ἐκχέων αἷμα ἀνθρώπου] will be poured out [ἐκχυθήσεται] in exchange for that person's blood [ἀντὶ τοῦ αἵματος

αὐτοῦ] because I have made humanity in the image of God." Blood's being "poured out" (ἐκχέω) is thus a famous metaphorical image for murder in scripture (see also Ezek. 22:6, 9, 12), and Mark here overtly intertwines the referents Paul assumes (covenant sacrifice [Ex. 24:6–8] and manslaughter [Isa. 53:12]) via the imagery of Christ's blood being "poured out" (τὸ ἐκχυννόμενον). As Collins, *Mark*, 657, has rightly suggested, "The naming of Jesus' death as a 'pouring out of his blood for many' may result from the combination of the terminology of sacrifice with the poem about the suffering servant of the Lord in Isaiah 53."

45 Despite Mark's displacement, I add that Christ's death "for the many" is conveyed implicitly through the breaking of bread, as well. Many commentators presume this (see e.g., Stein, *Mark*, 650; Donahue and Harrington, *Mark*, 395; Collins, *Mark*, 655–6; Mann, *Mark*, 577; Marcus, *Mark 8–16*, 964; Eckey, *Markusevangelium*, 452; Johnson, *Mark*, 231; Moloney, *Mark*, 285–6; Klaiber, *Markusevangelium*, 272). "Bread" (ἄρτος) is synecdochical. Insofar as the breaking of the bread symbolizes Jesus' body, beaten and then broken upon a cross (see Mk. 14:65; 15:16–20, 24, 34–37), Mark presumes his audience will recall, through that ritual action, what Jesus' body accomplishes: salvation "for the many" (ὑπὲρ πολλῶν).

46 So Pesch, *Abendmahl*, 49: "Die Anamnesisbefehle … schließlich, die nur in der Paulus-Fassung begegnen, zielen mit den Imperativen τοῦτο ποιεῖτε eindeutig auf eine wiederholbare liturgische Handlung, die zum Gedenken an Jesus (εἰς τὴν ἐμὴν ἀνάμνησιν …) vorgenommen werden soll; ihr Zuwachs im kultätiologischen Text ist leicht erklärbar, eine Streichung in der berichtenden Erzählung, die keinen Platz für die Befehle hat (da sie nicht auf Jesu Tod zurückschaut, sondern von der Situation vor seinem Tod erzählt), unwahrscheinlich ist." See also, Fitzmyer, *Corinthians*, 440.

47 On this point, see Marxsen, *Mark*, 129–31; see also Elizabeth V. Dowling, "'Do This in Remembrance of Me': Last Supper Traditions in Paul and Mark," in Wischmeyer et al., *Paul and Mark*, 234–9.

48 The potential for verbal parallelism is quickly ruptured when the apostle employs "cup" (τὸ ποτήριον) at 11:25 as the correlate to "body" (τὸ σῶμα) at 11:24, rather than the more natural "blood." Other significant discrepancies occur between the two clauses, as well, including placement of the copula and the lack of a possessive pronoun at 11:25 (replaced instead by a possessive adjective).

49 It is because of the careful parallelism that scholars such as Cranfield, *Mark*, 426–7 suggest the Pauline formulation is older. For him, Mark represents a liturgical formula, and it is difficult to imagine Paul disrupting it. Therefore, Paul must be working with the older tradition. This judgment is, I suspect, largely correct. My contention is only that Mark's liturgical formulae could grow out of a familiarity with Paul's Eucharist tradition and then inflect the subsequent narrative he tells.

50 Many commentators perceive meaningful differences between Mark's and Paul's formulations vis-à-vis the cup. Conzelmann, for example, suggests that, "The corresponding formula is not bread and wine, but bread and cup. Thus, the interpretation attaches not to the elements as such, but to the act of administration" (*1 Corinthians*, 199). Alternatively, Jeremias (*Eucharistic Words*, 169–70) has argued that, while the essential meaning of Jesus' words over the cup for Mark and Paul is the same, Mark's formulation is the older on the basis of it being the more difficult reading (*lectio difficilior*). That is, because the idea of "drinking blood" would have been deeply offensive to first-century Jews, Mark, who presents Jesus' *blood* as that which is drunk, offers the older version of the tradition, while the words over the cup in Paul/Luke are an update, "occasioned by the intention of warding off the misunderstanding that the Lord's Supper was as Thyestian meal where blood was drunk" (Jeremias, *Eucharistic Words*, 170). For my part, I agree with Jeremias' general assessment that Mark's and Paul's words over the cup amount to much the same thing (see also Cranfield, *Mark*, 427). I disagree, however, that Mark's Last Supper is necessarily the older on the basis of its being the more offensive to

Jewish persons (see the good rebuttal to this line of reasoning in Jonathan Klawans, "Interpreting the Last Supper: Sacrifice, Spiritualization, and Anti-Sacrifice," *NTS* 48 [2002], 5–7).

51 France, *Mark*, 570; see also Collins, *Mark*, 656; Lane, *Mark*, 507. Other Markan scholars do not cite Jeremiah 38:31 LXX as a background text, but they nevertheless assume it. For example, Johnson, *Mark*, 231 writes, "A *new* relationship is to be inaugurated, or an old relation restored, between men and God." (emphasis added).

52 Rightly noted by Thiselton, *Corinthians*, 886.

53 Collins, *Corinthians*, 434; Ciampa and Rosner, *Corinthians*, 553–4; Keener, *1–2 Corinthians*, 98; Witherington III, *Conflict and Community*, 250–1; Thiselton, *Corinthians*, 887–8; Klauck, *1 Korintherbrief*, 83; etc.

54 On the eschatological undertones of the phrase "the Kingdom of God" (ἡ βασιλεία τοῦ θεοῦ), see Collins, *Mark*, 154–5. For scholars who hear eschatological overtones in Mk 14:25, see Collins, *Mark*, 657; Johnson, *Mark*, 232; Keener, *1–2 Corinthians*, 98; Lane, *Mark*, 508; Klaiber, *Markusevangelium*, 274; France, *Mark*, 571–2; Donahue and Harrington, *Mark*, 399–400.

55 The conceptual similarity of the Markan Jesus' proclamation to Paul's eschatological proclamation at 1 Cor. 11:26 is explicitly noted by Marcus, *Mark 8–16*, 967–8.

56 It can be added that the imminent eschatological expectation one sees present in Mark and Paul's Eucharist is noticeably altered in other Eucharistic accounts. It is not found at all in the tradition of the Didachist (*Didache* 9:2), and both Matthew and Luke soften the eschatological dimension. For example, Matthew adds μεθ' ὑμῶν at 26:29, which, when coupled with sayings of Jesus at Matt. 18:20 and 28:20, suggests a continual presence of Jesus with his followers after his death. As Luz aptly explains, "While Matthew knows that a time will come in which Jesus will no longer be with his disciples (9:15; 26:11), he also knows that the earthly Immanuel who has celebrated his last meal as a fellowship meal 'with' his disciples (26:18, 20) will be 'with' his church as the risen lord 'always' until the end of the world" (*Matthew*, 3.383; see also John Nolland, *The Gospel of Matthew* [NIGTC; Grand Rapids: Eerdmans, 2005, 1084–5]). Luke conceives of the Kingdom of God similarly. He displaces the eschatological proclamation to Lk. 22:16–18, and the words there may refer as much to the celebratory meals of the early Lukan communities as they do to the eschatological banquet at the final consummation (see Lk. 24:25–31, 41–48; see also I. Howard Marshall, *The Gospel of Luke* [NIGTC; Grand Rapids: Eerdmans, 1978] 396–9; Luke Timothy Johnson, *The Gospel of Luke*, [SP 3; Collegeville: Liturgical Press, 1991] 337, 341–2; cf. Francois Bovon, *Luke* [3 vols.; trans. Christine Thomas et al.; Hermeneia; Minneapolis, Fortress, 2012]; 2.297; 3.157–8; Robert C. Tannehill, *Luke* [ANTC; Nashville: Abingdon, 1996], 313).

57 On paraphrase in the ancient world, see the discussion of the late first century rhetor Theon: "'Paraphrase (*paraphrasis*) consists of changing the form of expression while keeping the thoughts. It is also called metaphrase.' There are four main kinds: variation in syntax, by addition, by subtraction, and by substitution, plus combinations of these:

Syntactical paraphrase: we keep the same words but transpose the parts, which offers numerous possibilities.

By addition: we keep the original words and add to them; for example, Thucydides (1.142.1) said, 'in war, opportunities are not abiding,' while Demosthenes (4.37) paraphrased this, 'opportunities for actions do not await our sloth and evasions.'

By subtraction: speaking in an incomplete way, we drop many of the elements of the original …

By substitution: we replace the original word with another; for example, a *pais* or *andrapodon* for *doulos* (slave), or the proper word instead of a metaphor or a metaphor instead of a proper word, or several words instead of one or one instead of several." The translation is taken from *Progymnasmata: Greek Textbooks of Prose*

Composition and Rhetoric (trans. George A. Kennedy; WGRW 10; Atlanta: Society of Biblical Literature, 2003), 70. See also Quintilian, *Inst.* 10.5.4–11. As I argued in Part I, the Eucharist Paul presents in 1 Cor. 11:23–26 is a rhetorically determined paraphrase along the lines of what Theon suggests. What I add now is that Mark has recognized it as such, and he attempts to compose for his community that event of which he takes Paul's story to be a summary.

58 This latter point is important to counter the critique of circularity in my argument. That is, if Paul has paraphrased the Eucharist in his presentation at 1 Cor. 11:23–26, and Mark presents a version of the Eucharist without Paul's expansions, who is to say that Mark has not simply reproduced an older (common) tradition to which both Mark and Paul are independently indebted? I offer two responses to this critique. First, while it is possible that Paul has moved "on behalf of you" (ὑπὲρ ὑμῶν) from the cup to the body in the course of his παράφρασις, exegetical grounds for making this argument are not especially strong (though see Jeremias, *Eucharistic Words,* 167 for an attempt to do precisely this). Mark's transposition therefore still requires Paul's Eucharist as a *Vorlage.*

Second (and more important), as has been demonstrated throughout this chapter, the rhetorical ends to which the words of institution are deployed in Mark and Paul are extraordinarily similar. Through the ritualized performance of Jesus' death in the Eucharist, Christ believers affirm their (universal) unity within the body of Jesus Christ (contrast this with the unity as imagined by Didache 9.1–3). This idea is seeded into Mark's gospel through the feeding narratives, and it is articulated explicitly in Paul's argument to the Corinthians. A (common) tradition from which Mark and Paul independently draw for their words of institution cannot easily accommodate this larger thematic overlap.

59 An echo of this sort has been noted by, amongst others, Collins, *Corinthians,* 379; Thiselton, *Corinthians,* 757–60; Keener, *1–2 Corinthians,* 87; and Ciampa and Rosner, *Corinthians,* 552.

60 See Part I, note 12 of this chapter.

61 I argued in the previous chapter (Chapter 2, note 50) that the reference to Ἀββα ὁ πατήρ in Mark 14:36 should be taken to recall baptism, due to the parallel phrasing of Mk. 10:38–39, where baptism and cup are explicitly linked. Given that Matthew and Luke are both reading the pages of Mark and could have easily replicated it, it is noteworthy that the connection between cup and baptism is not preserved in the other synoptic gospels. In the Matthean and Lukan parallels to Mk. 10:38–39, Matt. 20:22 is missing baptism ("And answering, Jesus said, 'You do not know what you are asking. Are you able to drink the cup which I am about to drink [πιεῖν τὸ ποτήριον ὃ ἐγὼ μέλλω πίνειν]?' They said to him, 'we are able [δυνάμεθα]'"), whereas Luke 12:50 is missing the cup ("But I have a baptism to be baptized [βάπτισμα δὲ ἔχω βαπτισθῆναι], and how I am constrained until it has been accomplished [πῶς συνέχομαι ἕως ὅτου τελεσθῇ]!" In the synoptic parallels to Mk. 14:36, Matt. 26:39 and Lk. 22:42 are both missing reference to the baptismal cry, αββα ὁ πατήρ (cf. Gal. 4:6; Rom. 8:15). Instead, Matt. 26:39 reads, "My father" (πάτερ μου), while Lk. 22:42 says simply, "Father" (πάτερ). It is probable that Mark creates an association between cup and baptism on the model of Paul that Matthew and Luke either miss or ignore.

62 See Chapter 2, Part II for my full argument.

63 Many commentators note a connection with the biblical "cup of wrath." See, for example, Collins, *Mark,* 496, 680; Johnson, *Mark,* 179, 236; France, *Mark,* 416, 585; Cranfield, *Mark,* 337, 433; Lane, *Mark,* 380, 517; Klaiber, *Markusevangelium,* 201, 280; Eckey, *Markusevangelium,* 343, 461–2.

4 Death "in accordance with the Scriptures"

In investigating the various "performances" of Christ's death that are found in Paul's letters and the means by which they are seeded into Mark's gospel, I have demonstrated, first, that Paul's imagination of himself as an embodied "icon" of Jesus Christ crucified is anticipated in the Markan Jesus, a figure who iconically and proleptically manifests his salvific death through the miracles of his earthly life (Chapter 1). Second, I have shown that Mark's baptismal narrative anticipates Paul's baptism into the "death" of Christ (Rom. 6:3), reinforcing Paul's insistence on the mimetic patterning of the believer on the person of the messiah (Chapter 2). Third, I have argued that Paul's Eucharist, which performs the Last Supper and Jesus' crucifixion, is both incorporated into and anticipated by Mark's gospel through linguistic modification and the accentuation of the rite's universal significance (Chapter 3). In this chapter, I will attend to Mark and Paul's use of scripture, particularly the prefigurative performances of Jesus' death that they find contained within it.[1]

As in previous chapters, this chapter will be divided into three main blocks of material. After a few preliminary remarks on the nature of Mark's and Paul's interaction with scripture, I will turn to a sustained analysis of the latter, and I will argue that, for the apostle, Jesus' death is paradigmatically prefigured in at least three biblical exemplars: the death of the suffering servant (Isa. 53), Abraham's near slaughter of his son (Gen. 22), and the sacrifice of the Paschal lamb (Ex. 12). Each of these stories is seen as a typological precursor to Jesus' death "in accordance with the scriptures" (κατὰ τὰς γραφάς [1 Cor. 15:3, 4]). At the same time, because Paul's consistent hermeneutical principle vis-à-vis scripture is that its full significance is only disclosed in and through the Christ event, in the act of performing one passage or another, Jesus' death and the promises associated with the full gospel narrative are brought forward. In other words, scriptural performances of Jesus' death synecdochically evoke all of salvation history.

Following my analysis of Paul, I will turn to Mark, and I will demonstrate that for him, too, three essential typological precursors to Jesus' death are the servant that is handed over (Isa. 53), the son that is bound (Gen. 22), and the lamb that is slaughtered (Ex. 12). These prefigurations are understood by Mark to be prospective and proleptic performances of Christ's death that synecdochically evoke the whole gospel plot. They form a part of the scriptural substructure to Mark's "passion narrative with an extended introduction."[2]

Finally, I will conclude by arguing that Mark has crafted his gospel such that the scriptural types of Jesus' death that Paul draws upon are harmoniously combined within a single figure, the earthly Jesus. What are ostensibly (though not necessarily) distinct typologies in Paul's letters, Mark has drawn together in his narrative of the death of Christ through their shared associations with a lamb that is slaughtered for the sake of the people (πρόβατον [Gen. 22:7–28; Ex. 12:3–5; Isa. 53:6–7]). If, in the previous chapters, Mark's concern was to bolster Paul's rhetorical claims of his person, the importance of *imitatio Christi*, and the oneness of the people of God, this chapter shows how Mark confirms the scriptural witnesses Paul uses to demonstrate the salvation-historical necessity of the cross.[3]

Preliminary remarks: The evocation of scripture in Mark's and Paul's communities

The purpose of this section is to set out, in brief, a few hermeneutic presuppositions vis-à-vis Mark's and Paul's engagement with scripture. First, as I noted in Chapter 1, I presume that Mark, Paul, and their audiences all read scripture in Greek. For some time, scholars have recognized this of Paul, and it is generally accepted of Mark.[4] Biblical citations in the following pages are thus taken from the Greek translation of the Hebrew Bible (the Septuagint).

Second, I take both Mark's and Paul's engagement with scripture to be what Hays has called "metaleptic." That is, both authors employ

> a literary technique of citing or echoing a small bit of a precursor text in such a way that the reader can grasp the significance of the echo only be recalling or recovering the original context from which the fragmentary echo came and then reading the two texts in dialogical juxtaposition.[5]

This literary technique aligns closely with the synecdochical poetics I have argued that Mark and Paul share. In order for a scriptural allusion to be understood properly, the whole of the literary unit to which it refers must be recalled and brought into conversation with the text in which that allusion was first perceived. The part, in other words, evokes the whole, and the whole is utilized to draw out and elucidate the significance or meaning of the part.

To assess the plausibility of a scriptural echo and avoid the dangers of exegetical excess,[6] Hays has also introduced methodological controls on this comparative process. He suggests the following seven criteria for evaluating the critical viability of an apparent metalepsis: (1) availability (was the source of the echo available to the author and readers?); (2) volume (are there substantial verbal or syntactical overlaps, or is the precursor text distinctive enough in scripture such that only few words are needed to evoke it?); (3) recurrence (does the author elsewhere allude to or cite the same scriptural passage?); (4) thematic coherence (does the echoed text fit thematically within the argument [or, in the case of Mark, the narrative]?); (5) historical plausibility (could the echo have been intended by its author or understood by his or her reader, or is it subject to the charge of anachronism?); (6) history of interpretation (have other readers [critical and pre-critical] perceived the echo?); and (7) satisfaction (does the proposed reading help to illuminate the broader discourse in which it is found?).[7] Though there have been attempts over the years to rework or update Hays' criteria, the substance of these controls has remained largely the same,[8] and, as will become apparent in the course of my argument that follows, the scriptural echoes I analyze satisfy all of Hays' individual criteria.[9]

Third and finally, I judge the performances of scripture discussed in this chapter to be what one might call "typological." In her *Biblical Exegesis and the Formation of Christian Culture*, Francis Young has made the important observation that typology is a modern scholarly category. That is, it is unrecognized by any ancient interpreter.[10] There are, however, "types" (τύποι) that prefigure later realities in early Christian thought (e.g., Rom. 5:14; 1 Cor. 10:6, 11; 1 Pet. 3:20–21; Ep. Barn. 7.7, 10, 11; etc.), and she suggests that these are discernable not so much by their character as historical events but by their "mimetic quality.[11] Building upon the works of Northrop Frye and Tibor Fabiny, Young notes that typology is also a form of intertextuality, and she suggests that

> the important element in a 'type' is its integrity, its 'reality' whether as event or simply as narrative or character or act, its autonomy, and yet its capacity significantly, often prophetically, to mirror another event or narrative, or character, or act. Typology permits both setting side by side.[12]

For the purposes of my argument, the conceptual framework provided by Young is a useful one. I presume that, when the scriptural passages investigated in this chapter—passages to which Mark and Paul allude via metalepsis—were performed within the apostle's and evangelist's communities, these performances would have maintained their own autonomy as well as having had a power to signify. In the case of Isaiah 53, for example, viewers would not see the narrative (re)presentation of Jesus' death, which is found in Mark 15; rather, they would see the *prophetic* (re)presentation of it. This is a fine distinction, but an important one. In the course of a performance of Isaiah 53, believers would see the death of Jesus prophetically prefigured, but they would not see the emplotted, causal sequence of events surrounding Jesus' death itself put on display. This occurs separately, in the retelling of that portion of the gospel narrative that (re)presents the earthly mission of Jesus Christ. Thus, the scriptural passages analyzed in this chapter would have been received as "types" (τύποι), according to Young's definition, that (re)present for the audience the crucifixion of the messiah. All three (Gen. 22, Ex. 12, Isa. 53), through performance, permit "both setting side by side."[13]

Part I: Scriptural prefigurations of Jesus' death in Paul

In his classic work, *Echoes of Scripture in the Letters of Paul*, Hays has argued that Paul's scriptural approach is "ecclesiocentric" rather than "Christocentric." That is,

What Paul finds in Scripture, above all else, is the prefiguration of the *church* as the people of God ... Paul uses Scripture primarily to shape his under-standing of the community of faith; conversely, Paul's experience of the Christian community—composed of Jews and Gentiles together—shapes his reading of Scripture. In short, Paul operates with an ecclesiocentric herme-neutic (emphasis original).[14]

Given the nature of Paul's correspondence—epistolary arguments written to correct factionalist behavior, alleviate doubts about apostolic authority, foster hope and endurance, and so forth—it is unsurprising that Paul does not often employ Christological readings of scripture to demonstrate that Jesus is the mes-siah who died and was raised on behalf of the many.[15] Instead, he is able to take it as given, as 1 Corinthians 15:3, 4's "according to the scriptures" (κατὰ τὰς γραφάς) clearly demonstrates. That said, there is some scriptural content to Paul's Christological assumptions that can be reconstructed from the laconic allusions in his letters.[16] In this section, I explore what Paul takes to be scrip-tural prefigurations of the death of Christ, specifically, Isaiah 53 (the death of the suffering servant), Exodus 12 (the slaughter of the Paschal lamb), and Genesis 22 (the aborted immolation of Isaac).[17] I will argue that these stories were performed in the context of early Christian worship and that they would have fostered for the listening community an epiphanic encounter with the deity through the use of Paul's gospel poetics.

(A) The suffering servant

Isaiah 53 opens with the proclamation that God's servant (ὁ παῖς) "will be exalted and glorified greatly" (ὑψωθήσεται καὶ δοξασθήσεται σφόδρα) and that "many nations will marvel at him" (θαυμάσονται ἔθνη πολλά ἐπ᾽ αὐτῷ [Isa. 52:13-15]). This exaltation, however, comes at a cost, as the audience is told that God "hands over" (παραδίδωμι) the servant to abuse and rejection for (the sake of) "our sins" (ταῖς ἁμαρτίαις ἡμῶν/διὰ τὰς ἁμαρτίας ἡμῶν [see Isa. 53:4-6]).[18] This servant, "led like a lamb to slaughter" (ὡς πρόβατον ἐπὶ σφαγὴν ἤχθη), is silent throughout this suffering ("he does not open his mouth [οὐκ ἀνοίγει τὸ στόμα αὐτοῦ]" [Isa. 53:7]), and, though free of lawlessness (ἀνομίας) and deceit (δόλος), he dies at the hands of the wicked and the wealthy (see Isa. 53:9: "I will put the wicked opposite his tomb [δώσω τοὺς πονηροὺς ἀντὶ τῆς ταφῆς αὐτοῦ] and the wealthy opposite his death [τοὺς πλουσίους ἀντὶ τοῦ θανάτου]" [see also Isa. 53:8]). In the end, however, the Lord vindicates his servant (he chooses to "justify the just one who serves the many well" (δικαιῶσαι δίκαιον εὖ δουλεύοντα πολλοῖς [Isa. 53:11]), and the Fourth Servant Song concludes with the following words:

> For this reason he will inherit many and he will divide the spoils of the strong, because [ἀνθ᾽ ὧν] his life [ἡ ψυχὴ αὐτοῦ] was handed over unto death [παρεδόθη εἰς θάνατον], and he was reckoned amongst the lawless

[ἐν τοῖς ἀνόμοις ἐλογίσθη]. And he himself took up [ἀνήνεγκεν] the sins of many [ἁμαρτίας πολλῶν], and, for the sake of their sins [διὰ τὰς ἁμαρτίας αὐτῶν], he was handed over [παρεδόθη]" (Isa. 53:12).

Isaiah's suffering servant plays no small role in Paul's thinking. Indeed, he quotes Isaiah 53:1 explicitly at Romans 10:16: "For Isaiah says, 'Lord, who has believed our report [τίς ἐπίστευσεν τῇ ἀκοῇ ἡμῶν]?'" This citation occurs within the masterful climax of Paul's letter (Rom. 9–11),[19] a rhetorical tour de force in which the apostle and his gospel dance between Jews and Gentiles, seeking to accommodate both groups in the salvation history of God. Yet, due to its seemingly incidental nature, the relationship of Paul's citation of Isaiah 53:1 to this broader argument, on one hand, and Jesus' death, on the other, needs to be unpacked.

Paul's argument in Romans 10–11 runs as follows: Paul moves from proper Jewish "zeal" (ζῆλος) for but improper "knowledge" (ἐπίγνωσις) of the deity (Rom. 10:2–3) to an assertion that there is no distinction (διαστολή,) between Jews and Gentiles (an earlier theme of the letter [see Rom. 3:22, 29]), as it is the same Lord who is ultimately over all (Rom. 10:12). He next admits that only a "remnant" (λεῖμμα) of Jews have come to believe (Rom. 11:4–5)—the majority have been "hardened" (ἐπωρώθησαν) by divine intention (Rom. 11:7–8)—but this allows him to make a transition from a notion of Gentile salvation as a merciful outpouring of God's love to Gentile salvation as a deliberate moment in God's plan to "provoke" (παραζηλῶσαι) his chosen people to jealousy (Rom. 11:11). Paul claims that the hardening (πώρωσις) of the hearts of the Jews has always been intended for the good of the Gentiles, since it is during its duration that space has been allotted by God for their "fullness" (πλήρωμα) to enter in (Rom. 11:25). Then, upon the completion of one epoch, there begins another: the salvation of *all* Israel (πᾶς Ἰσραήλ [Rom. 11:26]). In the end, in a spectacular paradox, Paul exclaims that all have been made to disbelieve in order that all can come to believe and be shown the immeasurable mercy of God (Rom. 11:32). At this moment, when he has exhausted the limits of dialectic and finds himself staring into the depths of God's unfathomable will, Paul leaves off exposition and resorts to doxology: "O depth of wealth and wisdom and knowledge of God! etc." (Rom. 11:33–36).[20]

Within this larger argument, Paul introduces his quotation of Isaiah 53:1 at Romans 10:16a with the following words: "But not all have obeyed [ὑπήκουσαν] the gospel [τῷ εὐαγγελίῳ]." To understand the role of the suffering servant in Romans 9–11, one must remember that, for Paul, the gospel's primary episode is Jesus' crucifixion in expiation for the sins of others ("Christ died [ἀπέθανεν] on behalf of our sins [ὑπὲρ τῶν ἁμαρτιῶν ἡμῶν]" [1 Cor. 15:3]). It is, moreover, the humiliating death of Christ that Paul labels the "stumbling block" (σκάνδαλον [1 Cor. 1:23]) for the Jewish people: "We proclaim Christ *crucified* [Χριστὸν ἐσταυρωμένον], a stumbling block for Jews [Ἰουδαίοις μὲν σκάνδαλον] and folly to Gentiles [ἔθνεσιν δὲ μωρίαν]" (1 Cor. 1:23). For Paul, Isaiah 53 thus functions as a scriptural witness to that death that has caused the Jewish people such distress, and his evocation of it at Romans

10:16 with the words, "Lord, who has believed our report [τίς ἐπίστευσεν τῇ ἀκοῇ ἡμῶν]?" (Isa. 53:1) serves as a subtle reminder to his audience that that which the Jewish people have rejected, that which has effected the hardening (πώρωσις) of their hearts, is prefigured within the scriptures themselves (see esp. Isa. 53:6, 12).[21]

The prefigurative status of Isaiah 53 is seen most clearly at Romans 4:23–25. At the end of Paul's extended discussion of Abraham's faith (Rom. 4), wherein its exemplary nature apart from circumcision and the law is framed by citations of Genesis 15:6 ("Abraham believed in God [ἐπίστευσεν Αβραμ τῷ θεῷ], and it was reckoned to him as righteousness [ἐλογίσθη αὐτῷ εἰς δικαιοσύνην]" [Rom. 4:3; 22]), Paul drives home the lesson of the patriarch with the following words:

> 23. But it was not written for his sake alone [δι' αὐτὸν μόνον] that "it was reckoned to him [ἐλογίσθη αὐτῷ]"; 24. but also for our sake [δι' ἡμᾶς], to whom it is about to be reckoned [μέλλει λογίζεσθαι], [we] who believe in the one who raised Jesus our Lord from the dead [τοῖς πιστεύουσιν ἐπὶ τὸν ἐγείραντα Ἰησοῦν τὸν κύριον ἡμῶν ἐκ νεκρῶν], 25. who was handed over for the sake of our sins [παρεδόθη διὰ τὰ παραπτώματα ἡμῶν], and who was raised for the sake of our justification [ἠγέρθη διὰ τὴν δικαίωσιν ἡμῶν] (Rom. 4:23–25).

Paul's language at Romans 4:25 evokes the description of the suffering servant at Isaiah 53:12. The prophet's words, "He was handed over for the sake of their sins [διὰ τὰς ἁμαρτίας αὐτῶν παρεδόθη]," map closely onto Paul's "he was handed over for the sake of our trespasses [παρεδόθη διὰ τὰ παραπτώματα ἡμῶν]" (Rom. 4:25). There is linguistic variation, but no difference in action ("handed over") or significance (redemption).[22]

Moreover, Isaiah 53 may have influenced the logic underlying Paul's argument in Romans 4 in more fundamental ways. If Abraham's faith is intended to create space for Gentiles to be incorporated into Paul's gospel narrative on the basis of faith, Isaiah's claim that "many nations will marvel" (θαυμάσονται ἔθνη πολλά) at the servant, and that they will "see" (ὄψονται) and "understand" (συνήσουσιν [Isa. 52:15]), must have served as a scriptural warrant for that Gentile mission. Paul's later citation of Isaiah 52:15 as justification for his continued mission to Spain confirms this (see Rom. 15:21: "but as it is written, 'those to whom no report was brought concerning him will see [οἷς οὐκ ἀνηγγέλη περὶ αὐτοῦ ὄψονται], and those who have not heard will understand [οἳ οὐκ ἀκηκόασιν συνήσουσ-ιν]'").[23] Similarly, if Paul intends to demonstrate that God justifies on the basis of faith rather than works (see esp. Rom. 4:5–8; 4:13–16), the justification that the servant receives (Isa. 53:11) may have been taken to anticipate God's subsequent justification of all believers through the faithfulness of, and faith in, Jesus Christ (see Rom. 3:22; Gal. 2:16). That is, for Paul, Christ is justified as a result of his faithfully dying for the sins of the many, and this, in turn, opens the way for others to be justified by faith in him.

In the end, then, there can be little doubt that the Fourth Servant Song is essential to Paul's Christological thinking. It stands in the background of his gospel narrative at 1 Corinthians 15:3 (Christ died "on behalf of our sins" [ὑπὲρ τῶν ἁμαρτιῶν ἡμῶν]), his Eucharist at 1 Corinthians 11:23–26 ("he was handed over [παρεδίδετο] … on behalf of you [ὑπὲρ ὑμῶν]" [1 Cor. 11:23–24]), in his justification for the primacy of faith (Rom. 4), and in Paul's argument for the temporary hardening of the Jewish people's hearts (Rom. 9–11).[24] Though Paul never explicates it as a scriptural witness to Christ's death, he assumes it (and his audience's familiarity it), and he allows it to inform the arguments he makes. For Paul, Isaiah 53 is a prefiguration of Jesus' death that occurs "in accordance with the scriptures" (κατὰ τὰς γραφάς [1 Cor. 15:3, 4]).

(B) The binding of Isaac

Genesis 22 (the Aqedah) tells the story of Isaac's binding and near immolation at the hands of his father, Abraham. At the opening of the story, "God tests Abraham" (ὁ θεὸς ἐπείραζεν τὸν Αβρααμ), and he calls him to take his beloved son ("Take your son, the beloved" [λαβὲ τὸν υἱόν σου τὸν ἀγαπητόν]) to a high land where the child would be offered as a whole burnt offering (ὁλοκάρπωσις [Gen. 22:1–2]). The patriarch obeys and sets out with his child and two servants. "On the third day" (τῇ ἡμέρᾳ τῇ τρίτῃ), they see from afar the spot that God had designated, and, leaving his servants behind, Abraham takes Isaac, and they head to the location alone (Gen. 22:3–6). Along the way, Isaac asks after the whereabouts of the sacrificial sheep (τὸ πρόβατον), to which Abraham gives his famous reply, "God will see to the sheep for himself" (ὁ θεὸς ὄψεται ἑαυτῷ πρόβατον [Gen. 22:7–8]). Abraham then builds the altar, binds Isaac, and "sets him upon the altar above the wood" (ἐπέθηκεν αὐτὸν ἐπὶ τὸ θυσιαστήριον ἐπάνω τῶν ξύλων [Gen. 22:9]). Just as Abraham is about to sacrifice his child, however, an angel of the Lord intervenes. The angel informs Abraham that, as a result of his willingness to slaughter his son, the patriarch's pious fear has been recognized (Gen. 22:12). Abraham then finds a ram caught in a thicket, and he offers that animal in place of the sheep that his son had himself come to replace (Gen. 22:13). Afterwards, the angel of the Lord appears once more and affirms the previous promise(s) God had made to the patriarch (e.g., Gen. 12:2–3; 17:2–8), saying,

> Because [οὗ εἵνεκεν] you have done this thing [τὸ ῥῆμα τοῦτο], and you did not spare your son, the beloved, for my sake [οὐκ ἐφείσω τοῦ υἱοῦ σου τοῦ ἀγαπητοῦ δι᾽ ἐμέ], 17. truly blessing I will bless you [εὐλογῶν εὐλογήσω σε], and multiplying I will multiply your seed [πληθύνων πληθυνῶ τὸ σπέρμα σου]; as the stars of heaven and as the sand that is along the shore of the sea, your seed will inherit the cities of its enemies [κληρονομήσει τὸ σπέρμα σου τὰς πόλεις τῶν ὑπεναντίων], 18. and all the nations of the earth will be blessed in your seed [ἐνευλογηθήσονται ἐν τῷ σπέρματί σου πάντα τὰ ἔθνη τῆς γῆς] because you have obeyed my voice [ἀνθ᾽ ὧν ὑπήκουσας τῆς ἐμῆς φωνῆς] (Gen. 22:16–18).

As with the Fourth Servant Song, the Binding of Isaac forms an important Christological backdrop to Paul's thinking about the salvation-historical necessity of the cross. At the same time, because Paul assumes its importance and his communities' familiarity with it, he never explicates his allusions fully. For example, though Abraham and Isaac play crucial roles in Galatians as both types of believers and of Christ,[25] the Aqedah is rarely recognized as forming a scriptural backdrop to the letter. The primary issue in Galatians is obedience to the law, particularly the necessity of circumcision (see Gal. 5:1–13). It seems that Paul's opponents have introduced Genesis 17:1–14, where God commands circumcision for Abraham and all his descendants, in order to bolster their calls for its adoption.[26] In scripting his counter argument, Paul presumes his communities' familiarity with a variety of scriptural exemplars upon which he draws and to which he alludes. At Galatians 3:6–14, where Paul musters biblical witnesses to demonstrate the truth of his assertion that righteousness is attained through faith rather than works of the law, Paul "quotes" scripture with the following words: "All the nations will be blessed in you" (ἐνευλογηθήσονται ἐν σοὶ πάντα τὰ ἔθνη [Gal. 3:8]).[27] This language finds no exact parallel in the Septuagint.[28] Though exegetes often consider it a conflation of Genesis 12:13 and 18:18,[29] it is more probably the promise of the Aqedah (Gen. 22:16–18) that is in view. I place below the passages side by side for comparison (Table 4.1).

It is easy to see why commentators select Genesis 18:18 as the second passage with which Genesis 12:3 is combined. After all, it looks as if Paul has merely exchanged "all the tribes of the earth" (πᾶσαι αἱ φυλαὶ τῆς γῆς) for "all the nations" (πάντα τὰ ἔθνη). This reading, however, does not take into account the wider context of Paul's discussion. For Paul, the "in you" (ἐν σοὶ) of Genesis 12:3 has a very particular referent. At Galatians 3:16 the apostle asserts: "But to Abraham and to his seed [τῷ σπέρματι αὐτοῦ] the promises have been spoken. It does not say, 'and to his seeds [τοῖς σπέρμασιν],' as if to many, but as if to one [ὡς ἐφ' ἑνός]: and to your seed [τῷ σπέρματί σου], which is Christ [ὅς ἐστιν Χριστός]." Nils Dahl has rightly pointed out that Paul is making an exegetical inference by analogy here: just as the "seed" (τὸ σπέρμα) of David is understood messianically in the early Jesus movement (see 2 Sam. 7:12), so too is Paul claiming that Abraham's "seed" must be understood: the "in you" refers to the seed (τῷ σπέρματί) of Abraham, and that seed is Jesus Christ.[30]

If the "in you" (Gal. 3:8) is the "seed" (Gal. 3:16a), and the "seed" is Jesus Christ (Gal. 3:16b), Paul's initial invocation of Abraham's blessing at Galatians 3:8 must be

Table 4.1 Galatians 3:8 and Genesis 12:3; 18:18; 22:18

Galatians 3:8	*Genesis 12:3*	*Genesis 18:18*	*Genesis 22:18*
"All the nations will be blessed in you."	"All the tribes of the earth will be blessed **in you**."	"All the nations of the earth will be blessed in him."	"All the nations of the earth will be blessed **in your seed**."
ἐνευλογηθήσονται **ἐν σοὶ** πάντα τὰ ἔθνη.	ἐνευλογηθήσονται **ἐν σοὶ** πᾶσαι αἱ φυλαὶ τῆς γῆς.	ἐνευλογηθήσονται ἐν αὐτῷ πάντα τὰ ἔθνη τῆς γῆς.	ἐνευλογηθήσονται **ἐν τῷ σπέρματί σου** πάντα τὰ ἔθνη τῆς γῆς.

the combination of Genesis 12:3 and Genesis 22:18. The promise contained within the Aqedah is not only the earliest moment at which "all the nations" (πάντα τὰ ἔθνη) are blessed in Abraham's "seed," but the locution used there, "in your seed" (ἐν τῷ σπέρματί σου [Gen. 22:18]) mirrors Paul's language at Galatians 3:16 almost exactly: "to your seed" (τῷ σπέρματί σου).[31] Because the "in him" (ἐν αὐτῷ) of Genesis 18:18 refers grammatically to Abraham and not to Isaac, it is at Genesis 22:18 that Paul finds clear scriptural warrant for interpreting the ἐν σοί of Genesis 12:3 messianically.[32]

Importantly, Paul does not evoke the near sacrifice of Isaac simply to provide scriptural warrant for reading the blessing that occurs in Abraham as referring to Christ. Rather, he perceives (and he expects his audience to perceive) a typological prefiguration of the crucifixion of the messiah within the Aqedah. Essential to Paul's argument for justification by faith in Galatians 3 is the fact that Christ *dies*. At Galatians 3:13, Paul equates Christ's death with a curse—"cursed [ἐπικατάρατος] is everyone who hangs upon a tree [ἐπὶ ξύλου]" (comp. Deut. 21:23: "Every person hanging upon a tree [κρεμάμενος ἐπὶ ξύλου] is cursed by God [εκατηραμένος ὑπὸ θεοῦ]")—and he claims that, because Christ became a "curse" on behalf of others (ὑπὲρ ἡμῶν κατάρα), he is able to redeem others from the "curse of the law" ("Christ redeemed us from the curse of the law" [Χριστὸς ἡμᾶς ἐξηγόρασεν ἐκ τῆς κατάρας τοῦ νόμου]). According to Paul, it is Christ's death that allows the blessing of Abraham to come to the nations, which they are then able to receive "through faith" (διὰ τῆς πίστεως [Gal. 3:14]). Paul thus evokes the Aqedah in Galatians 3 because, as a type of Christ's death, it prefigures two of his essential claims: (1) that the Gentiles will be blessed in Abraham, and (2) that blessing is rooted within and contingent upon death and sacrifice. Indeed, there may be an association in Paul's mind between Christ's hanging "upon the tree" (ἐπὶ ξύλου Gal. 3:13]) and Isaac's being set "upon the wood" (ἐπάνω τῶν ξύλων [Gen. 22:9]) that helped to facilitate Paul's allusion to Deuteronomy 21:23 at Galatians 3:13.[33]

When Paul composes his letter to the Romans some years later, the Aqedah appears once more. While more than one passage in that epistle has been thought to recall Isaac's binding, none has garnered as much support as Romans 8:32.[34] Paul's allusion comes at the end of a major block of material (Rom. 5:1–8:39) throughout which the apostle consistently circles back to the idea that there is now freedom for believers: "freedom from the wrath of God in chapter 5 (5:9–11); freedom from the power of sin in chapter 6 (6:14); freedom from the law in chapter 7 (7:4–6); and freedom from death in chapter 8 (8:9–11; 37–39)."[35] In his discussion of freedom from death, Paul touches upon sonship and inheritance, the sustaining power of the Spirit, and the anticipated (or "hoped for" [see Rom. 8:20, 24–25]) liberation of the whole cosmos that will occur in accordance with God's will (see esp. Rom. 8:14–30). Paul concludes his discussion by arguing that nothing will be capable of separating believers from the love of God (Rom. 8:31–9). He initiates this bold claim with a rhetorical question: "If God is for us [ὑπὲρ ἡμῶν], who can be against us [καθ᾽ ἡμῶν]?" (Rom. 8:31).[36] Then, on the heels of this first question, he asks a second: "He who did not even spare [ἐφείσατο] his own son [τοῦ ἰδίου υἱοῦ], but he handed him over [παρέδωκεν αὐτόν] on behalf of us all [ὑπὲρ ἡμῶν πάντων], how will he not also freely give [χαρίσεται] to us everything [τὰ πάντα] along with him?" (Rom. 8:32). Because God has already offered that which is beyond human comprehension (his own son [τοῦ ἰδίου υἱοῦ]), Paul's claim is that believers should be confident that God stands with them (indeed, with *all* creation [Rom. 8:22: πᾶσα ἡ κτίσις]), and that he will deliver on his promises.

The language Paul uses at Romans 8:32 clearly evokes Genesis 22:16: "Because [οὗ εἵνεκεν] you have done this thing [τὸ ῥῆμα τοῦτο], and you did not spare [οὐκ ἐφείσω] your son [τοῦ υἱοῦ σου], the beloved [τοῦ ἀγαπητοῦ] ..." (see also Gen. 22:12). Together with the larger thematic connection that sees father offer son upon the altar (see Gen. 22:9–10), there are verbal associations that bind the two texts together. On one hand, both share the same verb in the same tense (φείδομαι) with an emphasized "son" (τοῦ ... υἱοῦ) as the genitive object. On the other, both underscore the familial relationship between son and father.[37] The Aqedah does so through the use of a personal pronoun (σου) and the use of the affectionate title, ἀγαπητός. Paul does so through the possessive adjective (ἴδιον).[38]

As in Galatians, Paul here presumes that the near sacrifice of Isaac prefigures God's action taken vis-à-vis Christ, and, as before, Paul evokes the Aqedah as scriptural witness to the universal access to salvation granted through Christ's death. In the biblical narrative, "because of" (οὗ εἵνεκεν [Gen. 22:16]/ἀνθ᾿ ὧν [Gen. 22:18]) Abraham's obedient but aborted sacrifice, the covenant between God and Israel is established. Since Romans 8 opens with a discussion of freedom from the law (Rom. 8:1–4; comp. Gal. 3:10–14,) and continues with a discussion of the power of the baptismal Spirit that makes all believers children of God, regardless of ethnic background (Rom. 8:9–11, 14–17; comp Gal. 3:26–4:6), it comes as little surprise that Paul's allusion to the Aqedah at Romans 8:32 again recalls God's promise to Abraham at Genesis 22:16–18 ("because you obeyed this command and did not spare your son, the beloved ... all the nations of the earth [πάντα τὰ ἔθνη τῆς γῆς] will be blessed in your seed [ἐν τῷ σπέρματί σου]" [Gen. 22:16, 18; see Gal. 3:8]). Within the larger context of Paul's argument to the Romans, it appears that the apostle has inferred from the Abraham cycle that the patriarch's initial worthiness to attain "the oracles of God" (τὰ λόγια τοῦ θεοῦ) has resulted in a certain "advantage" (τὸ περισσόν) to the Jewish people (see Rom. 3:1–2; 4:11–12). In the wake of Christ's completed sacrifice, however, the advantage to the Jewish people as "first" (πρῶτον [Rom. 3:2; see also 1:16; 2:9–10]) remains, but the blessings that come to Abraham's biological seed, and the divine commandments (e.g., circumcision) imposed as a result, are transformed (see Rom. 3:21–30). Like in Galatians, then, the Aqedah is assumed to be a typological prefiguration of the cross that anticipates Gentile salvation. In the story's antitype, however, where God takes on the role of Abraham, the sacrifice is carried through to the end, and it results in expiation and access to salvation on a universal scale. As Jon Levenson has suggested of Romans 8:32, "the new aqedah, which is the crucifixion of Jesus, has definitively and irreversibly secured the blessings of which the angel there spoke."[39]

(C) The Passover lamb

In Exodus 12, God provides Moses and Aaron instruction on how the Israelites are to survive the impending deaths of the firstborn in Egypt. The deity explains that each household is to take a sheep (πρόβατον), a perfect (τέλειον) one-year-old male (ἄρσεν ἐνιαύσιον [Ex. 12:3–5]), and, on the fourteenth of the month, the household is to slaughter that sheep and set its blood upon the doorposts and lintel of their home (Ex. 12:7, 12–13). The sheep's flesh is to be consumed with unleavened bread (ἄζυμα) and its bones left unbroken ("You will not break a bone from it [ὀστοῦν οὐ συντρίψετε ἀπ᾽ αὐτοῦ]" [Ex. 12:10]), and, if anything should remain until morning, the leftovers are to be burned (Ex. 12:8–10). God then provides instructions for a yearly memorial festival built out of the Passover event (Ex. 12:14: "this day will be for you a memorial [μνημόσυνον], and you shall celebrate it as a feast for the Lord through all your generations [ἑορτάσετε αὐτὴν ἑορτὴν κυρίῳ εἰς πάσας τὰς γενεὰς ὑμῶν]"). He enjoins that, for seven days, the Israelites are to consume unleavened bread (ἄζυμα), beginning "on the evening of the 14th day [of the year's] first month" (τῇ τεσσαρεσκαιδεκάτῃ ἡμέρᾳ τοῦ μηνὸς τοῦ πρώτου) and ending "on the evening of the 21st day" (ἕως ἡμέρας μιᾶς καὶ εἰκάδος τοῦ μηνὸς ἕως ἑσπέρας [Ex. 12:18; see also Ex. 12:1]). During this period, the Israelites are to remove leaven from their homes (ἀφανιεῖτε ζύμην ἐκ τῶν οἰκιῶν ὑμῶν [Ex. 12:15a]), and anyone who consumes it is to be cut off from the congregation of Israel (Ex. 12:15b, 19–20). The account concludes with Moses calling the elders of the people together, commanding them to "sacrifice the Passover" (θύσατε τὸ πασχα [Ex. 12:21]), and providing instructions for how they are to do so (Ex. 12:21–28).

That Paul sees in the Passover lamb a prefiguration of the death of Christ is demonstrated by 1 Corinthians 5:7. There, the apostle writes, "Christ, our Passover [τὸ πάσχα ἡμῶν] has been sacrificed [ἐτύθη]" (comp. Ex. 12:21: "sacrifice the Passover" [θύσατε τὸ πασχα]). These words are spoken in the course of Paul's attempt to correct what he considers a particularly dangerous type of aberrant behavior within the Corinthian church: sexual malfeasance (πορνεία [1 Cor. 5:1a]). One of the believers is sleeping with his own stepmother ("someone has the wife of his father [γυναῖκά τινα τοῦ πατρός]" [1 Cor. 5:1b]).[40] Equally problematic, the community has arrogantly condoned this action (they have become "puffed up [πεφυσιωμένοι]" [1 Cor. 5:2]).[41] After Paul provides an unequivocal judgment on the matter—"hand this man over to Satan for the destruction of the flesh [εἰς ὄλεθρον τῆς σαρκός] so that the Spirit might be saved [τὸ πνεῦμα σωθῇ] on the day of the Lord" (1 Cor. 5:5)[42]—the apostle makes a transition into Paschal imagery, and he writes,

> 6. Your boasting [τὸ καύχημα ὑμῶν] is not a good thing. Do you not know that a little leaven [μικρὰ ζύμη] leavens the whole lump [τὸ φύραμα]? 7. Clean out [ἐκκαθάρατε] the old leaven [τὴν παλαιὰν ζύμην] in order that you become a new lump [νέον φύραμα], as you really are unleavened [ἄζυμοι]. For Christ, our Passover [τὸ πάσχα ἡμῶν], has been sacrificed

[ἐτύθη]. 8. So let us celebrate [ἑορτάζωμεν] not with old leaven [ἐν ζύμῃ παλαιᾷ], nor leaven of evil and wickedness [ἐν ζύμῃ κακίας καὶ πονηρίας], but with unleavened bread of sincerity and truth [ἐν ἀζύμοις εἰλικρινείας καὶ ἀληθείας] (1 Cor. 5:6–8).

This excerpt is replete with references to, or assumptions about, the Passover celebration. Beyond the obvious use of πάσχα, the Corinthians are called to "celebrate" (ἑορτάζω) with unleavened bread, as are the Israelites (Ex. 12:14–15), and the idea that the old leaven must be "cleaned out" (ἐκκαθαίρω) is precisely what the Passover celebration accomplishes (see Ex. 12:15, 19).[43] Indeed, so evident is the overlap that, when coupled with Paul's "I will come to you soon" (ἐλεύσομαι δὲ ταχέως πρὸς ὑμᾶς [1 Cor. 4:19]) and his statement that, "I will remain in Ephesus until Pentecost" (ἐπιμενῶ δὲ ἐν Ἐφέσῳ ἕως τῆς πεντηκοστῆς [1 Cor. 16:8]), some scholars have suggested that Paul may have written his letter during the Passover season.[44]

Regardless of when in the year one places the composition of Paul's letter, it is clear that Paul is here using the Passover lamb as a type of Christ's death. Just as the blood of the Passover sacrifice, when splashed upon the doorposts and lintels of the Israelite homes (Ex. 12:7, 13, 22–23), protects the Jewish people from the destroyer and grants them freedom from bondage in Egypt (Ex. 12:17, 31–32), so too does the blood of Christ, poured out upon the cross, grant access to freedom from the bondage of sin and death for all who were once enslaved to it (Rom. 6:20; see also 1 Cor. 7:22–23). Though the procedure may be inverted—that is, the Israelites have to clean out leaven from their homes in order to celebrate the Passover, while, for the Corinthians, the sacrifice has already been completed, and the unleavened Corinthians are called to clean out any fresh corrupting influences[45]—it is nevertheless clear that Paul sees in the Passover of Exodus 12 Christ's death on the cross prefigured. In a manner analogous to the Israelites' wilderness experiences prefiguring the situation of the Corinthian community (see 1 Cor. 10:1–13; comp. Ex. 13:21; 14:21–31; 16:4, 14–18; 17:6; 32:6; Num. 20:7--13; 25:9; etc.), that which was a salvific event for one nation, in its performance in Paul's lifetime, has become a salvific event for all.

To conclude: the suffering servant of Isaiah 53, the Aqedah of Genesis 22, and the sacrifice of the Paschal lamb in Exodus 12 are all scriptural prefigurations of Jesus' death for Paul. They proleptically manifest for the believing community the salvific crucifixion of the messiah. Paul presumes these types, and he alludes to them in the course of his arguments without ever fully explicating their significance. A few logical inferences can be made on the basis of these conclusions. First, presuming these passages form a part of a network of interconnected scriptural witnesses that Paul shares with his communities (thus his ability to assume their knowledge), the allusions Paul makes in the composition of his letters are recognizable *because* the passages under discussion were performed in early communal worship.[46] There was no written gospel in Paul's day; instead, scripture was read, and the (oral) story of Christ's death was discussed and interpreted in light of it. Second, though Hays rightly suggests that Paul's reading of scripture is primarily ecclesiological, it is nevertheless also Christological in the broader sense that all scripture points to or anticipates the Christ event and realities subsequent to it. To understand scripture properly requires reading it in light of the story of the death and resurrection of Jesus Christ that occurs "in accordance with the scriptures" (κατὰ τὰς γραφάς [1 Cor. 15:3, 4]). Thus, from Paul's perspective, these scriptural types are necessarily synecdochical: they require the full recollection of the gospel plot to be understood fully. Third and finally, scholars have noted that the recitation of scripture in the ancient world was thought to have had a mystical or "numinous" quality.[47] If true, in light of my arguments in the previous chapters, it can be hypothesized that, in the synecdochical evocation of the whole through the performance of one of its parts, Paul believes that an epiphanic encounter with the deity takes place. In other words, the reading of scripture in a Pauline community, as baptism or the consumption of the Eucharist, was presumed to be an epiphanic experience.

Part II: Scriptural prefigurations of Jesus' death in Mark

In what follows, I will argue that, as with Paul, three essential prefigurations of Christ's death upon which the Markan narrative is constructed are the suffering servant of Isaiah 53, the Aqedah of Genesis 22, and the Paschal sacrifice of Exodus 12. For Mark, these texts serve as scriptural witnesses to, and proleptic manifestations of, the crucifixion of the messiah. At the same time, because scripture is interpreted through the lens of the death and resurrection of Jesus Christ (see Mk. 8:31: "it is necessary [δεῖ]"), these stories are also synecdochical.[48] In the (re)presentation of one type (τύπος) or the other, the passion of Jesus and the whole remainder of salvation history is brought before the eye of the viewer.

(A) The suffering servant

It has long been recognized that Jesus' mission statement at Mark 10:45 alludes to the story of the suffering servant of Isaiah 53.[49] Jesus' claim that, "the Son of Man did not come to be served but to serve [διακονηθῆναι ἀλλὰ διακονῆσαι], and to give his life [δοῦναι τὴν ψυχὴν αὐτοῦ] as a ransom for many [λύτρον ἀντὶ πολλῶν]," bears close conceptual similarity to Isaiah 53:12:

> For this reason he will inherit many and he will divide the spoils of the strong, because [ἀνθ' ὧν] his life [ἡ ψυχὴ αὐτοῦ] was handed over unto death [παρεδόθη εἰς θάνατον], and he was reckoned amongst the lawless [ἐν τοῖς ἀνόμοις ἐλογίσθη]. And he himself took up [ἀνήνεγκεν] the sins of many [ἁμαρτίας πολλῶν], and, for the sake of their sins [διὰ τὰς ἁμαρτίας αὐτῶν], he was handed over [παρεδόθη].

To be sure, there are scholars who argue that Isaiah 53 neither stands behind Mark 10:45 nor the gospel narrative more broadly, but their arguments place undue weight on the lack of explicit verbal parallels between Mark 10:45 and Isaiah 53:12, or they read the passage too narrowly within its immediate literary context (or both).[50] Mark 10:45 is a summary of Jesus' purpose on earth, and the gospel of Mark, *as a whole*, is the story of Mark 10:45. The sentence stands in a synecdochical relationship to the entire narrative. In order to determine whether Isaiah 53 functions as a typological backdrop to Mark's gospel, one must investigate whether the Markan narrative broadly reflects the literary contours of the Fourth Servant Song. As I will demonstrate below, this can be answered in the affirmative.

First, both the Gospel of Mark and Isaiah 53 presume an encounter with Gentile nations. Isaiah 52:15a says, "Many nations [ἔθνη πολλά] will marvel [θαυμάσονται] at him," while Mark 13:10 says, "It is necessary [δεῖ] that the gospel first be proclaimed [κηρυχθῆναι] to all the nations [εἰς πάντα τὰ ἔθνη]." Isaiah, as scripture, anticipates the mission that Mark assumes must occur in accordance with scripture. The prophet then goes on to say that "those to whom no report was brought concerning him will see [οἷς οὐκ ἀνηγγέλη περὶ αὐτοῦ ὄψονται]," and "those who have not heard will understand [οἳ οὐκ ἀκηκόασιν συνήσουσιν]" (Isa. 52:15b). The dénouement of the theme of misunderstanding in Mark's gospel (encapsulated in Mark's paraphrase of Isaiah 6:9–10—"so that seeing they might see and not perceive [βλέπωσιν καὶ μὴ ἴδωσιν], and hearing they might hear and not comprehend [ἀκούωσιν καὶ μὴ συνιῶσιν], lest they turn and it be forgiven them" [Mk. 4:12; see also Mk. 6:42; 7:14, 18; 8:17, 21; etc.])—is thus anticipated in the Fourth Servant Song. For Mark, human misunderstanding is only resolved after the messiah's death and resurrection (see Mk. 14:28; 16:7) wherein full comprehension of these events (see Mk. 9:9–10), together with Jesus' purpose on earth (Mk. 10:45), is finally attained (cf. Mk. 8:31–38). It is no coincidence that Christological comprehension coincides with the commission to the Gentile nations (Mk. 13:10), which formally begins (i.e., as an institutional program facilitated by early missionaries) after Jesus' expiration. For an interpreter like Mark, Isaiah's story of the suffering servant affirms that it is only in the wake of the messiah's suffering and violent death that the nations "will see and understand." In other words, the mission to the Gentiles, as an activity that entails the proclamation of Jesus Christ *crucified*, finds its scriptural warrant in the servant of Isaiah 53. It is proof that the death of Christ and the mission to the Gentile nations is "necessary" (δεῖ).

Second, Isaiah's insistence that the servant is "handed over" (παραδίδωμι) for the sake of the sins of others[51]—both actively ("The Lord [κύριος] handed him over for our sins [παρέδωκεν αὐτὸν ταῖς ἁμαρτίαις ἡμῶν]" [Isa. 53:6]) and passively ("… because his soul was handed over to death [παρεδόθη εἰς θάνατον] … for the sake of their sins [διὰ τὰς ἁμαρτίας αὐτῶν] he was handed over [παρεδόθη]" [Isa. 53:12])—is pervasively represented in Mark's gospel.[52] Mark, like Isaiah, represents Jesus' "handing over" in the active (Mk. 3:19; 10:33; 14:10–11, 18; 21, 42, 44; 15:1, 10, 15) and in the passive (Mk. 9:31; 10:33; 14:21). Moreover, Mark not only affirms Isaiah's attribution of the servant's "handing over" to God (Isa. 53:6), but he clarifies the ambiguous roles that human beings appear to play in that process (see Isa. 52:14; 53:5, 7, 9). Because Mark takes the messiah's death to be anticipated in scripture, ultimate responsibility for it rests with the deity (see Mk. 14:21: "just as it is written [καθὼς γέγραπται] concerning him ... the Son of Man is handed over [παραδίδοται]"). Yet, because Mark's story tells the earthly mission of the Jewish savior of the world, a figure whose death occurs within a human sphere of activity that includes individual persons, communities, and institutions, he fills out Isaiah's suggested but undetermined roles for human agents (see Judas [Mk. 3:19; 14:10–11, 18, 42, 44]; the ruling authorities [Mk. 15:1, 10, 15]).[53] Jesus Christ, savior of the human race who dies for the forgiveness of sins, is thus handed over actively and passively, by human beings and by God. For Mark, Isaiah 53 again serves as scriptural proof that Jesus' death for the forgiveness of sin was "necessary" (δεῖ).

Finally, it is regularly noted that Jesus' silence before the chief priests and Sanhedrin during the first trial scene of Mark 14:55–65 ("And he was silent [ἐσιώπα] and saying nothing [οὐκ ἀπεκρίνατο οὐδέν]" [Mk. 14:61; see also Mk. 15:5]) may echo Isaiah 53:7: "And he, because of his mistreatment [διὰ τὸ κεκακῶσθαι], does not open his mouth [οὐκ ἀνοίγει τὸ στόμα αὐτοῦ] ... as a lamb is silent before its shearer [ὡς ἀμνὸς ἐναντίον τοῦ κείροντος αὐτὸν ἄφωνος], he does not open his mouth [οὐκ ἀνοίγει τὸ στόμα αὐτοῦ]."[54] What is not often perceived, however, is the larger thematic mapping of the trial of Mark 14 onto Isaiah 53.

In describing the events leading up to Jesus' execution, Mark is careful to highlight the centrality of deceit (δόλος; see Mk. 14:1: "And the chief priests and scribes were seeking how, once they had caught him by deceit [αὐτὸν ἐν δόλῳ κρατήσαντες], they might kill him"). The deceit by which the authorities seek to destroy Jesus is a consistent theme throughout chapter 14 (see Mk. 14:1–2, 10–11, 18–20, 44), and it recurs in the false testimony brought against Jesus by the chief priests and Sanhedrin at his first trial (Mk. 14:55–59). After Jesus' (apparent) silence during their lies and the High Priest's initial line of inquiry (Mk. 14:60–61), Jesus finally responds to the question of his messianic status with a striking declaration, "I am [ἐγώ εἰμι]" (Mk. 14:62), a possible signal of his divine status (comp. Ex. 3:14; see also Gen. 17:1; 31:13; Ex. 3:6; etc.).[55] Whereas the witnesses have lied about what Jesus has done so as to foreshadow what will occur (the destruction and resurrection of his body after three days [Mk. 14:58]), Jesus (finally) speaks the unadulterated truth about his messianic status (he is the Christ, the Son of God, who will sit at the right hand of the deity and will return with the clouds of heaven [Mk. 14:61–62]) to persons who are all but guaranteed to take him for a liar. The scene is masterfully ironic, and it draws on the Fourth Servant Song for more than just the silence motif. At Isaiah 53:9, the prophet claims that the servant is without deceit (δόλος): "nor was any deceit discovered in his mouth [οὐδὲ εὑρέθη δόλος ἐν τῷ στόματι αὐτοῦ]." When coupled with Isaiah's prediction that the wicked and powerful will take a central role in the servant's death ("and I will put the wicked opposite his tomb [δώσω τοὺς πονηροὺς ἀντὶ τῆς ταφῆς αὐτοῦ] and the wealthy opposite his death [τοὺς πλουσίους ἀντὶ τοῦ θανάτου]" [Isa. 53:9]), which results in his being "reckoned amongst the lawless" (ἐν τοῖς ἀνόμοις ἐλογίσθη [Isa. 53:12]), there is strong reason to believe that more of Isaiah 53 stands behind Jesus' trial(s) than has heretofore been noticed. Jesus is famously counted amongst the lawless (he is associated with Barabbas, an "insurrectionist" [στασιαστής; Mk. 15:7], and he is crucified with two "brigands" [λῃσταί; Mk. 15:27]),[56] and those who are responsible for the crucifixion are the wicked and wealthy ruling classes of Palestine (the chief priests and Sanhedrin [Mk. 14:55]; the scribes and council of elders [Mk. 15:1], Pilate [Mk. 15:15]; the soldiery of the praetorium [Mk. 15:16]; etc.). That which Isaiah 53 predicts in general terms, Mark weaves into his story and fleshes out with specific details.

(B) The binding of Isaac

Of course, Isaiah 53 is not the only scriptural prefiguration of the death of Christ in Mark. An equally important witness is the Aqedah of Genesis 22. In Chapter 2 of this monograph, I argued that a verbal echo of the binding of Isaac is present in Jesus' baptism. I suggested that God's words, "You are my son [σὺ εἶ ὁ υἱός μου], the beloved [ὁ ἀγαπητός], in you I am well pleased [ἐν σοὶ εὐδόκησα]" (Mk. 1:11) not only recall Psalm 2:7; they recall Genesis 22:2. There, God says, "Take your son [λαβὲ τὸν υἱόν σου], the beloved [τὸν ἀγαπητόν], whom you love [ὃν ἠγάπησας]." Through the self-conscious connection of "beloved" (ἀγαπητός) with "son" (υἱός), Mark evokes the entirety of the Aqedah by way of synecdoche. In so doing, Mark invites his audience to read his story of the mission and death of Jesus Christ in light of Genesis 22, and, because Mark maps the sequence of events at Jesus' death (Mk. 15:37–39) upon the baptismal sequence (Mk. 1:9–11), the Aqedah, recalled at Mark 1:11, logically stands in the background of Mark 15:37–39, as well.[57]

That said, unlike Isaac's binding, Jesus' sacrifice is not aborted; it is carried through to the end. Mark's passion narrative is peppered with possible allusions to and reversals of the Aqedah, but the most important occurs on the cross itself: Jesus *dies*.[58] In the Genesis narrative, Abraham acts unhesitatingly to take the life of his son. He wordlessly comes to the allotted place, builds the altar, sets the wood upon it, binds the feet of Isaac, and takes the knife to slaughter his child (Gen. 22:9–10). If the reader is to expect God's imminent intervention in the sacrifice (see Abraham's ironic statement, "God will see to the sheep for himself [ὁ θεὸς ὄψεται ἑαυτῷ πρόβατον]" [Gen. 22:8]), the characters at the level of the story are not. That intervention does occur, however—"an angel of the Lord called him out from heaven and said to him, 'Abraham! Abraham! … Do not cast your hand against your little boy [τὸ παιδάριον]!'" (Gen. 22:11–12)—and Abraham is informed that it is "because of" (οὗ εἵνεκεν [Gen. 22:16]; ἀνθ' ὧν [Gen. 22:18]) his obedient action that "all the nations of the earth will be blessed in your seed" (ἐνευλογηθήσονται ἐν τῷ σπέρματί σου πάντα τὰ ἔθνη τῆς γῆς [Gen. 22:18]).

In the Markan crucifixion, one sees this scene inverted. The audience knows that there is to be no rescue from the cross—Mark has repeatedly made it clear that "it is necessary" (δεῖ [Mk. 8:31]) that Christ die—but the witnesses within the story (mockingly?) expect an intervention of the sort that occurs in Genesis 22. Immediately after Christ's cry of dereliction (Mk. 15:34; comp. Ps. 22:2), Mark says,

> 35. And some of those who were standing there [τινες τῶν παρεστηκότων] when they heard, were saying, "Look! He calls Elijah [ἴδε Ἠλίαν φωνεῖ]." 36. And someone, having run and filled a sponge with sour wine, after setting it upon a reed, was attempting to give him drink, saying, "Leave him [ἄφετε]![59] Let us see if Elijah is coming to take him down [ἴδωμεν εἰ ἔρχεται Ἠλίας καθελεῖν αὐτόν]" (Mk. 15:35–36; see also Ps. 69:22).[60]

This expectation for aid is, of course, disappointed. In the very next verse, Mark's audience is told that Jesus has died ("And Jesus, having let out a loud cry [ἀφεὶς φωνὴν μεγάλην], breathed out his Spirit [ἐξέπνευσεν]" [Mk. 15:37]), and the temple veil is rent in two ("the veil of the temple was torn in two [ἐσχίσθη εἰς δύο] from top to bottom" [Mk. 15:38]). This "rending" marks an epochal shift in salvation history. God's presence ceases to be located in the temple and a new and universal access to redemption becomes available. Eugene Boring nicely summarizes Mark's symbolism with the following words: "Jesus' death is the removal of a barrier, the opening of the way into God's presence for both Jews and Gentiles, as the eschatological temple not made by hands becomes a house of prayer for all nations."[61]

If this reading is correct, the reprisal of the narrative of Isaac's slaughter is an essential component in Mark's justification for the Gentile mission. The death of the messiah fulfills that which was prefigured in the Abrahamic narrative: the blessing of all nations in Abraham's seed. For Mark, the promises of God that were originally gifted to Israel as a result of the near sacrifice of Isaac have become universalized through the death of God's own beloved child upon the cross. Fulfilling the sacrifice is the necessary modification of the type that results in the antitype's expansion to the Gentile nations. What was true of Paul is thus equally true of Mark: "the new aqedah, which is the crucifixion of Jesus, has definitively and irreversibly secured the blessings of which the angel there spoke."[62]

(C) The Passover lamb

Finally, as with the Aqedah and Isaiah 53, the slaughter of the Paschal lamb (Ex. 12) also stands behind the crucifixion in the Gospel of Mark. To be sure, within the canonical gospels, it is John who most clearly maps Christ's sacrifice onto that of Exodus 12.[63] (If the fourth evangelist was familiar with the Gospel of Mark, however, it may be that he drew out and embellished the allusions to Passover he perceived in Mark's narrative.[64]) Nevertheless, Mark also presumes that the Paschal sacrifice prefigures the death of Christ, an association first signaled through the evangelist's labeling Christ's death a "ransom for the many" (λύτρον ἀντὶ πολλῶν [Mk. 10:45]). In the Septuagint, the noun "ransom" (λύτρον) and its corresponding verb "to redeem" (λυτρόω) are regularly connected with the freeing of the

Israelites from slavery in Egypt. Early in the Exodus narrative, for example, God commands Moses to "Go, speak to the children of Israel, saying, 'I am the Lord, and I will lead you from the tyranny of the Egyptians, and I will rescue you from slavery [ῥύσομαι ὑμᾶς ἐκ τῆς δουλείας], and I will redeem [λυτρώσομαι] you with an uplifted arm and great judgment'" (Ex. 6:6; see also Ex. 15:13; Deut. 7:8; 9:26; 13:6; 15:15; 2 Sam. 7:23; etc.). In response to this redemption, the Israelites are then obligated to sacrifice the firstborn male of all their flocks, and they are told that they must redeem their firstborn sons:

> 13. … You will redeem [λυτρώσῃ] every firstborn person among your sons [πᾶν πρωτότοκον ἀνθρώπου τῶν υἱῶν σου]. 14. And if your son should ask you afterwards, saying, "Why is this [τί τοῦτο]?" you will also say to him, "With a strong hand the Lord led us out of Egypt [ἐξήγαγεν ἡμᾶς κύριος ἐκ γῆς Αἰγύπτου], out of the house of bondage [ἐξ οἴκου δουλείας]. 15. And when Pharaoh hardened [himself] against sending us away, [God] killed every firstborn in Egypt [ἀπέκτεινεν πᾶν πρωτότοκον ἐν γῇ Αἰγύπτῳ], from the firstborn of human beings to the firstborn of beasts. Because of this, I am sacrificing to the Lord everything that opens the womb [θύω τῷ κυρίῳ πᾶν διανοῖγον μήτραν], the males, and I will redeem [λυτρώσομαι] every firstborn of my sons [πᾶν πρωτότοκον τῶν υἱῶν μου]" (Ex. 13:13–15; see also Ex. 34:18–20; Num. 3:11–13).

One is thus invited to relate Mark 10:45 to a constellation of themes found in the Passover narrative. Sacrifice, redemption, and the firstborn male have all become associated with the person of Jesus Christ. For Mark, he is the messiah, God's only (and therefore "firstborn") child, who will soon supplant the sacrificial lamb in order to redeem the many from the bondage of sin.

This invitation to thematic mapping is confirmed when Jesus dies on Nisan 15—Passover—the day on which the Israelite's redemption from Egypt was celebrated. At Mark 14:12, the evangelist says that the first day of Unleavened Bread coincides with the sacrifice of the Paschal lamb ("And on the first day of Unleavened Bread [τῇ πρώτῃ ἡμέρᾳ τῶν ἀζύμων], when they sacrifice the Passover [τὸ πάσχα] …"). There is a calendrical difficulty here. Conventionally, Jews of the Second Temple period would have reckoned days from evening to evening rather than from morning to morning. For them, the slaughter of the Paschal lamb would have occurred on the day *before* the first day of the Feast of Unleavened Bread rather than upon it (afternoon of Nisan 14 = Day of Preparation; evening of Nisan 15 = first day of the Feast of Unleavened Bread).[65] Mark, however, appears to be counting days from morning to morning, which results in his claiming that the sacrifice of the Paschal lamb, which occurs in the afternoon, takes place on the same day as the feast of Unleavened Bread, which begins at sundown (they are, in other words, both Nisan 14 for him). After Jesus' prayer at the Garden of Gethsemane (Mk. 14:32–34), his betrayal and arrest (Mk. 14:43–52), and his first trial (Mk. 14:53–65), the day is concluded, and Jesus is handed over to Pilate on the following morning (see Mk. 15:1: "and immediately in the morning [καὶ εὐθὺς πρωΐ] …").[66] *This* is Nisan 15, the day that Israel's redemption is formally celebrated. Mark here makes it une-quivocally clear that the redemption the Passover recalls coincides with the day on which Jesus is crucified.

Jesus' death on Passover suggests that, though John may map the figure of Jesus on the Passover lamb more accurately than does Mark, the typological logic of the two evangelists is the same. The slaughter of the lamb that results in the redemp-tion of the Israelites from Egypt prefigures the shedding of the blood of the mes-siah in expiation for the sins of the many. The sacrifice and consequence of the one prefigures the sacrifice and consequence of the other.

To conclude: I have argued in this section that three essential scriptural types prefiguring the death of Jesus in Mark are the suffering servant (Isa. 53), the bind-ing of Isaac (Gen. 22), and the Paschal sacrifice (Ex. 12). These stories are assumed by the evangelist and his community to bear witness to Jesus' death that must hap-pen in accordance with the scriptures (Mk. 8:31: "it is necessary" [δεῖ]). Presuming that these stories were read in worship, they would have synecdochically evoked in their auditors Jesus' crucifixion and the larger gospel narrative of which the cross is an episode. I suggest, then, that Mark, in composing his story of the mission and death of Jesus Christ, has attempted to weave references to these witnesses into his narrative in order to demonstrate that what the community has come to believe scripture prefigures is, in fact, fulfilled in the person of the messiah.

Part III: Combining Pauline types in the Markan Jesus

In this final section, I will argue that the three scriptural prefigurations of Jesus' death shared by Mark and Paul (Isa. 53; Gen. 22; and Ex. 12) are the result of the former's dependence upon the latter. Mark seeks to show within his story that the disparate biblical types (τύποι) of the crucifixion to which Paul alludes are simul-taneously and harmoniously fulfilled within the person of Jesus Christ. Through the use of an etiological hermeneutic, Mark seeds into his story the biblical pre-figurations of Christ's death that Paul understands scripture to provide, and, by (re)presenting their fulfillment within his story of the mission and death of the messiah, Mark affirms the gospel "in accordance with the scriptures" (κατὰ τὰς γραφάς [1 Cor. 15:3, 4]) that Paul presumes.

Importantly, the harmonization that Mark creates is built upon more than just the biblical interpretation of Paul. Other Second Temple exegetical traditions also play important roles in his construction. For example, ancient Jewish interpret-ers had already come to associate the Aqedah with Paschal sacrifice in order to demonstrate that God's redemptive process works consistently across biblical narratives. On this reading, the firstborn son, Isaac, who takes the place of the lamb (Gen. 22:7-8), is understood to be redeemed for the cost of a ram (Gen. 22:13), which prefigures God's redemptive action in Exodus.[67] At the same time, as Jews reflected upon recent and horrific experiences of persecution and death in the lives of their people, the narrative of Isaac's binding also came to be linked with expiation. Because the Temple Mount, where atonement sacrifices were offered, was already linked to Mount Moriah (2 Chr. 3:1;[68] see also Jubilees 18.13;

Josephus, *A.J.* 1.226), the narrative of the Aqedah could readily be connected with the expiatory system of ancient Israel. Isaac's aborted sacrifice thus came to be seen as a type of atonement sacrifice, one which found its fulfillment in the subsequent martyrdoms of the sons and daughters of Israel, persons whose self-sacrifices were capable of washing away the sins of the people.[69]

Both of these interpretive traditions likely informed Mark's thought. Indeed, they may have also informed Paul's. As I argued in Part I of this chapter, the child whom Paul says God did not "spare" (οὐκ ἐφείσατο [Rom. 8:32]) evokes the son whom Abraham did not "spare" (οὐκ ἐφείσω) at Genesis 22:12, 16. Paul's saying that God "handed him over" (actively: παρέδωκεν αὐτόν), however, may echo Isaiah 53:6, where God hands over the servant (κύριος παρέδωκεν αὐτόν). If this is the case, it is possible that undergirding Paul's conviction that Isaac's binding is a prefiguration of the death of Christ is the Second Temple interpretive tradition that associates the Aqedah with expiation.

Regardless, because the gospel narrative "in accordance with the scriptures" (κατὰ τὰς γραφάς [1 Cor. 15:3, 4]) is already assumed within Paul's epistolary correspondence, the apostle feels no need to explain how Christ can at the same time be antitype to the suffering servant, Isaac, and the Paschal sacrifice. In a story that presents the mission and death of Jesus Christ wherein those types are ful-filled, however, some meaningful attempt at their synthesis must be made. Mark's gospel does precisely this, and he uses the associations already established in the Second Temple period between the Aqedah and redemption and the Aqedah and expiation, on one hand, and the language of the sacrificial "sheep" (πρόβατον) that appears in all three witnesses (Gen. 22:7–8; Ex. 12:3–5; Isa. 53:7), on the other, to bind the types together.

I argued in the previous section that, for Mark, Christ is a new Isaac, and his death fulfills the aborted sacrifice that occurs in Genesis 22. At the same time, because Mark narrates Jesus' death as occurring on Nisan 15, the evangelist des-ignates him as the new Passover that redeems the many from bondage. Since the Aqedah was already thought to prefigure the Paschal sacrifice in Second Temple exegetical tradition, Mark's suggestion that both stories find their typological ful-fillment within a single antitype would have seemed a logical exegetical inference. Similarly, because Isaac's near sacrifice had come to be associated with atonement, the human self-sacrifice it was taken to prefigure, and the human sacrifice Isaiah 53 prophesies, could also have been seen as fulfilled within the death of Jesus Christ (an exegetical inference Mark may have shared with Paul [Rom. 8:32]). For Mark, this triangle of biblical types is chained together by their shared language. Isaac takes the place of the sacrificial sheep (πρόβατον [Gen. 22:7–8]) and is then redeemed for the cost of one (κριός [Gen. 22:13]). Each firstborn son of Israel in Egypt is redeemed for the cost of a sheep (πρόβατον [Ex. 12:3–5]), and the suffer-ing servant is likened to one (πρόβατον [Isa. 53:7]) in the course of his dying for the sins of the many.[70] If the Aqedah is the anchor to which the themes of expiation (Isa. 53) and redemption (Ex. 12) are tied, the sacrificial sheep that Genesis 22, Isaiah 53, and Exodus 12 all share is the metaphorical image upon which Mark reflects in order to put forth Christ as the single eschatological antitype to them all.

Narratively, the fulfillment of the three types occurs in the unfolding of Mark's plot. Mark begins by associating the mission of Jesus with Isaac's (near) slaughter by designating the messiah as God's beloved son (Mk. 1:11; see also Gen. 22:2; Mk. 12:6–9). Mark then associates Jesus with Isaiah 53 through literary echoes of the servant's mission and experiences (Mk. 10:45; 14:24, 61; etc.). Finally, he maps the death of the messiah that occurs on Passover back onto the sequence of baptism wherein Jesus' sonship is disclosed (comp. Mk. 1:9–11 with Mk. 15:38–39). Three of the chief scriptural witnesses to the cross that Paul invokes are thus enfolded within one coherent plot, with the underlying narrative progression seeming to work as follows: the sheep (πρόβατον) that the beloved son (Isaac) replaced (Gen. 22:7–8) is now replaced by a new beloved son (Mk. 1:11). This son (Jesus) is simultaneously the suffering servant who, like the sheep (πρόβατον [Isa. 53:7]), must be slaughtered (Mk. 15:37–39). The slaughter of this servant/beloved son effects a new redemption for the many (Mk. 10:45) on the pattern of the redemption from Egypt that the slaughter of a sheep secured (πρόβατον [Ex. 12:3–5]).

Importantly, as a result of Jesus' death "for many" (ἀντὶ πολλῶν [Mk. 10:45]/ ὑπὲρ πολλῶν [Mk. 14:24]), the rhetorical and theological ends towards which Paul deploys his scriptural witnesses to the cross (esp. to establish the validity of the Gentile mission [see Part I above]) are affirmed in Mark's gospel. The evangelist shows narratively that Jesus' Passover sacrifice, which effects redemption from sin, expands God's promises—once restricted to Israel as a result of Abraham's near-sacrifice of Isaac—to all who choose to believe in the messiah. Mark, in threading throughout his text those scriptural performances of Jesus' death that he and Paul share, creates additional narrative precedent for Paul's universal claims. The significances Paul derives from scriptural witnesses to the death of Christ are now echoed within the narrative (re)presentation of the messiah's earthly career.

Conclusion

Throughout his letters, Paul presumes scriptural prophecies about, or typological prefigurations of, Jesus' death. In this chapter, I have attempted to unearth some of those witnesses. The three paradigmatic examples I analyzed are the suffering servant of Isaiah 53, the binding of Isaac at Genesis 22, and the slaughter of the Paschal lamb at Exodus 12. Because Paul assumes rather than explicates the scriptural types with which he works, the stories in which these prefigurations are contained must have represented some of the narratives that were performed within Pauline communal worship. Moreover, because they would have been understood in relation to the Christ event, they necessarily (and synecdochically) evoke the entirety of the gospel narrative of which they are a part. They thus operate using the same epiphanic logic as the other phenomena discussed in this monograph: they bring the death of the messiah before the eyes of the community. In this case, however, they function as the "literary icons" of Jesus Christ crucified (to use the language of Mitchell) prior to the composition of Mark's gospel.[71]

Mark, then, in composing his own literary icon, seeds within his narrative those scriptural witnesses to Jesus' death that Paul presumes. Three of the same proleptic manifestations of the crucifixion found in Paul (Isa. 53, Gen. 22, and Ex. 12) reappear in Mark's story. The evangelist goes further than the apostle, however, as he attempts to show *how* these prefigurations are fulfilled within the person of Jesus, on one hand, and he affirms the significances Paul has attached to them for the believing community, on the other. Thus, Mark tells a story in which God's replaying the sacrifice of Isaac results in a new and universal access to deliverance because Christ has died in order that the many might be redeemed. Jesus, as scriptural antitype, unlocks the mission to the Gentile nations through his death.

Notes

1 On the centrality of scripture in early Christian thought, see Gamble, *Books and Readers*, 23–32. See also, Margaret M. Mitchell, "The Emergence of the Written Record," in eadem, *The Emergence of Christian Textuality*, 1–18; repr. from *The Cambridge History of Christianity: Volume 1, Origins to Constantine* (eds. Margaret M. Mitchell and Francis M. Young; Cambridge: Cambridge University Press, 2006), 177–94.

2 Kähler, *The So-Called Historical Jesus*, 80 n. 11.

3 Importantly, I am not claiming that this chapter presents an exhaustive investigation into the typological prefigurations of Jesus' death that Mark and Paul find in scripture. For example, both Paul and Mark also presume a Davidic Christology (see Rom. 1:3; Mk. 10:47–48) wherein the experiences of the sufferer in the Psalms of Lament typologically prefigure the suffering and death of Jesus. This is apparent at both Mk. 15:34, where the evangelist puts Ps. 22:2 (21:2 LXX) on the lips of Jesus, and at Rom. 15:3, where Paul does the same with Ps. 69:10 (68:10 LXX). An investigation into Mark's understanding of and potential engagement with Paul's Davidic Christology is beyond the scope of the current investigation. Instead, I have selected a thematically interrelated and linguistically overlapping complex of scriptural witnesses to the death of Christ that Paul presumes and Mark attempts to synthesize within his narrative. I do not wish to foreclose on the possibility of Mark's or Paul's using additional scriptural types to elucidate the meaning of Jesus' death, but I do contend that there is an interconnectedness between Isa. 53, Ex. 12, and Gen. 22 in the thought of Paul and Mark that warrants their shared investigation. For Mark's use of Ps. 22 in his passion narrative, see the good discussion of Holly J. Carey, *Jesus' Cry from the Cross: Towards a First-Century Understanding of the Intertextual Relationship between Psalm 22 and the Narrative of Mark's Gospel* (LNTS 398; London: T&T Clark, 2009). For an analysis of Mark's use of the Psalms of Lament more generally, see Stephen P. Ahearne-Kroll, *The Psalms of Lament in Mark's Passion: Jesus' Davidic Suffering* (SNTSMS; Cambridge: Cambridge University Press, 2007). On Paul's use of Ps. 68:10 LXX at Rom. 15:3, see, for example, Jewett, *Romans*, 879–80.

4 For discussion, see Chapter 1, note 96.

5 Hays, *Echoes of Scripture in the Gospels*, 11. For his earlier definition, see idem, *Echoes of Scripture in the Letters of Paul* (New Haven: Yale University Press, 1989), 20; see also John Hollander, *The Figure of an Echo: A Mode of Allusion in Milton and After* (Berkeley: University of California Press, 1981), 113–32.

6 One such excess might be a form of "parallelomania" wherein any given word, sentence, or phrase of the New Testament is thought to be dependent upon some previous biblical precursor (on the dangers of this phenomenon generally, see Samuel Sandmel, "Parallelomania," *JBL* 81 [1962], 1–13). Though tightly argued and, at

times, deeply insightful, one cannot help but wonder if Queller's intertextual investigation into Mk. 3:1-6 falls into precisely this trap (see Queller, "Echo and Metalepsis," 737–58).

7 Hays, *Echoes of Scripture*, 29–32.

8 See e.g., Jeannine K. Brown, "Metalepsis," in *Exploring Intertextuality: Diverse Strategies for New Testament Interpretation of Texts* (eds. B. J. Oropeza and Steve Moyise; Eugene: Cascade Books, 2016), 29–41, esp. 30–3. For a critical assessment of Hays' contribution, see David Allen, "The Use of Criteria: The State of the Question," in *Methodology in the Use of the Old Testament in the New: Context and Criteria* (eds. David Allen and Steve Smith; LNTS 579; London: T&T Clark, 2020), 129–41. On scriptural reuse more broadly, see William A. Tooman, "Scriptural Reuse in Ancient Jewish Literature: Comments and Reflections on the State of the Art," in Allen and Smith, *Methodology*, 23–39; see also the pioneering work of Michael Fishbane: *Biblical Interpretation in Ancient Israel* (Oxford: Clarendon Press, 1985).

9 Because Mark's and Paul's satisfaction of Hays' individual criteria will be obvious, and consistent reference back to them would be disruptive to my larger argument, I trust the reader to keep these criteria in mind and recall them where appropriate.

10 Francis Young, *Biblical Exegesis and the Formation of Christian Culture* (Cambridge: Cambridge University Press, 1997), 152, see also 193 n. 20.

11 "The word *typos* may be used for any 'model' or 'pattern' or 'parable' foreshadowing its fulfillment, whether an event or an oft-repeated ritual. It is not its character as historical event which makes a 'type'; what matters is its mimetic quality" (Young, *Biblical Exegesis*, 153. See also the good discussion in Robert M. Grant, *The Letter and the Spirit* [Eugene: Wipf & Stock, 1957], 137–9).

12 Young, *Biblical Exegesis*, 154. See also Northrop Frye's *The Great Code: The Bible and Literature* (New York: Harcourt Brace Jovanovich, 1981) and Tibor Fabiny's *The Lion and the Lamb: Figuralism and Fulfilment in the Bible, Art and Literature* (London: Macmillan, 1992).

13 One might add here that distinctions between prophecy and narrative, at least for Paul, are somewhat overdrawn. For the apostle, "in accordance with the scriptures" (κατὰ τὰς γραφάς [1 Cor. 15:3, 4]) enfolds both biblical narrative and biblical prophecy, and the result is that there is not always a clear distinction between type/antitype and prophecy/fulfillment in the apostle's letters. For example, at Gal. 3:8 Paul writes, "Scripture [ἡ γραφή], foreseeing [προϊδοῦσα] that God justifies the Gentiles by faith [ἐκ πίστεως], announced the gospel message beforehand to Abraham [προευηγγελίσατο τῷ Ἀβραάμ], saying: 'All the nations will be blessed in you'" (Gal. 3:8; see also Gen. 12:3; 18:18; 22:18). This pronouncement is both prophetic and typological. It is prophetic insofar as Paul appears to circumvent Isaac entirely as the recipient of the promises at Gal. 3:16: "It [i.e., scripture] does not say, 'to your seeds [ὡς ἐπὶ πολλῶν],' as if to many, but as to one [ὡς ἐφ' ἑνός], 'to your seed [καὶ τῷ σπέρματί σου],' which is Christ [ὅς ἐστιν Χριστός]." Here, one might argue that Paul reads scripture according to a prophecy-fulfillment pattern wherein the prophecy is fulfilled through the Christ event that occurs externally to the narrative. That said, this 'prophecy' simultaneously (and paradoxically) takes place and is concluded *within* the biblical narrative, with the result that Paul also reads Isaac typologically. In Paul's famous "allegory" of Gal. 4:21–31, Isaac is designated as the (or a) child of the promise: "you, brothers and sisters, are children of the promise [ἐπαγγελίας τέκνα], just as Isaac [κατὰ Ἰσαάκ]" (Gal. 4:28). If Isaac does not stand as a type of Christ for Paul (though I argue in this chapter that he does), he at least stands as "type" (τύπος) for all believers (see Rom. 9:7–10; see also Dunn, *Galatians*, 255–6; Martyn, *Galatians*, 348, 443–4; Matera, *Galatians*, 177–9; Betz, *Galatians*, 249). Prophecy and "type" are thus not clearly distinguished or compartmentalized in Paul's mind.

14 Hays, *Echoes of Scripture*, 86. See also his thoroughgoing analysis of Paul's use of scripture in Romans, where he makes this case fully (34–83).

15 See Hays: "Perhaps the genre of Paul's surviving writings obviates overt attention to Christological prophecy: he writes pastoral letters to Christian communities, not evangelistic or apologetic treatises. Paul's readers do not need to be convinced that Jesus was and is the messiah. In that case, the messianic exegesis might be assumed as the presuppositional background to Paul's interpretations" (*Echoes of Scripture,* 86).

16 Hays, *Echoes of Scripture,* 84–6 notes, for example, Paul's allusions to Ps. 110:1 and Ps. 8:6 in 1 Cor. 15:25–27, amongst others.

17 Interestingly, Hays alludes to Gen. 22 and Isa. 53 as scriptural types of Jesus' death, but he interprets them as embedded within Paul's larger ecclesiological argument about the suffering the community undergoes in the period before the end (see Hays, *Echoes of Scripture,* 61–3). The community's suffering is modeled upon the suffering of the messiah as a vicarious means to bring redemption to others.

18 Suggesting that διά here should be translated as "for the sake of" is not without controversy. Cilliers Breytenbach ("The Septuagint Version of Isaiah 53 and the Early Christian Formula, 'He was Delivered for Our Trespasses,'" *NovT* 51 [2009], 344–9), for example, argues that the διά of Isa. 53 should be translated causally. He goes on to argue that there is no reason to see Isa. 53 standing behind texts like Rom. 4:25 or 1 Cor. 15:3 due to the fact that, in the former, the servant dies "because of their sins" (διὰ τὰς ἁμαρτίας αὐτῶν [Isa. 53:12; see also Isa. 53:5]), while, in the latter, Christ dies, "for the sake of" (διά) or "on behalf of" (ὑπέρ) the people's sins. This reading, however, too strongly fixes the semantic range of διά to a causal "because in Isaiah." As is well known, when paired with the accusative, διά can convey a broader range of meanings, which includes both causality ("because of" or "on account of") and purpose ("for the sake of" [see Smyth, *Greek Grammar,* 375, § 1685b–c]), and the multi-valency of διά would have allowed a Christ-believing reader such as Paul or Mark to read Isa. 53:1–12 messianically ("for the sake of"). Indeed, "for the sake of," "because of," and "on behalf of" form a network of interconnected descriptions of the purpose of Jesus' death in Paul's thought. They should not be taken to be mutually exclusive. It is a part of Paul's divine economy that Christ is sent *because of* the rampant sin that has consumed the world, and he comes in order to free humanity from its bondage by paying the ultimate price *on their behalf* (see Rom. 7:7–8:4). In other words, Christ dies both because of and on behalf of the sins of the people. Drawing stark dividing lines does not do sufficient justice to the flexibility of Paul's rhetorical poetics. The case is equally true of Mark (see note 51 below). Thus, insofar as I am attempting to read Isa. 53 through the eyes of Mark, Paul, and their communities, I judge it appropriate to translate Isaiah's διά objectively.

19 I concur with Fitzmyer who sees chapters 9–11 as the rhetorical climax towards which Paul is working (*Romans,* 541); Tobin, *Paul's Rhetoric,* 352 limits chapter 11 to climactic status; cf. Heinrich Schlier, *Der Römerbrief* (HThKNT 6; Freiburg im Breisgau: Herder, 1977), 282, who says of these chapters, "Wenn man auch nicht von einem Exkurs reden kann, so ist doch zu bedenken, dass es, während der zweite Teil des Römerbriefes (5, 1–8, 39) formal und inhaltlich als Konsequenz des ersten (1, 8–4, 25) eng mit diesem verbunden ist, zwischen dem dritten und zweiten Teil keinen ausgesprochen Zusammenhang gibt."

20 For a similar summary, see Roetzel, *Man and the Myth,* 126–9. For a comprehensive treatment of these chapters, with special attention paid to their relationship to the book of Isaiah, see J. Ross Wagner, *Heralds of the Good News: Isaiah and Paul "in Concert" in the Letter to the Romans* (NTSupp 101; Leiden: Brill, 2002), 43–305.

21 On this, see Wagner, *Heralds of the Good News,* 178–80.; see also Jewett, *Romans,* 640–1.

22 See Hultgren, *Romans,* 191–2; Jewett, *Romans,* 342–4; Fitzmyer, *Romans,* 389–90. For good discussion of Rom. 4 generally, see Hultgren, *Romans,* 178–92.

23 See Wagner, *Heralds of the Good News,* 332–6.

24 On Isa. 53's connection to 1 Cor. 15:3, see Thiselton, *Corinthians*, 1189–90, who notes an allusion but rightly cautions against equating Paul's words with any single biblical reference. According to him, Christ's death "for our sins" (ὑπὲρ τῶν ἁμαρτιῶν ἡμῶν) is the heart of the gospel, and Isa. 53 presents one instantiation of Christ's atoning death "in accordance with the scriptures," but it is not the only one. On the connection between Isa. 53 and Paul's Eucharist, see my discussion in Chapter 3, Part I.

25 On Abraham as type, see Hays, "πίστις and Pauline Christology," 35–60 (discussed in detail in Chapter 2, note 10). On Isaac as a type of Christ, see this chapter, note 13.

26 Hays, "πίστις and Pauline Christology," 47. This interpretive stance is adopted by many scholars. See e.g., Betz, *Galatians*, 142; Martyn, *Galatians*, 117–26 (esp. 125), 297–306; Dunn, *Galatians* (London: A&C Black, 1993), 15–17; Sam K. Williams, *Galatians* (ANTC; Nashville: Abingdon, 1997), 86–7; Matera, *Galatians* 122; Simon Légasse, *L'Épître de Paul aux Galates* (LDC 9; Paris: Les Éditions du Cerf, 2000), 220–2; cf. Pheme Perkins, *Abraham's Divided Children: Galatians and the Politics of Faith* (Harrisburg: Trinity Press International, 2001), 65–7; Alfred Loisy, *L'Épître Aux Galates* (Paris: E. Nourry, 1916), 144–5; Wilfried Eckey, *Der Galaterbrief: ein Commentar* (Neukirchener Theologie; Neukirchen-Vluyn: Neukirchener Verlag, 2010), 188–9.

27 As Légasse (*Galates*, 227) rightly says of these words, "Le text est introduit sans formule de citation, mais par une phrase qui indique le register dans lequel Paul entend conduire ses lecteurs." On Gal. 3:6–14 generally, see Betz, *Galatians*, 137–54.

28 Noted by, amongst others, Betz, *Galatians*, 142; Martyn, *Galatians*, 301; Eckey, *Galaterbrief*, 194; Matera, *Galatians*, 118; Dunn, *Galatians*, 164.

29 See e.g., Dunn, *Galatians*, 164; Martyn, *Galatians*, 301; Matera, *Galatians*, 118.

30 Nils Alstrup Dahl, *Studies in Paul: Theology for the Early Christian Mission* (Minneapolis: Augsburg, 1977), 130. 2 Sam. 7:12 (2 Kgdms. 7:12) reads as follows: "And I will raise up your seed [τὸ σπέρμα σου] after you, who will be from your womb, and I will prepare his kingdom [ἑτοιμάσω τὴν βασιλείαν αὐτοῦ]." As is well-known, Davidic Christologies are peppered throughout New Testament Texts. See, for example, Rom. 1:3: "from the seed of David" (ἐκ σπέρματος Δαυίδ); Mk. 10:47: "Jesus, son of David [υἱὲ Δαυίδ], have mercy on me!" (see also Mk. 11:10); Matt. 1:1: "A Book of the origin of Jesus Christ, son of David [υἱοῦ Δαυίδ], son of Abraham;" Lk. 1:32: "This one will be great and he will be called the son of the Highest, and the Lord God will give to him the throne of David, his father [τὸν θρόνον Δαυίδ τοῦ πατρὸς αὐτοῦ];" 2 Tim. 2:8: "Remember Jesus Christ who has been raised from the dead, from the seed of David [ἐκ σπέρματος Δαυίδ], in accordance to my gospel"; etc.

31 While the words τῷ σπέρματι occur with some regularity in God's promises to Abraham, they are almost always linked with the reception of *land*, not with the blessing of nations (e.g., Gen. 12:7; 13:15; 15:18; 17:8). For scholars who also hear an echo of the Aqedah in Gal. 3:8 or 3:16 or both, see Dahl, *Studies in Paul,* 130–1; idem, "The Atonement: Adequate Reward for the Akedah?" in *Neotestamentica et Semitica: Studies in Honour of Matthew Black* (eds. E. Earle Ellis and Max Wilcox; Edinburgh: T&T Clark, 1969), 23; Hays, *Faith of Jesus Christ*, 180; Sigve K. Tonstad, "Inscribing Abraham: Apocalyptic, the Akedah, and 'Abba! Father!' in Galatians," in *Galatians as Examined by Diverse Academics in 2012* (ed. Heerak Christian Kim; Newark: The Hermit Kingdom Press, 2013), 18; Scott W. Hahn, "Covenant, Oath, and the Aqedah: Διαθήκη in Galatians 3:15–18," in *CBQ* 67 (2005), 90–4; Hans Joachim Schoeps, "The Sacrifice of Isaac in Paul's Theology," in *JBL* 65 (1946), 391; Calvin J. Roetzel, *The Letters of Paul: Conversations in Context* (5th edn.; Louisville: Westminster John Knox, 2009), 50; and Jon Levenson, *The Death and Resurrection of the Beloved Son: The Transformation of Child Sacrifice in Judaism and Christianity* (New Haven: Yale University Press, 1993), 212–13.

32 Genesis 18:18 reads as follows: "And Abraham will truly become a great and mighty nation [Αβρααμ δὲ γινόμενος ἔσται εἰς ἔθνος μέγα καὶ πολύ], and all the tribes of the earth [πάντα τὰ ἔθνη τῆς γῆς] will be blessed in him [ἐνευλογηθήσονται ἐν αὐτῷ]."

33 See Hahn, "Covenant, Oath, and the Aqedah," 93; see also Dahl, "Atonement," 23.

34 Scholars who hear some echo of the binding of Isaac in Rom. 8:32 include (but are not limited to) Levenson, *Death and Resurrection*, 221–2; Dahl, "Atonement," 16–20 and passim; Schoeps, "The Sacrifice of Isaac," 390; Barrett, *Romans*, 172; Käsemann, *Romans*, 247; Simon Légasse, *L'Épître de Paul aux Romains* (LDC 10; Paris: Les Éditions du Cerf, 2002), 549–50; Gignac, *Romains*, 330; Michael Theobald, *Der Römerbrief* (EF 294; Darmstadt: Wissenschaftliche Buchgesellschaft, 2000), 175; Dunn, "Once More, πίστις Χριστοῦ," 76; Schmithals, *Römerbrief*, 307–8; cf. Fitzmyer, *Romans*, 531–2; Jewett, *Romans*, 536–8; Schlier, *Römerbrief*, 277.

35 Hultgren, *Romans*, 197.

36 Hultgren has suggested that "God is for us" is, in fact, "a massive summary of what has been said in the previous chapters. God is for us, Paul can say, because we are justified, reconciled, saved from the wrath of God, and freed from the power of sin, the law, and death itself (Rom. 5:1–8:30)" (Hultgren, *Romans*, 336–7).

37 In his discussion of Abraham in Rom. 8, Levenson (*Death and Resurrection*, 221–2) also suggests that there may lie behind Paul's belief that "for those who love God [τοῖς ἀγαπῶσιν τὸν θεόν], all things work together for good [πάντα συνεργεῖ εἰς ἀγαθόν]" (Rom. 8:28) the tradition of Abraham as the archetypal lover of God, who willingly chooses love of God over love of son (see Jub. 17.16; 18) and receives a nation in return.

38 Additionally, though Paul never uses the adjective ἀγαπητός to describe Christ, it is likely that, for him, Christ is God's beloved child. At Rom. 5:8, for example, Paul says, "But God commends [συνίστησιν] his love for us [τὴν ἑαυτοῦ ἀγάπην εἰς ἡμᾶς] because, while we were still sinners [ἔτι ἁμαρτωλῶν ὄντων ἡμῶν], Christ died on our behalf [Χριστὸς ὑπὲρ ἡμῶν ἀπέθανεν]." According to the apostle, Christ is the expression of God's love made manifest. *Mutatis mutandis,* the depthless love God has for humanity as adopted siblings of Christ plausibly extends to and encompasses that eldest child. Indeed, within Pauline epistolary literature, it would not be long before this connection is made explicit (see Col. 1:13: "... [the Father], who rescued us from the power of darkness and transferred us into the kingdom of his beloved son [τοῦ υἱοῦ τῆς ἀγάπης αὐτοῦ] ..."

39 Levenson, *Death and Resurrection*, 222.

40 As commentators rightly note, it is improbable that Paul is here referring to a concubine. Because prostitution is not illegal in the ancient world, Paul's statement that the type of sexual malfeasance under discussion is something that "does not even occur among the Gentiles" (οὐδὲ ἐν τοῖς ἔθνεσιν [1 Cor. 5:1]) must have a different referent. Intercourse with one's mother or stepmother was universally prohibited. In the early third century C.E., Aelian notes that even beasts do not willingly copulate with their own mothers (*Nat. an.* 3.47), while the second century C.E. Roman jurist, Gaius, says the following about marrying one's stepmother: "moreover, it is not permitted to take a wife who was for me, at one time, a mother-in-law [*socrus*] or daughter-in-law [*nurus*] or stepdaughter [*priuigna*] or stepmother [*nouerca*]" (*Inst.* 1.63; see also *Inst.* 1.59 for his prohibition of marriage between direct biological relations. The Latin text has been taken from Gaius, *The Institutes* [trans. W. M. Gordon and O. F. Robinson; Ithaca: Cornell University Press, 1988]). Alternatively, in Jewish thought, the prohibition against sexual intercourse with one's mother or stepmother is articulated explicitly at Lev. 18:17–8 ("You shall not reveal the shame [i.e., nakedness] of your mother [ἀσχημοσύνην μητρός] ... you shall not reveal the shame of your father's wife [ἀσχημοσύνην γυναικὸς πατρός σου]") and Deut. 27:20 ("Cursed is the one who lies with his father's wife" [ἐπικατάρατος ὁ κοιμώμενος μετὰ γυναικὸς τοῦ

πατρὸς αὐτοῦ]). For good discussions of the πορνεία that is occurring amongst the Corinthian community, see Thiselton, *Corinthians*, 385–7; Fitzmyer, *Corinthians*, 233–5.

41   Fitzmyer, *Corinthians*, 229 suggests that this is, in fact, the larger problem: "[Paul] is annoyed that the Corinthian Christian church has tolerated such a situation in its midst. Paul is not reacting so much against what the individual Corinthian Christian has done as against the image that the Corinthian community is projecting on itself." See also Michel Quesnel, *La première épître aux Corinthiens* (CBNT 7; Paris: Les Éditions du Cerf, 2018), 124.

42   What Paul means by "the Spirit might be saved [τὸ πνεῦμα σωθῇ]" is debated. On one hand, it could refer to the Spirit of the individual (Malina and Pilch, *Letters of Paul*, 80; Witherington III, *Conflict and Community*, 158–9; Calvin J. Roetzel, *Judgment in the Community: a Study of the Relationship between Eschatology and Ecclesiology in Paul* [Leiden: Brill, 1972], 115–16). On the other, it could refer to the Spirit of the community (Fitzmyer, *Corinthians*, 239–40; Collins, *Corinthians*, 212–13; Dale Martin, *The Corinthian Body* [New Haven: Yale University Press], 168–74). Given that Paul will quickly turn his attention to the effects that sexual malfeasance has on the community as a whole (1 Cor. 5:6–8), the latter interpretation is perhaps the more likely. In the end, however, I agree with those who emphasize that both the preservation of the community *and* the salvation of the individual are in view. τὸ πνεῦμα σωθῇ enfolds both semantic possibilities (for good discussions, see Garland, *Corinthians*, 169–77, esp. 174–7; Thiselton, *Corinthians*, 395–400).

43   Leaven is not the same thing as yeast. Rather, a piece of dough was held over from one week's baking to the next. It was then stored away in fermenting juices and used in the new dough as a rising agent. This practice ran the risk of contamination, however, as bacteria and disease could be passed on from week to week. Part of Passover's purpose, then, was to begin the cycle all over again with fresh, unleavened bread (see Thiselton, *Corinthians*, 400–1, Fitzmyer, *Corinthians*, 240–1).

44   So Klauck, *1 Korintherbrief*, 43; see also Thiselton, *Corinthians*, 407–8. For a more recent argument, see Michael A. Daise, "'Christ Our Passover' (1 Corinthians 5:6–8): The Death of Jesus and the Quartodeciman Pascha," *Neot* 50.2 (2016), 507–26, esp. 517–20.

45   Astutely noted by Fitzmyer, *Corinthians*, 241–2.

46   On the communal performance of texts generally in the ancient world, see Pieter J. J. Botha, *Orality and Literacy in Early Christianity* (BPC 5; Eugene: Wipf and Stock, 2012), 89–112. On the possible means by which scripture was performed in early Christian worship, see Gamble, *Books and Readers*, 211–31.

47   See Richard A. Horsley, *Text and Tradition in Performance and Writing* (BPC 9; Eugene: Wipf and Stock, 2013), 5–7, 38–42, whence comes my use of the term "numinous." In their discussion of the difference between the prophet and the scribe, William Doan and Terry Giles (*Prophets, Performance, and Power: Performance Criticism of the Hebrew Bible* [New York: T&T Clark, 2006], 29) make the following incisive suggestion: "The prophet *himself* was the presence through which God appeared to the people of Israel. This was more than a linguistic moment; it was a moment of full sensory engagement for both the prophet and the spectators. The scribe, both as writer and speaker of the prophetic text, cannot create that moment. He must impersonate the prophet by creating the prophetic character, in order to create the illusion of the prophetic experience. In this sense he creates the prophetic drama. He impersonates the prophet in order to bring forth the presence of God. Though the scribe writes, 'Thus says the LORD,' his words are meant to be spoken and heard; the prophet is brought forth so that God can be made present" (emphasis original; see also their discussion of "scribe as performer" at 30–3). This understanding of the scribal activity nicely reflects my claim. The reading of scripture in the ancient

world is not solely for the purposes of instruction or entertainment; in the act of its performance, the presence of the deity is brought forth, and, in the act of listening, the audience is made to experience it.

48 Peter-Ben Smit ("Questioning Divine δεῖ: On Allowing Texts *not* to Say Everything," *NovT* 61 [2019], 40–54) has sought to challenge the consensus that "it is necessary" (δεῖ) refers to God's predetermined plan for salvation mapped out within scripture in the Gospel of Mark. He argues that such a reading goes beyond what the text itself indicates ("Questioning Divine δεῖ," 49). His argument, however, contains some logical difficulties. Smit suggests, for example, that, if a statement of necessity such as that found in Mk. 8:31 is a post-Easter formulation, "it becomes more attractive to view δεῖ as an indication of a divine plan that, having been unrolled now, can be seen in retrospect and Jesus can be made to speak accordingly" ("Questioning Divine δεῖ," 50). But the Gospel of Mark *is* a post-Easter narrative. Though the traditions Mark incorporates and adapts may predate him, they are all read in light of the death and resurrection of Jesus Christ. One cannot know what the historical Jesus meant when (or if) he made a statement like "it is necessary that the Son of Man suffer greatly …" (Mk. 8:31), but, for the evangelist and his audience, who are reflecting on the significance of the Christ event well after the fact, it almost certainly would have evoked God's divine plan. Indeed, when one looks at the other evidence that the Gospel of Mark provides, an interpretation of this sort is confirmed. For example, Jesus says at Mk. 14:21, "The Son of Man goes just as it is written concerning him [καθὼς γέγραπται περὶ αὐτοῦ], but woe to that man through whom [δι᾽ οὗ] the Son of Man is handed over [παραδίδοται]. It would be better for that man if he had not been born." The death of Jesus is here clearly in view, signaled by Mark's use of παραδίδοται (see Mk. 9:31; 10:33), and Jesus' "handing over" is explicitly related to scriptural fulfillment ("The Son of Man goes *just as it is written* concerning him [καθὼς γέγραπται περὶ αὐτοῦ]"). Smit is certainly correct to caution against narrowly reading all uses of δεῖ in Mark as conveying divine necessity, but this should not be taken to mean that Mark does *not* use δεῖ in this way.

49 An incomplete list of commentators who hear the Suffering Servant echoed at Mk. 10:45 includes Collins, *Mark,* 500–4, Lane, *Mark,* 383–4; France, *Mark,* 420–1; Eckey, *Markusevangelium,* 346; Mann, *Mark,* 416; Marcus, *Mark 8–16,* 755–6; Benoît Standaert, *Marc,* 2.773; Donahue and Harrington, *Mark,* 315; Stein, *Mark,* 488–9; Schenke, *Markusevangelium,* 252; cf. Focant, *Marc,* 402–3. For a sustained argument that Isa. 53 stands as a typological backdrop for Mark's gospel, see Rikki E. Watts, "Jesus' Death, Isaiah 53, and Mark 10:45: A Crux Revisited," in *Jesus and the Suffering Servant: Isaiah 53 and Christian Origins* (eds. William H. Bellinger Jr. and William R. Farmer; Harrisburg: Trinity International Press, 1998), 125–52; see also Joel Marcus, "Mark and Isaiah," in *Fortunate the Eyes that See: Essays in Honor of David Noel Freedman in Celebrating His Seventieth Birthday* (eds. A.B. Beck et al.; Grand Rapids: Eerdmans, 1995) 449–66; cf. C. K. Barrett, "The Background to Mark 10:45," in *New Testament Essays: Studies in Honour of T. W. Manson* (ed. A. J. B. Higgins; Manchester: Manchester University Press, 1959), 1–18.

50 See e.g., Morna Hooker, *Jesus and the Servant: The Influence of the Servant Concept of Deutero-Isaiah in the New Testament* (London: S.P.C.K., 1959), 62–102, esp. 74–9. See also Barrett, "The Background to Mark 10:45," 1–18; Hays, *Echoes of Scripture in the Gospels,* 86–7.

51 As I argued vis-à-vis Paul earlier in this chapter (note 18), I do not take the objective and causal translations of διά to be mutually exclusive. Mark most likely imagines that Jesus Christ both dies "because of" the sins of humanity and "for" the sins of humanity. Indeed, both senses are implied in Mark's use of "ransom" (λύτρον [Mk. 10:45). The "ransom" is that which is paid to redeem someone or something from debt (that is its *purpose*), but it would not need to be paid at all if the debt had not been accrued in the first place (it is paid *because* of the debt). For a good discussion

of λύτρον, see Collins, *Mark,* 500–4. Mark's awareness that διά is multivalent is additionally suggested by the fact that he uses the preposition to express both causality (eg. Mk. 2:4; 6:14) and purpose (e.g., Mk. 2:27; 13:20) at different points in his narrative.

52   On the centrality of the forgiveness of sins in Mark, see Mk. 1:4-5; 2:1–12; 10:45; 14:24.

53   Interestingly, this observation raises questions about the historical existence of Judas. Paul betrays no clear awareness of such a figure (he refers to the apostles as "the twelve" [1 Cor. 15:5]; he gives no indication that one of the members may have been replaced [cf. Acts 1:12–26]), and he regularly ascribes Jesus' death to God rather than to human beings (e.g., Rom. 4:25; 8:32; 1 Cor. 11:23 [?]; cf. Gal. 2:20, which describes Jesus as giving *himself* up: "... the Son of God who loved me and gave himself up for me [παραδόντος ἑαυτὸν ὑπὲρ ἐμοῦ]"). A possible exception may be found in 1 Thess. 2:14–16, but this passage is sometimes considered a later interpolation (see Birger A. Pearson, "1 Thessalonians 2:13–16: A Deutero-Pauline Interpolation," *HTR* 64 [1971] 79–94). If Mark takes it upon himself to flesh out the undetermined roles of human agents in Isa. 53, and Paul displays no knowledge of a Judas figure, the possibility that the betrayer is a figment of Mark's own literary imagination must be allowed.

54   See, for example, Douglas J. Moo, *The Old Testament in the Gospel Passion Narratives* (Sheffield: Almond Press, 1983), 148–51; see also Marcus, *Mark 8–16,* 1004; Donahue and Harrington, *Mark,* 422; Gnilka, *Markus,* 2.281. (For his part, Focant, *Marc,* 567 hears the echo of the Servant's silence at Mk. 15:5, where it also fits.) Hays, *Echoes of Scripture in the Gospels,* 86 counters claims that the silence of the suffering servant is heard in Mark by suggesting that, "any possible parallel is compromised by the fact that as the scene unfolds, Jesus *does* speak emphatically in the very next verse, declaring himself to be the Christ, the Son of the Blessed One and the Son of Man who will be seated in glory at the right hand of God (Mk. 14:62)." This reading, however, does not take into consideration the iterative nature of the imperfects (ἐσιώπα; ἀπεκρίνατο), which suggests an extended period of silence. Moreover, it is a highly literalist reading of the narrative context (surprising, given the body of work of the exegete who makes the claim!), and one that does not sufficiently address the question of whether or not there are additional echoes of Isa. 53 in this scene that might facilitate an association between Jesus' death and the suffering servant within the minds of Mark or his audience.

55   Commentators generally do not go so far as to see Jesus' statement as an unqualified assertion of his divinity (see, for example, Donahue and Harrington, *Mark,* 423; Moloney, *Mark,* 304 n. 144; Collins, *Mark,* 704 n. 60), but it should remain a possibility.

56   On the meanings of these terms, see Marcus, *Mark 8–16,* 1029–30 and 1043–4.

57   See Chapter 2, Part II. Mark's invitation to read Jesus' mission and death in light of the Aqedah may find additional support in the episode that immediately follows Jesus' baptism in the River Jordan. After Jesus is identified as the beloved son (Mk. 1:11), he is cast out (ἐκβάλλει) into the wilderness (Mk. 1:12). There, he spends the next 40 days of his life, tested continuously (πειραζόμενος) by the devil (Mk. 1:13). For its part, the Aqedah opens as follows: "And it came to pass after these things [that] God tested [ἐπείραζεν] Abraham ..." (καὶ ἐγένετο μετὰ τὰ ῥήματα ταῦτα ὁ θεὸς ἐπείραζεν τὸν Αβρααμ ... [Gen. 22:1]). To be sure, the primary biblical model for Jesus' wilderness testing is Adam, who was tempted by the serpent, found disobedient to God, and expelled from Paradise (see Marcus, "Son of Man as Son of Adam," 55–6, 371–7; see also idem, *Mark 1–8,* 167–71; Collins, *Mark,* 153; France, *Mark,* 85–7; Haenchen, *Weg,* 64–5; cf. Boring, *Mark,* 47–8). Yet the first use of "test" (πειράζω) in the Septuagint occurs at Gen. 22:1. Though the primary purpose of Jesus' temptation in the wilderness is to replay and overturn Adam's initial disobedience in order to

prepare the way for his trials and victory yet to come, the evangelist's choice to use the participle πειραζόμενος ("being tested") invites his audience to recall the binding of Isaac. πειραζόμενος, like "you are my son, the beloved" (σὺ εἶ ὁ υἱός μου ὁ ἀγαπητός), is doubly allusive. It is an accurate description of Adam's and Eve's experience in the garden (though nowhere is the word used in that story), and it evokes God's first explicit "test" in the scriptures—Abraham's commanded immolation of his beloved son. Because the story does not end with Christ's victory over Satan at Mk. 1:12–13, Mark's audience is called to look beyond it, to that which will be Christ's final victory: his death and resurrection upon the cross.

On this reading, one cannot help but wonder whether or not Mark, like Paul, takes "death" to be a hypostasized entity that must be defeated (see 1 Cor. 15:26: "The last enemy [ἔσχατος ἐχθρός], death [ὁ θάνατος], is abolished [καταργεῖται]"). Rhoads et al. understand Mk. 1:12–13 as follows: "The resolution of the conflict with Satan occurs in the testing at the beginning of the story. While there are escalations within specific episodes of exorcism, there is no developing conflict with the demons across the story. Subsequent exorcisms are simply a consequence of the initial resolution, a mopping-up operation. Thus in Mark's depiction, Satan is not the last enemy to be defeated but the first" (*Mark as Story*, 82–3). If Satan is the "first" enemy to be defeated in Mark's gospel, is death the last? There may not be enough evidence to make a certain determination, but, at the least, there is nothing in Mark that precludes such a reading. This, in turn, may bring Mark close to Paul once again.

58 Other possible allusive reversals include the following: Abraham leaves dutiful servants to await his return (Gen. 22:5, 19), but Christ's disciples turn and flee, and the reader is left to wonder about their ultimate fate (Mk. 14:50; 16:7); Abraham and Isaac's purpose in their sacrifice is to render obeisance (προσκυνήσαντες) to God (Gen. 22:5), but Christ, as sacrifice, is object of mock obeisance (προσεκύνουν) by the soldiers (Mk. 15:19; see also Mk. 14:65; 15:29–32); and Isaac bears his own vehicle of sacrifice (Gen. 22:6), but Christ is incapable of doing the same (Mk. 15:21).

59 ἄφετε—the Greek here is famously problematic. I prefer the translation of France, *Mark*, 654 n. 51, who explains, "it is possible to take ἄφετε not as a request to leave Jesus alone but as introducing the deliberative subjunctive ἴδωμεν (so BDF, 364[2]) so that the whole phrase means 'let us see'… though the only NT parallel to use ἀφίημι [in this way] is the singular ἄφες ἐκβάλω in Matt. 7:4/Lk. 6:42. Mark is certainly capable of redundancy, but where the imperative has an appropriate sense of its own in the context this interpretation seems unnecessary." To further support France's reasoning, though Matthew *can* use the word to introduce a deliberative subjunctive, in the Matthean parallel to Mk. 15:35 (Matt. 27:49), the first evangelist does not appear to do so. Instead, he changes Mark's text to have the crowds watching the crucifixion be the speakers, and he changes what is said to a second person singular ("And the remainder were saying, 'leave him!'" [οἱ δὲ λοιποὶ ἔλεγον· ἄφες …] [Matt. 27:49]). Logically, then, the crowd seems to be trying to *stop* the one with the sponge from giving Jesus drink.

60 For discussions of the expectation of Elijah in Second Temple apocalyptic thought, see Marcus, *Mark 8–16*, 644; cf. Collins, *Mark*, 429–30.

61 Boring, *Mark*, 432; see also Marcus, *Mark 8–16*, 1066–7; Focant, *Marc*, 583–4; Klaiber, *Markusevangelium*, 308.

62 Levenson, *Death and Resurrection*, 222.

63 Jesus is designated as the "Lamb of God" (ὁ ἀμνὸς τοῦ θεοῦ) at Jn. 1:29, 36. The Last Supper takes place on the day *before* the Day of Preparation (it occurs "before the feast of the Passover [πρὸ δὲ τῆς ἑορτῆς τοῦ πάσχα]" [Jn. 13:1], rather than on it (see Mk. 14:12). As with the Paschal lamb, Jesus dies prior to the official beginning of the holiday (see Jn. 19:14, 31); and, in accordance with God's injunction at Ex. 12:10, 46, none of Jesus' bones are broken ("These things occurred in order that scripture

might be fulfilled [ἡ γραφὴ πληρωθῇ]: 'his bone will not be broken [ὀστοῦν οὐ συντριβήσεται αὐτοῦ]'" [Jn. 19:36]). For a good discussion, see Levenson, *Death and Resurrection*, 206–10.

64   On the potential dependence of John upon Mark, see Raymond E. Brown, *The Death of the Messiah from Gethsemane to the Grave: A Commentary on the Passion Narratives in the Four Gospels* [2 vols. New York: Doubleday, 1994], 1.75–7; M. E. Glasswell, "The Relationship between John and Mark" *JSNT* 23 [1985], 99–115; Ian D. Mackay, *John's Relationship with Mark: an Analysis of John 6 in Light of Mark 6–8* [WUNT 182; Tübingen : Mohr Siebeck, 2004]; cf. Robert Fortna, "Jesus and Peter at the High Priest's House: A Test Case for the Question of the Relation between Mark's and John's Gospels," *NTS* 24 [1978], 371–83).

65   For a helpful summary, see Collins, *Mark*, 646–7; see also Focant, *Marc*, 519–20.

66   Marcus (*Mark 8–16*, 932–3, 1070) has provocatively suggested that Mark has even shifted the traditional date of Jesus' crucifixion from Nisan 14 to Nisan 15. He uses Mk. 15:42 as evidence, which states, "And when evening had come, since it was the day of preparation [ἐπεὶ ἦν παρασκευή]—that is, the day before the Sabbath [ὅ ἐστιν προσάββατον] ..." This verse occurs just after Jesus' death and just prior to Joseph of Arimathea's seeking the body of Jesus from Pilate (Mk. 15:43). Notably, Mark inserts an editorial gloss that translates "day of preparation" (παρασκευή) as "the day before the Sabbath" (προσάββατον), rather than as the day before the Passover, which it also could mean (see Jn. 19:14). According to Marcus, it is possible that Mark has transposed Jesus' death from the Day of Preparation *for* Passover to the day of Passover itself, and he then interprets παρασκευή in a more general way.

67   See, for example, the 2nd century B.C.E. *Book of Jubilees* (17–18), which, through a carefully choreographed chronology, argues that the Aqedah takes place at the same time of the year as the Passover, thereby making the one an etiology for the other (for discussion, see Levenson, *Death and Resurrection*, 176–7; see also, James C. Vander-Kam, "The Aqedah, Jubilees, and PseudoJubilees," in *The Quest for Context and Meaning: Studies in Biblical Intertextuality in Honor of James A. Sanders* [eds. Craig A. Evans and Shemaryahu Talmon; BIS 28; Leiden: Brill, 1997], 244–8; Stanislas Lyonnet and Léopold Sabourin, *Sin, Redemption, and Sacrifice: A Biblical and Patristic Study* [Rome: Biblical Institute, 1970], 265). Similarly, throughout Pseudo-Philo's *Liber Antiquitatum Biblicarum* (1st century C.E.), one finds scattered references to the Aqedah (LAB 18.5; 32.2–4; 40.2), and the themes emphasized therein strongly echo those running throughout the Passover narrative (lamb sacrifice, redemption, the fourteenth of the month, etc.), which underscores the proleptic redemptive significance of that story (on Pseudo-Philo, see Bruce N. Fisk, "Offering Isaac Again and Again: Pseudo-Philo's use of the Aqedah as Intertext," *CBQ* 62 [2000] 481–507; Frederick James Murphy, *Pseudo-Philo: Rewriting the Bible* [New York: Oxford University Press, 1993]; Howard Jacobson, *A Commentary on Pseudo-Philo's Liber Antiquitatum Biblicarum with Latin Text and English Translation* [2 vols.; AGAJU 31; Leiden: Brill, 1996]; Christian Dietzfelbinder, *Pseudo-Philo: Antiquitates Biblicae* [JSHRZ II.2; Gütersloh: Gerd Mohn, 1975]). Later, in Rabbinic thought, lines of continuity are again drawn between Isaac's (near) sacrifice and the slaughter of the Paschal lamb. See, for example, Pisḥa 7 of *Mekhilta de-Rabbi Ishmael* (ed. Jacob Z. Lauterbach; Philadelphia: Jewish Publication Society, 2004, 40), where Isaac's blood preserves the Israelites and Jerusalem from the wrath of the destroyer (see also Levenson, *Death and Resurrection*, 180). In each case, what stands behind the association is the idea that the Aqedah proleptically manifests God's redemptive process: "the Father's refusal to spare his son has become a paradigm of the saving act, and the Paschal lamb has become a cipher for the beloved son" (Levenson, *Death and Resurrection*, 180).

68   The Chronicler writes at 3:1: "And Solomon began to build the house of the Lord [בֵּית־יְהוָה] in Jerusalem on the hill of Moriah [בְּהַר הַמּוֹרִיָּה]."

69 Nowhere is this clearer than in the 1st century C.E. document 4 Maccabees. Throughout the text, the Maccabean martyrs understand their deaths to be a means of atoning for the sins of the people (see, for example, 4 Macc. 6.27–29; 9.23–25; 12.16–17; 17.20–22). Indeed, at 4 Macc. 17.22, ἱλαστήριον is used to describe the sacrifice of martyrs, a word which translates "mercy seat" (כפרת), the gold slab covering the Arc of the Covenant that is cleaned with blood on the Day of Atonement. At the same time, they understand their deaths to be patterned upon the willing sacrifice of Isaac (see 4 Macc. 7.13–14; 13.12–13; 16.20). For the author of 4 Maccabees, then, the willing death of the beloved son functions as a type of martyr's death on behalf of the people's sins. Though the slaughter of Isaac, as Abraham's seed (σπέρμα [see Gen. 22:17]), would ostensibly preclude the fulfillment of God's covenantal promises with Abraham, in 4 Macc. it is the beloved son's willingness to die that has, in fact, established them, and it is the Maccabean martyrs' willingness to do the same that preserves them. The author of 4 Macc. takes the view that the Aqedah has proleptically anticipated expiation on behalf of the people. For good introductions to 4 Maccabees, see David A. DeSilva, *4 Maccabees* (Sheffield: Sheffield Academic Press, 1998), 11–28; Hans-Josef Klauck, *4 Makkabäerbuch* (JSHRZ III.6; Gütersloh: Gerd Mohn, 1989) 647–80; Jan Willem van Henten, *The Maccabean Martyrs as Saviours of the Jewish People: A Study of 2 and 4 Maccabees* (JSJSupp 57; Leiden: Brill, 1997), 58–82.

70 An association between the suffering servant and the Paschal lamb may appear, at first, problematic, as the servant of Isa. 53 is far from the "perfect lamb" (πρόβατον τέλειον) that Moses is commanded to sacrifice (Ex. 12:5). (On the inappropriateness of the suffering servant's death as a temple sacrifice, see Jeremy Schipper, "Interpreting the Lamb Imagery in Isa. 53," *JBL* 132 [2013] 315–25.) Nevertheless, because Mark is reading Isa. 53 through the lens of the death of Jesus Christ, whom he no doubt understands to be perfect, the evangelist may have understood the blemishes upon the person of the servant to be indicative of the new standards of perfection that result from Christ's death setting worldly standards upon their heads (see Mk. 2:16–17; see also 1 Cor. 1:27–30).

71 See Mitchell, "Epiphanic Evolutions," 194.

5 Conclusion

Part I: Summation

The goal of this monograph has been to make a plausible case for the literary dependence of the Gospel of Mark on select letters of the apostle Paul (Romans, 1 Corinthians, and Galatians). Taking as a starting point the incisive observations of Joel Marcus—the range of theological, Christological, and ecclesiological overlaps shared between the evangelist and apostle and his own conclusions vis-à-vis the centrality of the cross for each—I have sought to explore on one hand the ways in which Jesus' death is constructed and performed in Pauline communities, and on the other the ways in which Mark attempts to anticipate and justify those Pauline performances within his own story.

With Dodd, I agree that Paul's "gospel" (εὐαγγέλιον) is an episodic narrative that covers the life, death, resurrection, and second coming of Jesus Christ "in accordance with the scriptures," and, with Hays, I presume that, to understand Paul's theological argumentation, one must recognize that this narrative undergirds all of Paul's thought. It is the foundation upon which Paul's variable argumentation is built. Finally, with Mitchell, I concur that Mark and Paul interface with that gospel narrative via a shared synecdochical poetics.

My work expands upon the contributions of these scholars by arguing that Mark and Paul not only share a synecdochical poetics, but that they also share a sacred story, and that this sacred story contains a shared episode: the epiphany of Jesus Christ to Paul himself (1 Cor. 15:8). Within the telling of a circumscribed portion of the gospel narrative (the earthly mission and death of Jesus Christ), Mark regularly anticipates and evokes episodes that occur beyond his 16 chapters (Jesus' resurrection appearances [Mk. 14:28; 16:7]; the destruction of the Second Temple [Mk. 13:1–2]; the second coming of the messiah [Mk. 13:26–27]; etc.), and I have made the case that Paul and his mission should be numbered amongst them. Mark's hermeneutical principle vis-à-vis Paul is, in other words, etiological. The evangelist, who shares his gospel with the apostle, seeks to seed the apostle and his teachings into his text.

In order to demonstrate this claim, I examined select media by which the death of Christ is performed in Pauline communities, and I established that Paul's person, the baptismal and Eucharistic rites, and the reading of select passages of scripture are all considered (by the apostle and by his communities) to be epiphanic performances of the death of Jesus Christ that synecdochically evoke the whole gospel plot. I compared these results to the Gospel of Mark, and I showed that, in parallel phenomena in Mark's narrative (the person of Jesus, the baptisms of John, the Last Supper, scripture), the evangelist presents proleptic performances of Christ's death. I then argued that Mark's narrative is self-consciously crafted to anticipate the various mediated epiphanies of Jesus' death contained within the apostle's letters. Though Mark's strategies may vary (predictably) depending upon whether or not a Pauline performance is primarily prospective (scripture, the Eucharist) or retrospective (baptism, Paul's person) vis-à-vis its historical orientation to the cross, the evangelist nevertheless maintains a thoroughgoing project of establishing concordance between the episodes of Jesus' earthly mission, his sacrificial death, and the unique significances attached to performances of that death by the apostle.

Part II: Expanding the investigation

To this point, my argument for Mark's dependence on Paul has, of necessity, been limited in scope. It is my hope, however, that I have opened up a new and useful avenue of inquiry in the longstanding debate about the Paulinism of Mark's gospel, namely Mark as etiology.[1] The aim of this section is to present evidence for the utility of this approach in the investigation of a broader range of thematic overlaps between Mark and Paul.[2]

On can use this approach, for example, in analyzing the negative characterization of the disciples found in both authors. Mark's problematic portrayal of these figures has been a locus of scholarly controversy for many years. In particular, exegetes debate whether Peter, James, and John (Jesus' "inner circle" [Mk. 5:37; 9:2; 14:33; etc.]; possibly also Paul's "pillar" apostles [Gal. 2:9][3]) are persons with whom the Markan audience is supposed to sympathize, or against whom they ought to position themselves.[4] Particularly if the evangelist composes his story at Rome, the location at which both Peter and Paul lost their lives (according to tradition), one might wonder why Mark would draft a narrative that seems so overtly hostile to Peter within a city and at a time at which the pillar apostle would have been elevated to the status of apostolic hero.[5] Mark's use of an etiological hermeneutic vis-à-vis Paul provides an answer: Mark does not seek to reject Peter's authority *per se*; rather, his goal is to make clear that whatever authority Peter does have rests upon the vision he received from the resurrected Christ, irrespective of his familiarity with the earthly messiah. In other words, Mark has, in attempting to seed Paul and his mission into his story, sought to level the apostolic playing field to the authority of Peter and Paul upon the same epiphanic foundation.

To demonstrate this, I will analyze two incisive but incompatible studies on Mark's characterization of the disciples, and I will suggest that their seemingly incongruous theses can be brought together if one presumes Mark's goal is to anticipate Paul as a part of a larger story within which Peter and the other disciples play important roles. First, Finn Damgaard, in his "Persecution and Denial—Paradigmatic Apostolic Portrayals in Paul and Mark,"[6] argues that the negative portrayal of Peter in Mark is, in fact, based upon Paul's negative portrayal of himself. He explains,

> Mark might have focused especially on Peter's failings because he wanted to create a paradigmatic apostolic portrayal comparable to Paul's self-portrayal … For all his criticism of the disciples and Peter in particular, Mark actually employed the figure of Peter to connect the gospel to an apostolic authority. In so doing, he probably rescued his gospel from just being absorbed into Matthew, Luke and John and thereby consigned to oblivion.[7]

Damgaard admits that Peter is portrayed negatively throughout Mark's gospel (he is called Satan [Mk. 8:32]; he misjudges the transfiguration [Mk. 9:1–13]; he falls asleep at Gethsemane [Mk. 14:32–42]; etc.), but he also argues that Peter is, through this, turned into a "rounder" character, one who "encourages the audience to construct him as an individual."[8] Insofar as he is said to have a mother in law and a home [Mk. 1:29–30], and he is given a special name [Mk. 3:16], Peter becomes a person with whom Mark's audience can identify. This allows Damgaard to claim that "though Mark's portrayal of Peter primarily focuses on his mistakes, the narrator does not turn his readers against Peter, nor does he portray Jesus as someone who parts company with Peter."[9]

Instead, Damgaard suggests that Mark has based his characterization of Peter upon the literary model of Paul.[10] Damgaard points out that crucial to Paul's self-understanding is a then and now dichotomy in which Paul was *once* a persecutor but is *now* an apostle, imbued with Spirit and bearing divine authority (Gal. 1:23; see also Gal. 1:13–16; Phil. 3:6–11; 1 Cor. 15:9–10).[11] This "biography of reversal" eventually becomes a model for all Christians to follow (witnessed elsewhere in the New Testament, as, for example, at 1 Tim. 1:16), and, according to Damgaard, Mark adapts Peter's story to this same narrative structure. Because Peter could not be portrayed as a persecutor of the church, Mark portrays him as a dullard and coward, and he creates a "Petrine version" of the Pauline biography of reversal.[12] Damgaard thus concludes that "Mark may have been a Paulinist … but if he was, it was in spite of Paul's negative attitude to Peter. Instead, it was under the influence of Paul's complicated portrayal of himself."[13]

Alternatively, David C. Sim, in his "The Family of Jesus and the Disciples of Jesus in Paul and Mark: Taking Sides in the Church's Factional Dispute," contends that Mark is overtly hostile to Jesus' family and the disciples, reflecting Paul's antagonistic relationship with the Jerusalem apostles.[14] Sim argues that Paul's subversive title for them in Galatians (the "so-called pillars [οἱ δοκοῦντες στῦλοι εἶναι]" [Gal. 2:2, 6, 9]), coupled with his accusation against Peter of outright hypocrisy (Gal. 2:14), and his calling those affiliated with Jerusalem "false brothers" (ψευδαδέλφους [Gal. 2:4]), "provides clear evidence that in the late '40s and the early '50s Paul's relationship with the Jerusalem authorities, especially James and Peter, was one of bitter conflict."[15] Indeed, based upon the (unknown) fate of Paul's collection to Jerusalem, Sim suggests that the rift between Paul and the Jerusalem church was never bridged.[16]

Because this apostolic conflict is not resolved within the lifetime of Paul, Sim claims that later Christian authors were forced to align themselves with one figure or the other, and he argues that Mark chooses to position himself with Paul. Sim first looks at Mark's attitude towards Jesus' family. At Mark 3:20–35, which opens with Jesus' returning "home" (ἔρχεται εἰς οἶκον [Mk. 3:20], likely a reference to the place he was staying at Capernaum [see Mk. 2:1]), Mark informs his audience that Jesus' family (οἱ παρ' αὐτοῦ) attempts to restrain him (κρατῆσαι αὐτόν) because they believe that he is "out of his mind" (ἔλεγον γὰρ ὅτι ἐξέστη [Mk. 3:21]). Sim takes Mark's use of ἐξέστη ("out of his mind") to imply that Jesus' family believes him to be possessed by a demon.[17] Because the Beelzebul controversy with the scribes (Mk. 3:22–30) immediately follows, Sim infers that, with his pronouncing blasphemy against the Holy Spirit an eternal sin (Mk. 3:29), Jesus implicitly declares his family guilty of the same sin as the scribes. By calling him mad, they have blasphemed the Holy Spirit within his person.[18]

Sim next looks at the characterization of the disciples, and he claims that they are predominantly identified by their various shortcomings: their lack of faith (e.g., Mk. 4:35–51); their exclusion of children (Mk. 10:13–16); their rejection of the foreign exorcist (Mk. 9:38–41); their persistent inability to understand (e.g., Mk. 4:10–13; 6:51–52; 8:32–33); their cowardice (Mk. 14:50); Peter's denial (Mk. 14:66–72); and so forth.[19] So comprehensive are their failings that, at the conclusion of the gospel, where the youth at the tomb predicts a reunion between the twelve and Jesus (Mk. 16:7), Sim argues that such a reunion never takes place.[20] On Sim's reading, like the family of Jesus, the disciples of Jesus have severed themselves entirely from the messiah. For Mark, it is Paul, and Paul alone, who propagates the true message of Jesus Christ.

In my judgment, presuming Mark's use of an etiological (and synecdochical) hermeneutic, the evangelist's reason for portraying the disciples in the way that he does lies somewhere between the poles of Damgaard's and Sim's theses. On one hand, *pace* Damgaard, the idea that Mark seeks to portray Peter as a new Paul is difficult to establish on exegetical grounds. On the other, *pace* Sim, it goes too far to say that Mark categorically rejects the authority of Peter and the other disciples, given that the disciples are expected to encounter the risen messiah in Galilee (see Mk. 14:28; 16:7). Instead, Mark attempts to demonstrate that the authority of the disciples does not rest upon their knowledge of the earthly Christ. They, like Paul, must first encounter the risen Lord.

Thus, despite the disciples' occasional exemplary action (such as Simon [Peter] and Andrew immediately dropping their nets to follow Jesus [Mk. 1:16–18]), Sim is right to argue that Mark's characterization of these men during the period of Jesus' earthly mission is an emphatically negative one. When one compares the evangelist's characterization of the disciples with the requirements for praise (ἐγκώμιος/*laus*) and vituperation (ψόγος/*vituperatio*) in ancient rhetorical theory, Mark's negative portrait is confirmed.[21] Peter rebukes (ἐπιτιμάω) Jesus and is called "Satan" (σατανᾶς [Mk. 8:32–33]) for doing so, he suggests the construction of tents for spirits (Mk. 9:5), he makes a declaration he fails to keep (Mk. 14:29), he shows an inability to stay awake in the garden (Mk. 14:33–38), he flees with the other disciples (Mk. 14:50), and, in the end, he denies Jesus during the trial before the Sanhedrin (Mk. 14:66–72).[22] Similarly, James and John are shown unable to understand the transfiguration (Mk. 9:2–10, esp. 9:5–6, 10), and they too fall asleep at Gethsemane (Mk. 14:33–41). Moreover, John, speaking for all the disciples, rejects the authority of the foreign exorcist on the grounds that "he does not follow us" (οὐκ ἠκολούθει ἡμῖν [Mk. 9:38]), and James and John together inappropriately ask to be given positions of authority on the right and left of Jesus "in his glory" (ἐν τῇ δόξῃ σου [Mk. 10:36]), a clear embarrassment to Matthew, who puts the request on the lips of their mother instead (see Matt. 20:20–21).

All of these failures are exemplary of traits considered worthy of reproach in ancient rhetorical theory.[23] The flight from Gethsemane and Peter's threefold denial demonstrate cowardice (*ignavia*/δειλία).[24] Foolishness (ἀφροσύνη, contrary to wisdom [*prudentia*/φρόνησις]) is displayed in Peter's words at the transfiguration.[25] Peter's rebuke of Jesus, and James and John's request for glorification, show presumptiveness (*audacia*).[26] Meanness of spirit (μικροψυχία, contrary to generosity [μεγαλοφροσύνη]) is seen in John's rejection of the foreign exorcist,[27] and falsehood (*mendacium*, contrary to truth [*veritas*]) is presumed in Peter's failed vow.[28] Sim is correct, then, to find in Mark's characterization of the disciples a deep suspicion of their authority, particularly that of Peter, James, and John. During the earthly mission of the messiah, Mark depicts their actions as thoroughly ignoble.

Yet, as noted above, Mark also presumes that the disciples will ultimately encounter the risen Lord (Mk. 14:28; 16:6–7), a presumption rooted, I suggest, in Mark's sharing his gospel narrative with Paul. The revelation of the messiah to Peter and the other disciples is an episode that must be anticipated if the whole story is to be evoked synecdochically (see 1 Cor. 15:5–7). To the degree that Mark takes for granted the disciples' encounter with the risen Christ, then, Damgaard's "biography of reversal" carries a certain descriptive force. Within the larger story of the disciples that continues beyond Mark's 16 chapters, proper understanding of the nature and purpose of Jesus' mission is attained, and a turning from past mistakes is effected.

I stop short, however, of suggesting that Mark intends perfect apostolic parity. Mark's Peter is not the rock upon which the church is founded (see Matt. 16:18), and he is not the first to evangelize the nations (see Acts 10). Paul still remains, for Mark, the "last of all" (ἔσχατον δὲ πάντων [1 Cor. 15:8]) to whom the resurrected Christ appears. If the authority of the disciples is dependent upon the same revelation as is Paul's, Paul, by virtue of his position in the gospel narrative, functions as the final arbiter of God's salvific story.[29]

Thus, Mark does not reject the authority of the disciples. He attempts to level the apostolic playing field and grant to Paul a status of first amongst equals. Presuming

Mark wrote at Rome, and presuming Peter's death also took place there, it may be that Mark's negative characterization of Peter is the result of some within the Markan community aligning themselves with Peter over Paul (see 1 Cor. 1:10–17) on the grounds that the former knew the earthly Christ.[30] Mark's etiological approach is thus carefully calibrated to recognize subsequent disputes over Pauline authority and to enshrine within his story Paul's own solution to them. For Mark, as for Paul, what makes an apostle is a resurrection appearance (see 1 Cor. 9:1; 15:3–11; see also Gal. 1:1, 13–24; 2 Cor. 11:21–12:5 [esp. 12:1–5]).

Part III: The middest

I began this monograph with Frank Kermode's claim that "In the middest, we look for a fullness of time, for beginning, middle, and end in concord."[31] Mark is, in my judgment, one "in the middest." He is a writer alive at the ending of the world, and he seeks to bring (for himself and for his community) the past into concord with his present in anticipation of that future he knows will soon appear on the horizon with the clouds and great power and glory (see Mk. 13:26). By way of ending, then, I return briefly to the idea of the "middest." In conceptualizing the process by which the past is bound concordantly with the present in Mark and in the other synoptic gospels, I have found the hermeneutical procedure Paul Ricoeur labels threefold mimesis particularly illuminating.[32] According to Ricoeur, "the composition of plot is grounded in a preunderstanding of the world of action, its meaningful structures, its symbolic resources, and its temporal character" (mimesis one).[33] This preunderstanding is then imaginatively (re)configured by an author and mediated through emplotted narrative (mimesis two)[34] to readers who "receive it according to their own receptive capacity" and integrate it into own their lived experiences (mimesis three).[35] On my reading, Mark has also taken a "preunderstanding of the world of action" (to use Ricoeur's language), one that is informed by his familiarity with and particular conception of Paul's gospel narrative, traditional stories about Jesus, the various exigencies of his community at the time of his composition, and so forth, and he has configured a narrative about the earthly mission of the messiah that both participates in and reconfigures that world for the needs of his community living at a particular historical moment (with one of those needs being an elucidation of the connection between the person of Jesus and the teachings of the apostle Paul). Mark's story, then, does not attempt to (re)present the "that" of history (i.e., that which actually happened); rather, the "that" of the past has been fictively transformed for a community whose interests reside in the present and who look expectantly to the future. Ultimately, when that future does not arrive, the process begins again.[36] Matthew and Luke, from their different geographic locations and at their different historical moments, take up Mark's narrative, and, understood in relation to their own preunderstandings of the world, they configure the story anew. The end result is that the gospel that Paul proclaimed, reconfigured by Mark, is interwoven into their own gospels in profound and unexpected ways; but that, of course, is the subject of a different study.

Notes

1   As I noted in my introduction, I do not use "etiology" as a generic classification. Instead, I take Mark's project to be the crafting of a literary epiphany that combines traditional legends about Christ with the teachings of the apostle Paul in order to (re)-present on earth Jesus Christ crucified for Mark's community. The seeding of Paul and his mission is thus an essential *aspect* of Mark's literary project—one that is born of the fact that Mark's understanding of the nature and significance of the Christ event has occurred within the context of a Pauline community (most probably in Rome)—but I do not judge Mark's sole purpose in his composition to be the justification of Paul or the creation of an etiology for Paul's missionary journey.

2   Marcus, "Interpreter of Paul," 30-2. It can be added here that the etiological hermeneutic I have presented in this monograph can be used to support or even strengthen previous contributions to the debate over Mark's use of Paul. For example, Jesper Svartvik ("'East is East and West is West:' The Concept of Torah in Paul and Mark," in Wischmeyer et al., *Paul and Mark,* 157-85), draws a distinction between Mark's emphasis on "causality" and Paul's emphasis on "finality" ("Concept of Torah," 174), and he suggests that Mark's "entire narrative, all its sixteen chapters, constitute the beginning [of the gospel]. By the time of his writing his narrative account, everyone knew the end—the death of Jesus on the cross and the inclusion of the Gentiles—but the question that he wishes to give a lengthy answer to is how it all began" ("Concept of Torah," 184). Though I would dispute the idea that Paul's gospel "ends" with the death of Christ and the inclusion of the Gentiles, or that Paul's prevailing interest is in "finality" over "causality" (after all, the apostle is perfectly capable of making "causal" arguments of his own [e.g., Rom. 4:1-25; Gal. 2:16-4:31]), Svartvik's notion that Mark seeks to present a narrative beginning that provides reasons for a (Pauline) "way things are now" aligns closely with my own approach. Similarly, Engberg-Pedersen's reading of Mk. 8:34-9:1, wherein "what Mark has done in 8:34-37 ... is to generalize what Paul had said of himself so as to make it cover all Christ followers and then to put that generalization back into the mouth of Jesus" ("Paul in Mark 8:34-9:1," 206, see also 208) is thoroughly concordant with an etiological way of reading: Mark's generalization on the lips of Jesus is deliberately designed to anticipate and justify Paul's radical claims of his own calling (e.g., Gal. 2:19-20; see also Engberg-Pedersen, "Paul in Mark 8:34-9:1," 202-3), a calling which, importantly, is also itself a model for all Christ believers, insofar as Paul is someone whom they are called to imitate (1 Cor. 11:1). In other words, one could argue that Mark has understood a phrase like "I have been co-crucified with Christ" (Χριστῷ συνεσταύρωμαι [Gal. 2:19]) to be normative for all Christ believers, not just Paul, precisely because they are called to be imitators of the apostle (1 Cor. 11:1), and, in Mk. 8:34-37, Mark has sought to draw out the universal significance implicit in Paul's words. Thus, Engberg-Pedersen's suggestion may, in fact, be another example of Markan etiological hermeneutics at work, even if this scholar does not label it as such.

3   There is an obvious difficulty with this identification. For Paul, James the "pillar" of Gal. 2:9 is almost certainly to be identified with "James, the brother of the Lord" (Ἰάκωβον τὸν ἀδελφὸν τοῦ κυρίου) at Gal. 1:19 (see also 1 Cor. 15:7). While *a* James is the fraternal brother of the Lord in Mark (see Mk. 6:3), this James stands apart from the twelve. He is unrelated to the James of Jesus' inner circle, who is, instead, a child of Zebedee and the brother of John (see Mk. 3:17). Thus, it appears that Mark's "inner circle" and Paul's "pillars apostles" do not consist of the same persons.

That said, Paul explicitly refers to James as the "brother" of the Lord only once (Gal. 1:19), and Paul's encounter with this man is temporally removed from his subsequent encounter with the Jerusalem authorities by some 14 years (see Gal. 2:1). At that later meeting, (a) James is mentioned, but he does not have a fraternal attribute. Instead, he, together with Peter and John, are labeled the "so-called pillars" (οἱ δοκοῦντες στῦλοι εἶναι [Gal. 2:9]). It may be the case, then, that Mark simply did not recognize that James "the pillar" and James the "Lord's brother" are one and the same, and he inferred instead that Paul was referring to two different persons: James, the brother of the Lord (Gal. 1:19; 1 Cor. 15:7[?]) and James the "pillar," who was numbered amongst the twelve (Gal 2:9, 12; 1 Cor. 15:5, 7[?]). Though certainty is precluded, if this reading is accurate, Mark's "inner circle" and Paul's "pillar apostles" would then be comprised of the same persons.

4   Among important contributions, see Werner H. Kelber, "Mark 14:32–42: Gethsemane; Passion Christology and Discipleship Failure," *ZNW* 63 (1972), 166–87; idem, *Story of Jesus*, 30–42; Robert C. Tannehill, "The Disciples in Mark," 386–405; Tyson, "The Blindness of the Disciples," 261–8; Goulder, "Those Outside," 289–302; Elizabeth Struthers Malbon, "Texts and Contexts: Interpreting the Disciples in Mark," in eadem, *In the Company of Jesus*, 100–30, esp. 114–24; Telford, *Theology of the Gospel of Mark*, 127–37; Rhoads, et al., *Mark as Story*, 123–9.

5   On the location of Mark's composition, see Chapter 1, Part II(A).

6   Finn Damgaard, "Persecution and Denial—Paradigmatic Apostolic Portrayals in Paul and Mark," in Becker et al., *Mark and Paul*, 195–210.

7   Damgaard, "Persecution and Denial," 310.

8   Damgaard, "Persecution and Denial," 300.

9   Damgaard, "Persecution and Denial," 301.

10   Damgaard, "Persecution and Denial," 301.

11   Damgaard, "Persecution and Denial," 302.

12   Damgaard, "Persecution and Denial," 305.

13   Damgaard, "Persecution and Denial," 310.

14   David C. Sim, "The family of Jesus and the Disciples of Jesus in Paul and Mark: Taking Sides in the Church's Factional Dispute," in Wischmeyer, et al., *Paul and Mark*, 73–97.

15   Sim, "Family of Jesus," 82–3.

16   Sim, "Family of Jesus," 83–4.

17   "The relatives of Jesus believe him to be possessed by a demon … in the ancient world insanity was often associated with demon-possession (cf. the close connection in John 10:20), and the charge of demonic influence almost certainly underlies this tradition" (Sim, "Family of Jesus," 86–7).

18   Sim, "Family of Jesus," 88.

19   Sim, "Family of Jesus," 91–2.

20   "Even though the angel [sic] states that Jesus will go to Galilee to meet with the disciples, there is no indication in the narrative that this meeting ever takes place. In fact the opposite is implied insofar as the women who run from the tomb say nothing of their experience or the angelic message: the implication is that the disciples never receive this instruction to return to Galilee and so never meet the risen Christ" (Sim, "Family of Jesus," 93). A problem with this reading is, of course, that the disciples *do* receive this instruction at Mk. 14:28: "but after I have been raised [μετὰ τὸ ἐγερθῆναί με], I will go before you into Galilee [προάξω ὑμᾶς εἰς τὴν Γαλιλαίαν]." Jesus' prophesies that this will occur, and Mark consistently makes clear that Jesus' prophecies ultimately come true (for fuller discussion on how prophecy functions in Mark, see Chapter 1, note 21).

21   Importantly, characters within narratives are expected to participate in and conform to these requirements. For example, in his lecture "On Narrative" (Περὶ Διηγήματος), Aelius Theon (a rhetorical teacher of the late first or early second C.E.), claims that stories should make clear whether an action (πρᾶγμα) is just or unjust (δίκαιον ἢ ἄδικον), or honorable or dishonorable (ἔνδοξον ἢ ἄδοξον [Theon, *Progym.* 78]). (All Greek citations are taken from Theon, *Progymnasmata* [CUF; trans. Michel Patillon and Giancarlo Bolognesi; Paris: Belles Lettres, 1997]. The previous reference can be found on pages 38–9 of this edition.) He then connects the causes (αἰτία) of

actions with human motivations, and he claims that a narrative should make clear whether an action is undertaken for the sake of the good (ἕνεκεν ἀγαθῶν) or rescue from evil (χάριν κακοῦ ἀπαλλαγῆς), or whether it is done on account of the passions (διὰ τὰ πάθη), such as anger (θυμόν), desire (ἔρωτα), hatred (μῖσος), and envy (φθόνον), and so forth (Theon, *Progym.* 79 [Patillon, 39–40]). For Theon, then, subjects of narrative (διήγημα, used interchangeably with διήγησις [for a later attempt at disambiguation, see Aphthonius, *Progym.* 2]) must be presented in such a way as to be judged according to the prevailing ethical standards of the day, and the causes of their actions must be attributed to human motivations such that they can be categorized as either virtuous or reprobate. For a brief introduction to Theon, see Kennedy, *Progymnasmata*, xii, 1–3.

22   Additionally, should one posit that episodes focusing on Peter in the other gospel narratives contain traditional materials to which Mark may have had access but chose not to use, it is worth noting that Peter is not the "rock" upon which the church is founded (see Matt 16:18), nor is he the one who draws his sword in defense of Jesus (see Jn. 18:10).

23   The list of parallels that follows is drawn primarily from Cicero's *De Inventione*, a work that represents a conventional ancient Graeco-Roman rhetorical curriculum close to the time of Mark's composition. According to H. M. Hubbell (introduction to *De Inventione, De Optimo Genere Oratorum, Topica*, by Cicero [trans. H. M. Hubbell; LCL; Cambridge: Harvard University Press, 1949], vii), it is "hardly more than an elaborate note-book in which he recorded the dictation of his teacher." The various virtues and vices I discuss are pulled from Cicero's discussion of deliberative rhetoric [*deliberatio*], but they should not be thought exclusive to this rhetorical genre (for discussion of the overlaps in *topoi* in the various types of speech, see Quintilian, *Inst.* 3.4.12–16). All subsequent citations of Cicero's Latin are taken from the Hubbell edition.

24   See Cicero, *Inv.* 2.54.165. For his discussion of courage (*fortitudo*), see *Inv.* 2.54.163. See also Aristotle's discussion of virtues and their corresponding vices at *Rhet.* I.9.1366b.

25   On prudence (*prudentia*), see Cicero, *Inv.* 2.53.160; see also Theon, *Progym.* 110 (Patillon, 74–5).

26   See Cicero, *Inv.* 2.54.165.

27   Generosity is one of the ethical virtues (ἠθικά) singled out by Theon in his lecture, "On Praise and Vituperation" (Περὶ Ἐγκωμίου καὶ Ψόγου). See Theon, *Progym.* 110 (Patillon, 75); see also Aristotle, *Rhet.* I.9.1366b.

28   Cicero, *Inv.* 2.53.161.

29   An interpretation I share with Sim, who suggests that, because Paul describes himself as "last of all" (ἔσχατον δὲ πάντων [1 Cor. 15:8]), the apostle effectively becomes the final revelatory word, immune to those who might claim "that they were later visited by Jesus who communicated a message that differed from that of the apostle" ("Family of Jesus," 77).

30   An interesting (though much later) text that may provide an analogue is the third-century *Kerygmata Petrou*. In this document, "Peter" attempts to undermine Paul's apostolic authority on the grounds that he does not act in accordance with the teachings of the earthly Christ. Pseudo Peter says, "But how can someone think that, on account of a vision [δι' ὀπτασίαν], he has been educated for the purpose of instruction [πρὸς διδασκαλίαν σοφισθῆναι]? And if you will say, 'it is possible,' then why did the teacher [i.e., Jesus] associate with those who are awake, remaining with them for a whole year [ὅλῳ ἐνιαυτῷ ἐγρηγορόσιν παραμένων ὡμίλησεν]? And if it is the case that he appeared to you [κἂν ὅτι ὤφθη σοι], how will we even believe you on this point [πῶς δέ σοι καὶ πιστεύσομεν αὐτό]? And how could he even have appeared to you [πῶς δέ σοι καὶ ὤφθη], when you think things that are exactly opposite to his teaching [αὐτοῦ τὰ ἐναντία τῇ διδασκαλίᾳ φρονεῖς]? But if you had

been visited and taught by that man for even one hour [ὑπ᾽ ἐκείνου μιᾶς ὥρας ὀφθείς καὶ μαθητευθείς], then be an apostle [ἀπόστολος ἐγένου]! Proclaim his words [τὰς ἐκείνου φωνὰς κήρυσσε]! Expound his teachings [τὰ ἐκείνου ἑρμήνευε]! Love his apostles [τοὺς ἐκείνου ἀποστόλους φίλει]! Do not battle against me, who lived with him [ἐμοὶ τῷ συγγενομένῳ αὐτῷ μὴ μάχου]! For you have set yourself in opposition against me, the firm rock, the foundation of the church [πρὸς γὰρ στερεὰν πέτραν ὄντα με, θεμέλιον ἐκκλησίας, ἐναντίος ἀνθέστηκάς μοι]!" (H XVII 19.1–5; the Greek text is taken from Ps. Clement, *Die Pseudoklementinen I: Homilien* [GCS 42; 2nd edn.; eds. Johannes Irmscher, Georg Strecker, et al.; Berlin: Akademie Verlag, 1969]). For a good introduction to this document, see Johannes Irmscher and Georg Strecker, "The Pseudo-Clementines," in *New Testament Apocrypha* (2 vols.; ed. Wilhelm Schneelmelcher; trans. R. McL. Wilson; Cambridge: James Clarke & Co. Ltd, 1991–2), 2.483–93.

31 Kermode, *Sense of an Ending*, 58.

32 See Paul Ricoeur, *Time and Narrative* (3 vols.; trans. Kathleen McLaughlin and David Pellauer; Chicago: University of Chicago Press, 1983). Indeed, the Gospel of Mark makes for an interesting conversation partner with Ricoeur in a variety of different ways. For example, the second gospel occupies an intermediary space between the ancient figures that Ricoeur places in a dialogue to set up his entire project: Augustine (*Time and Narrative* 1.5–30) and Aristotle (*Time and Narrative* 1.31–51). Not only is the Gospel of Mark written in the first century, right in the middle of the temporal divide that separates the philosopher (4th century B.C.E.) from the theologian (4th–5th century C.E.), but it is also a Greek (i.e., Eastern) narrative written in the western half of the Roman empire, it draws upon tragedy for its themes without itself being tragedy (as a literary genre) or tragic (as a descriptive adjective for its final sequence of events [i.e., though Christ dies, his resurrection is nevertheless assured: Mk. 8:31; 9:31; 10:33–34; 14:28; etc.]), and it self-consciously invites the "filling in" or retelling of the narrative as a result of its abrupt ending (something which doubtlessly encouraged Matthew's and Luke's own reworkings). In other words, the ideas of the figures Ricoeur juxtaposes in order to lay the foundation for his theory of threefold mimesis find a certain synthesis in the Gospel of Mark, and this, in turn, invites further exploration of the ways in which Mark may be used to elucidate the thought of Ricoeur and vice versa. I am indebted to my conversations with Prof. Richard Rosengarten for these insights. Any errors or oversimplifications are my own.

33 Ricoeur, *Time and Narrative*, 1.54.

34 Ricoeur, *Time and Narrative*, 1.64–70.

35 Ricoeur, *Time and Narrative*, 1.70–87. The partial citation is taken from *Time and Narrative*, 1.77.

36 This renewal is what Ricoeur refers to as the hermeneutic spiral: "That the analysis is circular is indisputable. But that the circle is a vicious one can be refuted. In this regard, I would rather speak of an endless spiral that would carry the mediation past the same point a number of times, but at different altitudes" (Ricoeur, *Time and Narrative*, 1.72).

Bibliography

Primary sources

Aelian. *On Animals*. Translated by A. F. Scholfield. 3 vols. Loeb Classical Library. Cambridge: Harvard University Press, 2014.

The Apostolic Fathers: Greek Texts and English Translations. Translated by Michael W. Holmes. 3rd edn. Grand Rapids: Baker Academic, 2007.

Aphthonius. *Aphthonii Progymnasmata*. Edited by Hugo Rabe. Leipzig: Teubner, 1926.

Aristotle. *Poetics*. Translated by Stephen Halliwell. Loeb Classical Library. Cambridge: Cambridge University Press, 1995.

Aristotle. *The Art of Rhetoric*. Translated by John Henry Freese. Loeb Classical Library. Cambridge: Cambridge University Press, 1967.

Augustine. *The Confessions*. Translated by Henry Chadwick. Oxford: Oxford University Press, 2008.

Biblia Hebraica Stuttgartensia. Edited by K. Elliger and W. Rudolph. Stuttgart: Deutsche Bibelgesellschaft, 1977.

Cicero. *De Inventione, De Optimo Genere Oratorum, Topica*. Translated by H. M. Hubbell. Loeb Classical Library. Cambridge: Harvard University Press, 1949.

Clement. *Épître Aux Corinthiens*. Edited by A. Jaubert. Sources Chrétiennes 167. Paris: Les Éditions du Cerf, 1971.

Corpus Fabularum Aesopicarum. Edited by Augustus Hausrath and Herbert Hunger,. 2nd edn. Leipzig: Teubner, 1970.

Demetrius. *On Style*. Edited by Doreen C. Innes. Loeb Classical Library. Cambridge: Cambridge University Press, 1995.

Eusebius. *Ecclesiastical History*. Translated by Kirsopp Lake and J. E. L. Oulton. 2 vols. Loeb Classical Library. Cambridge: Harvard University Press, 1926–32.

Gaius. *The Institutes*. Translated by W. M. Gordon and O. F. Robinson. Ithaca: Cornell University Press, 1988.

Josephus. *The Jewish War*. Translated by H. St. John Thackeray. 3 vols. Loeb Classical Library. Cambridge: Harvard University Press, 1997.

Josephus. *Jewish Antiquities*. Translated by H. St. John Thackeray, Ralph Marcus, and Louis H. Feldman. 9 vols. Loeb Classical Library. Cambridge: Harvard University Press, 1993.

Josephus. *The Life, Against Apion*. Translated by H. St. John Thackeray. Loeb Classical Library. Cambridge: Harvard University Press, 1926.

Ignace d'Antioche, Polycarpe de Smyrne. Lettres. Martyre de Polycarpe. Edited by P. T. Camelot. 4th edn. Sources Chrétiennes 10. Paris: Les Éditions du Cerf, 1969.

Irenaeus of Lyons. Translated by Robert Grant. The Early Church Fathers London: Routledge, 1997.

Libanius. *Selected Orations*. Translated by A. F. Norman. 2 vols. Loeb Classical Library. Cambridge: Cambridge University Press, 1969.

Longinus. *On the Sublime*. Translated by W. H. Fyfe. Loeb Classical Library. Cambridge: Cambridge University Press, 1995.

Mekhilta De-Rabbi Ishmael. Edited by Jacob Z. Lauterbach. Philadelphia: Jewish Publication Society, 2004.

New Testament Apocrypha. Edited by Wilhelm Schneemelcher. Translated by. R. McL. Wilson. 2 vols. Cambridge: James Clarke & Co. Ltd, 1991–2.

Novum Testamentum Graece. 28th edn. Edited by Kurt Aland, Johannes Karavidopoulos, Carlo M. Martini and Bruce M. Metzger. Stuttgart: Deutsche Bibelgesellschaft, 2012.

The Old Testament Pseudepigrapha. Edited by James H. Charlesworth. 2 vols. Peabody: Hendrickson, 1983.

Philo. Translated by F. H. Colson and G. H. Whitaker. 10 vols. Loeb Classical Library. Cambridge: Cambridge University Press, 1929–62.

Pliny. *Letters*. Translated by Betty Radice. 2 vols. Loeb Classical Library; Cambridge: Harvard University Press, 1969.

Progymnasmata: Greek Textbooks of Prose Composition and Rhetoric. Translated by George A. Kennedy. Writings in the Greco-Roman World 10. Atlanta: Society of Biblical Literature, 2003.

Pseudo Clement. *Die Pseudoklementinen I: Homilien*. Edited by Johannes Irmscher, Georg Strecker, Franz Pashke, and Bernhard Rehm. 2nd edn. Die griechischen christlichen Schriftsteller 42; Berlin: Akademie Verlag, 1969.

Pseudo Philo. *Les Antiquités Bibliques*. Edited by Daniel J. Harrington. Sources Chrétiennes 229. Paris: Les Éditions du Cerf, 1976.

Quintilian. *The Orator's Education*. Translated by Donald A. Russell. 5 vols. Loeb Classical Library. Cambridge: Harvard University Press, 2001.

Septuaginta. Edited by Alfred Rahlfs and Robert Hanhart. Stuttgart: Deutsche Bibelgesellschaft, 2006.

Suetonius. *Lives of the Caesars*. Translated by J. C. Rolfe. 2 vols. Loeb Classical Library. Cambridge: Cambridge University Press, 1997–8.

Tacitus. *Annals*. Translated by M. Hutton, W. Peterson, Clifford H. Moore, and John Jackson. Revised by R. M. Ogilvie, E. H. Warmington, and M. Winterbottom. 5 vols. Loeb Classical Library. Cambridge: Cambridge University Press, 1937–70.

Theon. *Progymnasmata*. Translated by Michel Patillon, and Giancarlo Bolognesi. Collection des Universités de France. Paris: Belles Lettres, 1997.

Secondary sources

Adamczewski, Bartosz. *Hypertexuality and Historicity in the Gospels*. Frankfurt am Main: Peter Lang, 2013.

_____ *The Gospel of Luke: A Hypertextual Commentary*. Frankfurt am Main: Peter Lang, 2016.

_____ *The Gospel of Mark: A Hypertextual Commentary*. Frankfurt am Main: Peter Lang, 2014.

Ahearne-Kroll, Stephen P. "Abandonment and Suffering." Pages 293–309 in *Septuagint Research: Issues and Challenges in the Study of the Greek Jewish Scriptures*. Edited by Wolfgang Kraus and R. Glenn Wooden. Septuagint and Cognate Studies 53. Atlanta: Society of Biblical Literature, 2006.

_____ *The Psalms of Lament in Mark's Passion: Jesus' Davidic Suffering.* Society of New Testament Studies Monograph Series. Cambridge: Cambridge University Press, 2007.

Allen, David. "The Use of Criteria: The State of the Question." Pages 129–41 in *Methodology in the Use of the Old Testament in the New: Context and Criteria.* Edited by David Allen and Steve Smith. Library of New Testament Studies 579. London: T&T Clark, 2020.

Alter, Robert. *The Art of Biblical Narrative.* New York: Basic Books, 1981.

Anderson, Janice Capel and Moore, Stephen D.. "Introduction: The Lives of Mark." Pages 1–27 in *Mark and Method: New Approaches in Biblical Studies.* Edited by Janice Capel Anderson and Stephen D. Moore. 2nd edn. Minneapolis: Fortress, 2008.

Auerbach, Erich. *Mimesis: The Representation of Reality in Western Literature.* Translated by Willard R. Trask. Princeton: Princeton University Press, 2003.

Barrett, C. K. "The Background to Mark 10:45." Pages 1–18 in *New Testament Essays: Studies in Honour of T.W. Manson.* Edited by A. J. B. Higgins. Manchester: Manchester University Press, 1959.

_____ *The Epistle to the Romans.* Harper's New Testament Commentaries. New York: Harper and Row, 1957.

Barton, John. "The Canonical Approach." Pages 77–88 in *Reading the Old Testament: Method in Biblical Study.* Edited by John Barton. Louisville: Westminster John Knox, 1996.

_____ *The Nature of Biblical Criticism.* Louisville: Westminster John Knox, 2007.

Bauckham, Richard. "For Whom Were the Gospels Written?" Pages 9–48 in *The Gospels for All Christians: Rethinking the Gospel Audiences.* Edited by Richard Bauckham. Grand Rapids: Eerdmans, 1998.

Bayer, Hans F. *Das Evangelium des Markus.* Historisch Theologische Auslegung 5. Witten: SCM R. Brockhaus, 2008.

Beavis, Mary Ann. *Mark's Audience: The Literary and Social Setting of Mark 4:11–12.* Sheffield: Sheffield Academic Press, 1989.

Becker, Eve-Marie. "Earliest Christian Literary Activity: Investigating Authors, Genres, and Audiences in Paul and Mark." Pages 87–105 in *Mark and Paul: Comparative Essays Part II, For and Against Pauline Influence on Mark.* Edited by Eve-Marie Becker, Troels Engberg-Pedersen, and Mogens Müller. Beihefte zur Zeitschrift für die neutestamentliche Wissenschaft 199. Berlin: de Gruyter, 2014.

_____ *The Birth of Christian History: Memory and Time from Mark to Luke-Acts.* New Haven: Yale University Press, 2017.

Becker, Eve-Marie, Engberg-Pedersen, Troels and Müller, Mogens. "Mark and Paul—Introductory Remarks." Pages 1–10 in *Mark and Paul: Comparative Essays Part II, For and Against Pauline Influence on Mark.* Edited by Eve-Marie Becker, Troels Engberg-Pedersen, and Mogens Müller. Beihefte zur Zeitschrift für die neutestamentliche Wissenschaft 199. Berlin: de Gruyter, 2014.

Behr, John. *The Way to Nicaea.* New York: St. Vladimir's Seminary Press, 2001.

Betz, Hans Dieter. *Galatians.* Hermeneia. Philadelphia: Fortress, 1979.

_____ "Transferring a Ritual: Paul's Interpretation of Baptism in Romans 6." Pages 84–118 in *Paul in His Hellenistic Context.* Edited by Troels Engberg-Pedersen. Minneapolis: Fortress, 1995.

Black, C. Clifton. "Christ Crucified in Paul and Mark: Reflections on an Intracanonical Conversation." Pages 184–206 in *Theology and Ethics in Paul and His Interpreters: Essays in Honor of Victor Paul Furnish.* Edited by Eugene H. Lovering, Jr. and Jerry L. Sumney. Nashville: Abingdon, 1996.

_____ *Mark*. Abingdon New Testament Commentaries. Nashville: Abingdon, 2011.

Boring, M. Eugene. *Mark: A Commentary*. New Testament Library. Louisville: Westminster John Knox, 2006.

Botha, Pieter J. J. *Orality and Literacy in Early Christianity*. Biblical Performance Criticism 5. Eugene: Wipf and Stock, 2012.

Bovon, Francois. *Luke*. Translated by Christine M. Thomas, Donald Deer, and James Crouch. 3 vols. Hermeneia. Minneapolis: Fortress, 2002–13.

_____ *Luke the Theologian*. 2nd edn. Waco: Baylor University Press, 2006.

Bradshaw, Paul F. *Eucharistic Origins*. Oxford: Oxford University Press, 2004.

Bradshaw, Paul F. and Johnson, Maxwell E.. *The Eucharistic Liturgies: Their Evolution and Interpretation*. Collegeville: Liturgical Press, 2012.

Breytenbach, Cilliers. "The Septuagint Version of Isaiah 53 and the Early Christian Formula, 'He Was Delivered for Our Trespasses.'" *Novum Testamentum* 51 (2009): 339–51.

Brown, Jeannine K. "Metalepsis." Pages 29–41 in *Exploring Intertextuality: Diverse Strategies for New Testament Interpretation of Texts*. Edited by B. J. Oropeza and Steve Moyise. Eugene: Cascade Books, 2016.

Brown, Raymond E. *The Death of the Messiah from Gethsemane to the Grave: A Commentary on the Passion Narratives in the Four Gospels*. 2 vols. New York: Doubleday, 1994.

Bultmann, Rudolf. *Die Geschichte der Synoptischen Tradition*. Göttingen: Vandenhoeck & Ruprecht, 1931.

Bundy, Walter E. "The Meaning of Jesus' Baptism." *The Journal of Religion* 7 (1927): 56–71.

Burridge, Richard A. *What Are the Gospels: A Comparison With Graeco-Roman Biography*. 2nd edn. Grand Rapids: Eerdmans, 2004.

Byrne, Brendan. *Romans*. Sacra Pagina 6. Collegeville: Liturgical Press, 1996.

Carey, Holly J. *Jesus' Cry from the Cross: Towards a First-Century Understanding of the Intertextual Relationship between Psalm 22 and the Narrative of Mark's Gospel*. Library of New Testament Studies 398. London: T&T Clark, 2009.

Chatman, Seymour. *Story and Discourse: Narrative Structure in Fiction and Film*. Ithaca: Cornell University Press, 1978.

Ciampa, Roy E. and Rosner, Brian S. *The First Letter to the Corinthians*. The Pillar New Testament Commentary. Grand Rapids: Eerdmans, 2010.

Cockerill, Gareth Lee. *The Epistle to the Hebrews*. The New International Commentary on the New Testament. Grand Rapids: Eerdmans, 2012.

Cohen, Shaye J. D. *From the Maccabees to the Mishnah*. Philadelphia: Westminster, 1987.

Collins, Adela Yarbro. *Mark: A Commentary*. Hermeneia. Minneapolis: Fortress, 2007.

_____ "Mark and the Hermeneutics of History Writing." Pages 231–44 in *Mark and Matthew II: Comparative Readings: Reception History, Cultural Hermeneutics, and Theology*. Edited by Eve-Marie Becker and Anders Runesson. Wissenschaftliche Untersuchungen zum Neuen Testament 304. Tübingen: Mohr Siebeck, 2013.

Collins, Raymond E. *I & II Timothy and Titus*. New Testament Library. Louisville: Westminster John Knox, 2002.

Collins, Raymond F. *First Corinthians*. Sacra Pagina 7. Collegeville: Liturgical Press, 1999.

Conzelmann, Hans. *1 Corinthians*. Translated by James W. Leitch. Hermeneia. Philadelphia: Fortress, 1974.

Cranfield, C. E. B.. *The Gospel According to Saint Mark*. Cambridge Greek Testament Commentary. Cambridge: Cambridge University Press, 1959.

Dahl, Nils Alstrup. *Studies in Paul: Theology for the Early Christian Mission*. Minneapolis: Augsburg, 1977.

_____ "The Atonement—Adequate Reward for the Akedah?" Pages 15–29 in *Neotestamentica et Semitica: Studies in Honour of Matthew Black*. Edited by E. Earle Ellis and Max Wilcox. Edinburgh: T&T Clark, 1969.

_____ "The Purpose of Mark's Gospel." Pages 52–65 in *Jesus in the Memory of the Early Church*. Edited by Nils Alstrup Dahl. Minneapolis: Augsburg, 1976.

Dahood, Mitchell. *Psalms 1–50*. Anchor Bible 16. New York: Doubleday, 1966.

Daise, Michael A. "'Christ Our Passover' (1 Corinthians 5:6–8): The Death of Jesus and the Quartodeciman Pascha." *Neotestamentica* 50.2 (2016): 507–26.

Daly, Robert J. "Eucharistic Origins: From the New Testament to the Liturgies of the Golden Age." *Theological Studies* 66 (2005): 3–22.

Damgaard, Finn. "Persecution and Denial—Paradigmatic Apostolic Portrayals in Paul and Mark." Pages 195–210 in *Mark and Paul: Comparative Essays Part II, For and Against Pauline Influence on Mark*. edited by Eve-Marie Becker, Troels Engberg-Pedersen, and Mogens Müller. Beihefte zur Zeitschrift für die neutestamentliche Wissenschaft 199. Berlin: de Gruyter, 2014.

Davidsen, Ole. "Adam-Christ Typology in Paul and Mark: Reflections on a Tertium Comparationis." Pages 243–72 in *Mark and Paul: Comparative Essays Part II, For and Against Pauline Influence on Mark*. Edited by Eve-Marie Becker, Troels Engberg-Pedersen, and Mogens Müller. Beihefte zur Zeitschrift für die neutestamentliche Wissenschaft 199. Berlin: de Gruyter, 2014.

de Boer, Martinus C. *Galatians: A Commentary*. New Testament Library. Louisville: Westminster John Knox, 2011.

de Bruyne, Dom Donatien. "Les plus anciens prologues latins des Évangiles." *Revue Bénédictine* XL (1928): 193–214.

Derrida, Jacques. "Literature in Secret." Pages 119–58 in idem, *The Gift of Death and Literature in Secret*. Translated by David Wills. 2nd edn. Chicago: The University of Chicago Press, 2008.

DeSilva, David A. *4 Maccabees*. Sheffield: Sheffield Academic Press, 1998.

_____ *Perseverance in Gratitude: A Socio-Rhetorical Commentary on the Epistle "to the Hebrews."* Grand Rapids: Eerdmans, 2000.

Dibelius, Martin. *James*. Translated by Michael A. Williams. Hermeneia. Philadelphia: Fortress, 1964.

_____ *From Tradition to Gospel*. Translated by B. L. Woolf. New York: Charles Scribner's Sons, 1934.

Dietzfelbinder, Christian. *Pseudo-Philo: Antiquitates Biblicae*. Jüdische Schriften aus hellenistisch-römischer Zeit II.2. Gütersloh: Gerd Mohn, 1975.

Doan, William and Giles, Terry. *Prophets, Performance, and Power: Performance Criticism of the Hebrew Bible*. New York: T&T Clark, 2006.

Dochhorn, Jan. "Man and the Son of Man in Mark 2:27–28: An Exegesis of Mark 2:23–28 Focusing on the Christological Discourse in Mark 2:27–28 With an Epilogue Concerning Pauline Parallels." Pages 147–58 in *Mark and Paul: Comparative Essays Part II, For and Against Pauline Influence on Mark*. Edited by Eve-Marie Becker, Troels Engberg-Pedersen, and Mogens Müller. Beihefte zur Zeitschrift für die neutestamentliche Wissenschaft 199. Berlin: de Gruyter, 2014.

Dodd, C. H. *The Apostolic Preaching and Its Developments: Three Lectures*. Chicago: Willett, Clark & Company, 1937.

Donahue, John R., S.J. "The Quest for the Community of Mark's Gospel." Pages 817–37 in vol. 2 of *The Four Gospels: Festschrift for Frans Neirynck*. Edited by F. van Segbroek, C. M. Tucker, G. van Belle, and J. Verheyden. 3 vols. Bibliotheca Ephemeridum Theologicarum Lovaniensium 100; Leuven: Leuven University Press, 1991.

Donahue, John R. S.J. and Harrington, Daniel J.. *The Gospel of Mark*. Sacra Pagina 2. Collegeville: Liturgical Press, 2002.

Dowling, Elizabeth V. "'Do This in Remembrance of Me': Last Supper Traditions in Paul and Mark." Pages 221–41 in *Paul and Mark: Comparative Essays Part I, Two Authors at the Beginnings of Early Christianity*. Edited by Oda Wischmeyer, David C. Sim, and Ian J. Elmer. Beihefte zur Zeitschrift für die neutestamentliche Wissenschaft 198. Berlin: de Gruyter, 2014.

Drescher, Richard. "Das Markusevangelium und seine Entstehung." *Zeitschrift für die Neutestamentliche Wissenschaft* 17 (1916): 228–56.

Duff, Paul Brooks. "Apostolic Suffering and the Language of Processions in 2 Cor. 4:7–10. *Biblical Theology Bulletin* 21 (1991): 158–65.

_____ "Metaphor, Motif, and Meaning: The Rhetorical Strategy Behind the Image 'Led in Triumph' in 2 Corinthians 2:14." *Catholic Biblical Quarterly* 53 (1991): 79–92.

Dunn, James D. G. *A Commentary on the Epistle to the Galatians*. Black's New Testament Commentaries. London: A&C Black, 1993.

_____ "Once More, πίστις Χριστοῦ." Pages 61–81 in *Pauline Theology Volume IV: Looking Back, Pressing On*. Edited by Elizabeth Johnson, E. and David M., Hay. Atlanta: Scholars Press, 1997.

_____ "The New Perspective on Paul." Pages 183–214 in *Jesus, Paul and the Law: Studies in Mark and Galatians*. Louisville: Westminster John Knox, 1990. Reprinted and expanded from *Bulletin of the John Rylands University Library of Manchester* 65 (1983): 95–122.

Dykstra, Tom E. "From Volkmar to Tarazi and Beyond: Mark as an Allegorical Presentation of the Pauline Gospel." Pages 99–120 in *Festschrift in Honor of Professor Paul Nadim Tarazi*. Edited by Bradley Nassif. 2 vols. New York: Peter Lang, 2015.

_____ *Mark, Canonizer of Paul*. St. Paul: OCABS Press, 2012.

Eckey, Wilfried. *Das Markusevangelium: Orientierung am Weg Jesu*. Neukirchen-Vluyn: Neukirchener Verlag, 1998.

_____ *Der Galaterbrief: ein Kommentar*. Neukirchener Theologie. Neukirchen-Vluyn: Neukirchener Verlag, 2010.

Edwards, James R. *Romans*. New International Biblical Commentary on the New Testament 6. Peabody: Hendrickson, 1992.

_____ *The Gospel According to Mark*. Pillar New Testament Commentary. Leicester: Apollos, 2002.

Engberg-Pedersen, Troels. "Paul in Mark 8:34–9:1: Mark on What It Is to Be a Christian." Pages 189–209 in *Mark and Paul: Comparative Essays Part II; For and Against Pauline Influence on Mark*. Edited by Eve-Marie Becker, Troels Engberg Pedersen, and Mogens Müller. Beihefte zur Zeitschrift für die neutestamentliche Wissenschaft 199. Berlin: de Gruyter, 2014.

Fenton, J. C. "Paul and Mark." Pages 89–112 in *Studies in the Gospels: Essays in Honor of R.H. Lightfoot*. Edited by D. E. Nineham. Oxford: Basil Blackwell, 1955.

Fishbane, Michael. *Biblical Interpretation in Ancient Israel*. Oxford: Clarendon, 1985.

Fisk, Bruce N. "Offering Isaac Again and Again: Pseudo-Philo's Use of the Aqedah as Intertext." *Catholic Biblical Quarterly* 62 (2000): 481–507.

Fiske, G. C. *Lucilius and Horace: A Study in the Classical Theory of Imitation*. Westport: Greenwood Press, 1971.

Fitzmyer, Joseph A. *First Corinthians*. Anchor Bible 32. New Haven: Yale University Press, 2008.

Fitzmyer, Joseph A. *Romans*. Anchor Bible 33. New York: Doubleday, 1993.

Focant, Camille. *L'évangile selon Marc*. Commentaire Biblique: Nouveau Testament 2. Paris: Les Éditions du Cerf, 2010.

Fortna, Robert. "Jesus and Peter at the High Priest's House: A Test Case for the Question of the Relation between Mark's and John's Gospels." *New Testament Studies* 24 (1978): 371–83.

Foster, Paul. *Colossians*. Black's New Testament Commentaries. London: Bloomsbury T&T Clark, 2016.

Fowler, Robert M. "Reader-Response Criticism: Figuring Mark's Reader." Pages 59–93 in *Mark and Method: New Approaches in Biblical Studies*. Edited by Janice Capel Anderson and Stephen D. Moore. 2nd edn. Minneapolis: Fortress, 2008.

France, R. T. *The Gospel of Mark: A Commentary on the Greek Text*. New International Greek Testament Commentary. Grand Rapids: Eerdmans, 2002.

Friedrich, Gerhard. "εὐαγγέλιον." Pages 721–37 in vol. 2 of *Theological Dictionary of the New Testament*. Edited by Gerhard Kittel. Translated by Geoffrey W. Bromiley. 10 vols. Grand Rapids: Eerdmans, 1964–76.

Furnish, Victor Paul. *II Corinthians*. Anchor Bible 32a. New Haven: Yale University Press, 1984.

Gamble, Harry. *Books and Readers in the Early Church: A History of Early Christian Texts*. New Haven: Yale University Press, 1995.

Garland, David E. *1 Corinthians*. Baker Exegetical Commentary on the New Testament. Grand Rapids: Baker Academic, 2003.

Genette, Gérard. *Palimpsestes: La littérature au second degré*. Paris: Seuil, 1982.

Gibson, Jeffrey B. "The Rebuke of the Disciples in Mark 8:14–21." *Journal for the Study of the New Testament* 27 (1986): 31–47.

Gignac, Alain. *L'Épître aux Romains*. Commentaire Biblique: Nouveau Testament 6. Paris: Les Éditions du Cerf, 2014.

Glasswell, M. E. "The Relationship between John and Mark." *Journal for the Study of the New Testament* 23 (1985): 99–115.

Gnilka, Joachim. *Das Evangelium nach Markus*. 2 vols. Evangelisch-katholischer Kommentar zum Neuen Testament. Solothurn und Düsseldorf: Benziger Verlag, 1994.

Goulder, Michael D. "Those Outside (Mk. 4:10–12)." *Novum Testamentum* 33 (1991): 289–302.

Grant, Robert M. *The Letter and the Spirit*. Eugene: Wipf & Stock, 1957.

Guelich, Robert A. *Mark 1–8:26*. Word Biblical Commentary 34a. Dallas: Word Books, 1989.

Gurtner, Daniel M. "LXX Syntax and the Identity of the NT Veil." *Novum Testamentum* 47 (2007): 344–53.

Haenchen, Ernst. *Der Weg Jesu: eine Erklärung des Markus-Evangeliums und der kanonischen Parallelen*. Berlin: Töpelmann, 1966.

Hahn, Scott W. "Covenant, Oath, and the Aqedah: Διαθήκη in Galatians 3:15–18." *Catholic Biblical Quarterly* 67 (2005): 79–100.

Halliwell, Stephen. "Pleasure, Understanding, and Emotion in Aristotle's *Poetics*." Pages 241–60 in *Essays on Aristotle's Poetics*. Edited by Amélie Oksenberg Rorty. Princeton: Princeton University Press, 1992.

Harris, Horton. *The Tübingen School: A Historical and Theological Investigation of the School of F. C. Baur*. Grand Rapids: Baker, 1990.

Hays, Richard B. *Echoes of Scripture in the Gospels*. Waco: Baylor University Press, 2016.

_____ *Echoes of Scripture in the Letters of Paul*. New Haven: Yale University Press, 1989.

_____ *First Corinthians*. Interpretation: A Bible Commentary for Teaching and Preaching. Louisville: John Knox, 1997.

_____ "ΠΙΣΤΙΣ and Pauline Christology: What Is at Stake?" Pages 35–60 in *Pauline Theology Volume IV: Looking Back, Pressing On*. Edited by Elizabeth Johnson, E. and Hay, David M.; Atlanta: Scholars Press, 1997.

_____ *The Faith of Jesus Christ: The Narrative Substructure of Gal 3:1–4:11*. 2nd edn. Grand Rapids: Eerdmans, 2002.

Hengel, Martin *Judaism and Hellenism*. Philadelphia: Fortress, 1974.

_____ *Studies in the Gospel of Mark*. Eugene: Wipf & Stock, 1985.

_____ *The Septuagint as Christian Scripture: Its Prehistory and the Problem of Its Canon*. Old Testament Studies. Edinburgh: T&T Clark, 2002.

Hilgert, Earle. *The Ship and Related Symbols in the New Testament*. Assen: van Gorcum, 1962.

Hollander, John. *The Figure of an Echo: A Mode of Allusion in Milton and After*. Berkeley: University of California Press, 1981.

Hooker, Morna D. "A Partner in the Gospel: Paul's Understanding of His Ministry." Pages 83–100 in *Theology and Ethics in Paul and His Interpreters: Essays in Honor of Victor Paul Furnish*. Edited by Eugene H. Lovering, Jr. and Jerry L. Sumney. Nashville: Abingdon, 1996.

_____ *Jesus and the Servant: The Influence of the Servant Concept of Deutero-Isaiah in the New Testament*. London: S.P.C.K., 1959.

_____ "ΠΙΣΤΙΣ ΧΡΙΣΤΟΥ." *New Testament Studies* 35 (1989): 321–42.

_____ *The Gospel According to Saint Mark*. Black's New Testament Commentaries. Peabody: Hendrickson, 1991.

_____ "'Who died for our sins, and was raised for our acquittal': Paul's understanding of the death of Christ." *Svensk exegetisk årsbok* 68 (2003): 59–71.

Horsley, Richard A. *1 Corinthians*. Abingdon New Testament Commentaries. Nashville: Abingdon, 1991.

_____ *Text and Tradition in Performance and Writing*. Biblical Performance Criticism 9. Eugene: Wipf and Stock, 2013.

Huizenga, Leroy A. *The New Isaac: Tradition and Intertextuality in the Gospel of Matthew*. Supplements to Novum Testamentum 131. Leiden: Brill, 2009.

Hultgren, Arland J. *Paul's Letter to the Romans*. Grand Rapids: Eerdmans, 2011.

_____ "The Pastoral Epistles." Pages 141–55 in *The Cambridge Companion to St. Paul*. Edited by James D. G. Dunn. Cambridge: Cambridge University Press, 2003.

Incigneri, Brian J. *The Gospel According to the Romans: The Setting and Rhetoric of Mark's Gospel*. Biblical Interpretation Series 65. Leiden: Brill, 2003.

Jacobson, Howard. *A Commentary on Pseudo-Philo's Liber Antiquitatum Biblicarum with Latin Text and English Translation*. 2 vols. Arbeiten zur Geschichte des antiken Judentums und des Urchristentums 31. Leiden: Brill, 1996.

Janko, Richard. "From Catharsis to the Aristotelian Mean." Pages 341–58 in *Essays on Aristotle's Poetics*. Edited by Amélie Oksenberg Rorty. Princeton: Princeton University Press, 1992.

Jay, Jeff. *The Tragic in Mark: A Literary-Historical Interpretation*. Hermeneutische Untersuchungen zur Theologie 66; Tübingen: Mohr Siebeck, 2014.

Jenkins, C. Ryan. "Faith and Work in Paul and James." *Bibliotheca Sacra* 159 (2002): 62–78.

Jeremias, Joachim. "Paul and James." *Expository Times* 66 (155): 368–71.

_____ *The Eucharistic Words of Jesus*. Translated by Norman Perrin. London: SCM Press, 1966.

Jewett, Robert. *Romans*. Hermeneia. Minneapolis: Fortress, 2007.

Johnson, Luke Timothy. *The Gospel of Luke*. Sacra Pagina 3. Collegeville: Liturgical Press, 1991.

Johnson, Sherman E. *A Commentary on the Gospel According to Saint Mark*. Harper's New Testament Commentaries 2. New York: Harper & Brothers, 1960.

Kähler, Martin. *The So-Called Historical Jesus and the Historic, Biblical Christ*. Translated by Carl E. Braaten. Philadelphia, Fortress, 1964.

Käsemann, Ernst. *Commentary on Romans*. Translated by Geoffrey W. Bromiley. Grand Rapids: Eerdmans, 1980.

Kierkegaard, Søren. *Fear and Trembling*. Translated by Alastair Hannay. London: Penguin Books, 1985.

Keck, Leander E. *Romans*. Abingdon New Testament Commentaries. Nashville: Abingdon, 2005.

Kee, Howard Clark. "The Function of Scriptural Quotations and Allusions in Mark 11–16." Pages 165–88 in *Festschrift Für Werner Georg Kümmel Zum 70. Geburtstag*. Edited by E. Earle Ellis and Erich Gräber. Göttingen: Vandenhoeck & Ruprecht, 1975.

Keener, Craig S. *1–2 Corinthians*. New Cambridge Bible Commentary. New York: Cambridge University Press, 2005.

Kelber, Werner H. "Mark 14:32–42: Gethsemane; Passion Christology and Discipleship Failure." *Zeitschrift für die neutestamentliche Wissenschaft* 63 (1972): 166–87.

_____ *Mark's Story of Jesus*. Philadelphia: Fortress, 1979.

Kermode, Frank. *The Sense of an Ending: Studies in the Theory of Fiction*. Oxford: Oxford University Press, 1966.

Klaiber, Walter. *Das Markusevangelium*. Die Botschaft des Neuen Testaments. Neukirchen-Vluyn: Neukirchener Verlag, 2010.

_____ *Der erste Korintherbrief*. Die Botschaft des Neuen Testaments. Neukirchen-Vluyn: Neukirchener Verlag, 2011.

Klauck, Hans-Josef. *4 Makkabäerbuch*. Jüdische Schriften aus hellenistisch-römischer Zeit III.6. Gütersloh: Gerd Mohn, 1989.

_____ *1 Korintherbrief*. Neue Echter Bibel 7. Würzburg: Echter Verlag, 1989.

_____ *Herrenmahl und hellenistischer Kult: Eine religionsgeschichtliche Untersuchung zum ersten Korintherbrief*. Münster: Aschendorff, 1982.

Klawans, Jonathan. "Interpreting the Last Supper: Sacrifice, Spiritualization, and Anti-Sacrifice." *New Testament Studies* 48 (2002): 1–17.

Kloppenborg Verbin, John S. "Egyptian Viticultural Practices and the Citation of Isa 5:1–7 in Mark 12:1–9." *Novum Testamentum* 44 (2002): 134–59.

Koch, Dietrich-Alex. *Die Schrift als Zeuge des Evangeliums: Untersuchungen zur Verwendung und zum Verständnis der Schrift bei Paulus*. Beiträge zur historischen Theologie 69. Tübingen: Mohr Siebeck, 1986.

Kok, Michael. "Does Mark Narrate the Pauline Kerygma of 'Christ Crucified?' Challenging an Emerging Consensus on Mark as a Pauline Gospel." *Journal for the Study of the New Testament* 37 (2014): 139–57.

Krentz, Edgar. *The Historical-Critical Method*. Philadelphia: Fortress Press, 1975.

Lane, William L. *Hebrews 1–8*. Word Biblical Commentary 47a. Dallas: Word Books, 1991.

_____ *The Gospel According to Mark*. New International Commentary on the New Testament 2. Grand Rapids: Eerdmans, 1974.

Larsen, Kasper Bro. "Mark 7:1–23: A Pauline Halakah?" Pages 169–88 in *Mark and Paul: Comparative Essays Part II, For and Against Pauline Influence on Mark*. Edited by Eve-Marie Becker, Troels Engberg-Pedersen, and Mogens Müller. Beihefte zur Zeitschrift für die neutestamentliche Wissenschaft 199. Berlin: de Gruyter, 2014.

Larsen, Matthew D. C. *The Gospels before the Book*. Oxford: Oxford University Press, 2018.

Lear, Jonathan "Katharsis." Pages 129–41 in *Essays on Aristotle's Poetics*. Edited by Amélie Oksenberg Rorty Princeton: Princeton University Press, 1992.

Légasse, Simon. *L'Épître de Paul aux Galates*. Lectio Divina Commentaires 9. Paris: Les Éditions du Cerf, 2000.

_____ *L'Épître de Paul aux Romains*. Lectio Divina Commentaires 10. Paris: Les Éditions du Cerf, 2002.

_____ *L'Évangile de Marc*. 2 vols. Lectio Divina Commentaires 5. Paris: Les Éditions du Cerf, 1997.

_____ *Naissance du Baptême*. Lectio Divina 153. Paris: Les Éditions du Cerf, 1993.

Levenson, Jon. *The Death and Resurrection of the Beloved Son: The Transformation of Child Sacrifice in Judaism and Christianity*. New Haven: Yale University Press, 1993.

Lietzmann, Hans. *An die Korinther I/II*. Handbuch zum Neuen Testament 9. Tübingen: J. C. B. Mohr (Paul Siebeck), 1969.

_____ *An die Galater*. Handbuch zum Neuen Testament 10. Tübingen: J.C.B. Mohr (Paul Siebeck), 1932.

Lincoln, Andrew T. *Ephesians*. Word Biblical Commentary 42. Nashville: Thomas Nelson Publishers, 1990.

Lindemann, Andreas. "Das Evangelium bei Paulus und im Markusevangelium." Pages 313–59 in *Paul and Mark: Comparative Essays Part I, Two Authors at the Beginnings of Early Christianity*. Edited by Oda Wischmeyer, David C. Sim, and Ian J. Elmer. Beihefte zur Zeitschrift für die neutestamentliche Wissenschaft 198. Berlin: de Gruyter, 2014.

_____ *Die Clemensbriefe*. Tübingen: J.C.B. Mohr (Paul Siebeck), 1992.

_____ "The First Epistle of Clement" Pages 47–70 in *The Apostolic Fathers: An Introduction*. Edited by Pratscher, Wilhelm. Waco: Baylor University Press, 2010.

Löhr, Hermut. "The Epistles of Ignatius of Antioch" Pages 91–116 in *The Apostolic Fathers: An Introduction*. Edited by Wilhelm Pratscher. Waco: Baylor University Press, 2010.

Lohse, Eduard. *Colossians and Philemon*. Translated by William R. Poehlmann and Robert J. Karris. Hermeneia. Philadelphia: Fortress, 1971.

Loisy, Alfred. *L'Épitre Aux Galates*. Paris: E. Nourry, 1916.

Longenecker, Bruce. "Galatians." Pages 64–73 in *The Cambridge Companion to Saint Paul*. Edited by James D. G. Dunn. Cambridge; Cambridge University Press, 2003.

Luz, Ulrich. *Matthew*. Translated by James E. Crouch. 3 vols. Hermeneia. Minneapolis: Fortress, 2001–7.

_____ "Matthew the Evangelist: A Jewish Christian at the Crossroads." Pages 3–17 in *Studies in Matthew*. Edited by Ulrich Luz. Grand Rapids: Eerdmans, 2005.

Lyonnet, Stanislas and Sabourin, Léopold. *Sin, Redemption, and Sacrifice: A Biblical and Patristic Study*. Rome: Biblical Institute, 1970.

MacDonald, Dennis R. *Does the New Testament Imitate Homer?: Four Cases from the Acts of the Apostles*. New Haven: Yale University Press, 2003.

_____ *The Homeric Epics and the Gospel of Mark*. New Haven: Yale University Press, 2000.

Mack, Burton L. *A Myth of Innocence: Mark and Christian Origins*. Philadelphia: Fortress, 1988.

Mackay, Ian D. *John's Relationship With Mark: an Analysis of John 6 in Light of Mark 6–8*. Wissenschaftliche Untersuchungen zum Neuen Testament 182. Tübingen: Mohr Siebeck, 2004.

Malbon, Elizabeth Struthers. "Disciples/Crowds/Whoever: Markan Characters and Readers." Pages 70–99 in *In the Company of Jesus: Characters in Mark's Gospel*. Louisville: Westminster John Knox, 2000. Reprinted from *Novum Testamentum* 28 (1986): 104–30.

_____ *Mark's Jesus: Characterization as Narrative Christology*. Waco: Baylor University Press, 2009.

_____ "The Major Importance of the Minor Characters in Mark." Pages 185–225 in *In the Company of Jesus: Characters in Mark's Gospel*. Louisville: Westminster John Knox, 2000. Reprinted from pages 58–86 in *The New Literary Criticism and the New Testament*. Edited by Elizabeth Struthers Malbon and Edgar V. McKnight. Sheffield: Sheffield University Press, 1994.

_____ "Narrative Criticism: How Does the Story Mean?" Pages 1–40 in *In the Company of Jesus: Characters in Mark's Gospel*. Louisville: Westminster John Knox, 2000. Reprinted from pages 23–49 in *Mark and Method: New Approaches in Biblical Studies*. Edited by Janice Cape Anderson and Stephen D. Moore. Minneapolis: Fortress, 1992.

_____ "Texts and Contexts: Interpreting the Disciples in Mark." Pages 100–30 in *In the Company of Jesus: Characters in Mark's Gospel*. Louisville: Westminster John Knox, 2000. Reprinted from *Semeia* 62 (1993): 81–102.

Mann, C. S. *Mark*. Anchor Bible 27. New York: Doubleday, 1986.

Marcus, Joel. "Mark and Isaiah." Pages 449–66 in *Fortunate the Eyes That See: Essays in Honor of David Noel Freedman in Celebration of His Seventieth Birthday*. Edited by Astrid B. Beck, Andrew H. Bartelt, Paul R. Raabe, and Chris A. Franke. Grand Rapids: Eerdmans, 1995.

_____ *Mark: 1–8*. Anchor Bible 27. New York: Doubleday, 2000.

_____ *Mark 8–16*. Anchor Bible 27a. New Haven: Yale University Press, 2009.

_____ "Mark—Interpreter of Paul." Pages 29–49 in *Mark and Paul: Comparative Essays Part II, For and Against Pauline Influence on Mark*. Edited by Eve-Marie Becker, Troels Engberg-Pedersen, and Mogens Müller. Beihefte zur Zeitschrift für die neutestamentliche Wissenschaft 199. Berlin: de Gruyter, 2014.

_____ "Son of Man as Son of Adam." *Revue Biblique* 110 (2003): 370–86.

Marshall, I. Howard. *The Gospel of Luke*. New International Greek Testament Commentary. Grand Rapids: Eerdmans, 1978.

Martin, Dale B. *The Corinthian Body*. New Haven: Yale University Press, 1995.

Martin, Richard P. "Ancient Theatre and Performance Culture." Pages 36–54 in *The Cambridge Companion to Greek and Roman Theatre*. Edited by Marianne McDonald and J. Michael Walton. Cambridge: Cambridge University Press, 2007.

Martyn, J. Louis. *Galatians*. Anchor Bible 33. New York: Doubleday, 1997.

Marxsen, Willi. *Mark the Evangelist: Studies on the Redaction History of the Gospel*. Translated by James Boyce, Donald Juel, William Poehlmann, and Roy A. Harrisville. Nashville: Abingdon, 1969.

_____ "Repräsentation im Abendmahl?" in *Monatsschrift für Pastoraltheologie* 41 (1952): 69–78.

Matera, Frank J. *Galatians*. Sacra Pagina 9. Collegeville: Liturgical Press, 1992.

Mauser, Ulrich W. *Christ in the Wilderness: The Wilderness Theme in the Second Gospel and Its Basis in the Biblical Tradition*. London: SCM Press, 1963.

Mauss, Marcel. *The Gift: The Form and Reason for Exchange in Archaic Societies*. Translated by W. D. Halls. New York: W. W. Norton, 1990.

Mazza, Enrico. *The Celebration of the Eucharist: The Origin of the Rite and the Development of Its Interpretation*. Translated by Matthew J. O'Connell. Collegeville: Liturgical Press, 1999.

McGowan, Andrew. "Rethinking Eucharistic Origins." *Pacifica* 23 (2010): 173–91.

Meier, Martin. *A Marginal Jew: Rethinking the Historical Jesus.* 5 vols. New York: Doubleday, 1991–2016.

Meiser, Martin. "Evangelien als faktuale Erzählungen—Narration und Geschichte." Pages 9–36 in *Literatur und Geschichte.* Edited by Sikander Singh and Manfred Leber. Saarbrücker literaturwissenschaftliche Ringvorlesungen 7. Saarbrücken: Universitätsverlag des Saarlandes, 2018.

Mitchell, Margaret M. "1 and 2 Thessalonians." Pages 51–63 in *The Cambridge Companion to Saint Paul.* Edited by James D. G. Dunn. Cambridge: Cambridge University Press, 2003.

_____ "Epiphanic Evolutions in Earliest Christianity." Pages 237–55 in *Paul and the Emergence of Christian Textuality.* Wissenschaftliche Untersuchungen zum Neuen Testament 393. Tübingen; Mohr Siebek, 2017. Reprinted from *Illinois Classical Studies* 29 (2004): 183–204.

_____ "Homer in the New Testament?" *Journal of Religion* 83 (2003): 244–60.

_____ "Patristic Counter-Evidence to the Claim That 'The Gospels Were Written for All Christians.'" *New Testament Studies* 51 (2005): 36–79.

_____ *Paul and the Rhetoric of Reconciliation: An Exegetical Investigation of the Language and Composition of 1 Corinthians.* Louisville: Westminster John Knox, 1991.

_____ *Paul, the Corinthians, and the Birth of Christian Hermeneutics.* Cambridge: Cambridge University Press, 2010.

_____ "Rhetorical Shorthand in Pauline Argumentation: The Functions of 'the Gospel' in the Corinthian Correspondence." Pages 111–32 in *Paul and the Emergence of Christian Textuality.* Wissenschaftliche Untersuchungen zum Neuen Testament 393. Tübingen; Mohr Siebek, 2017. Reprinted from pages 63–88 in *Gospel in Paul: Studies on Corinthians, Galatians, and Romans for Richard N. Longenecker.* Edited by L. Ann Jervis and Peter Richardson. Sheffield: Sheffield Academic Press, 1994.

_____ "The Emergence of the Written Record." Pages 1–18 in *Paul and the Emergence of Christian Textuality.* Wissenschaftliche Untersuchungen zum Neuen Testament 393. Tübingen; Mohr Siebek, 2017. Reprinted from pages 177–94 in *The Cambridge History of Christianity: Volume 1, Origins to Constantine.* Edited by Margaret M. Mitchell and Francis M. Young. Cambridge: Cambridge University Press, 2006.

_____ "The Letter of James as a Document of Paulinism?" Pages 75–98 in *Reading James With New Eyes: Methodological Reassessments of the Letter of James.* Edited by Robert L. Webb and John S. Kloppenborg. London: T&T Clark, 2007.

Moloney, Francis J. *The Gospel of Mark.* Grand Rapids: Baker Academic, 2002.

Moo, Douglas J. *The Old Testament in the Gospel Passion Narratives.* Sheffield: Almond Press, 1983.

Moss, Candida. "The Man With the Flow of Power: Porous Bodies in Mark 5:25–34." *Journal of Biblical Literature* 129 (2010): 507–19.

Müller, W. G. "Interfigurality: A Study on the Interdependence of Literary Figures." Pages 101–21 in *Intertexuality.* Edited by H. E. Plett. Berlin: de Gruyter, 1991.

Murphy, Frederick James. *Pseudo-Philo: Rewriting the Bible.* New York: Oxford University Press, 1993.

Murphy-O'Connor, Jerome. "1 and 2 Corinthians." Pages 74–90 in *The Cambridge Companion to St. Paul.* Edited by James D. G. Dunn. Cambridge: Cambridge University Press, 2003.

_____ *St. Paul's Corinth: Texts and Archaeology.* Good News Studies 6. Wilmington: Glazier, 1983.

Nelligan, Thomas P. *The Quest for Mark's Sources: An Exploration of the Case for Mark's Use of First Corinthians*. Eugene: Pickwick Publications, 2015.

Neyrey, Jerome H. *2 Peter, Jude*. Anchor Bible 37. New York: Doubleday, 1993.

Nickelsburg, George W. E. *Jewish Literature between the Bible and the Mishnah*. Minneapolis: Fortress, 2005.

Niederwimmer, Kurt. *The Didache*. Hermeneia. Minneapolis: Fortress, 1998.

Nolland, John. *The Gospel of Matthew*. New International Greek Testament Commentary. Grand Rapids: Eerdmans, 2005.

Nünning, Ansgar. "Making Events—Making Stories—Making Worlds: Ways of Worldmaking from a Narratological Point of View." Pages 191–214 in *Cultural Ways of Worldmaking: Media and Narratives*. Edited by Vera Nünning, Ansgar Nünning, and Birgit Neumann. Concepts for the Study of Culture 1. Berlin: De Gruyter, 2010.

Nünning, Vera. "Conceptualizing (Un)Reliable Narration and (Un)Trustworthiness." Pages 1–30 in *Unreliable Narration and Untrustworthiness: Intermedial and Interdisciplinary Perspectives*. Edited by Vera Nünning. Narratologia 44. Berlin: de Gruyter, 2015.

——————— "Reconceptualizing Fictional (Un)Reliability and (Un)Trustworthiness from a Multidisciplinary Perspective: Categories, Typology, and Functions." Pages 83–108 in *Unreliable Narration and Untrustworthiness: Intermedial and Interdisciplinary Perspectives*. Edited by Nünning, Vera. Narratologia 44. Berlin: de Gruyter, 2015.

——————— "The Making of Fictional Worlds: Processes, Features, and Function." Pages 215–43 in *Cultural Ways of Worldmaking: Media and Narratives*. Edited by Vera Nünning, Ansgar Nünning, and Birgit Neumann. Concepts for the Study of Culture 1. Berlin: De Gruyter, 2010.

Nussbaum, Martha C. "Tragedy and Self-Sufficiency: Plato and Aristotle on Fear and Pity." Pages 261–90 in *Essays on Aristotle's Poetics*. Edited by Amélie Oksenberg Rorty. Princeton: Princeton University Press, 1992.

Oestreich, Bernhard. *Performance Criticism of the Pauline Letters*. Translated by Lindsay Elias and Brent Blum. Biblical Performance Criticism 14. Eugene: Cascade Books, 2016.

Omerzu, Heike. "Paul and Mark—Mark and Paul: A Critical Outline of the History of Research." Pages 51–61 in *Mark and Paul: Comparative Essays Part II, For and Against Pauline Influence on Mark*. Edited by Eve-Marie Becker, Troels Engberg-Pedersen, and Mogens Müller. Beihefte zur Zeitschrift für die neutestamentliche Wissenschaft 199. Berlin: de Gruyter, 2014.

Orr, William F. and Walther, James Arthur. *1 Corinthians*. Anchor Bible 32. New York: Doubleday, 1976.

Pearson, Birger A. "1 Thessalonians 2:13–16: A Deutero-Pauline Interpolation." *Harvard Theological Review* 64 (1971): 79–94.

Perkins, Pheme. *Abraham's Divided Children: Galatians and the Politics of Faith*. Harrisburg: Trinity Press International, 2001.

Perrin, Norman. *What Is Redaction Criticism?* Philadelphia: Fortress, 1969.

Perrot, Charles and Bogaert, Pierre-Maurice. *Les Antiquités Bibliques II: Introduction Littéraire, Commentaire, et Index*. Sources Chrétiennes 230. Paris: Les Éditions du Cerf, 1976.

Pervo, Richard I. *Acts*. Hermeneia. Minneapolis: Fortress, 2009.

——————— *Dating Acts: Between the Evangelists and the Apologists*. Santa Rosa: Polebridge, 2006.

Pesch, Rudolph. *Das Abendmahl und Jesu Todesverständnis*. Breisgau: Herder, 1978.

Popkes, Wiard. "Two Interpretations of 'Justification' in the New Testament Reflections on Galatians 2:15–21 and James 2:21–25." *Studia Theologica* 59 (2005): 129–46.

Porter, Stanley E. *The Letter to the Romans: A Linguistic and Literary Commentary*. Sheffield: Sheffield Phoenix Press, 2015.

Powell, Mark Allan. "Narrative Criticism: The Emergence of a Prominent Reading Strategy." Pages 19–44 in *Mark as Story: Retrospect and Prospect*. Edited by Kelley R. Iverson and Christopher W. Skinner. Resources for Biblical Studies 65. Atlanta: Society of Biblical Literature, 2011.

Queller, Kurt. "'Stretch Out Your Hand!' Echo and Metalepsis in Mark's Sabbath Healing Controversy." *Journal of Biblical Literature* 129 (2010): 737–58.

Quesnel, Michel. *La première épître aux Corinthiens*. Commentaire Biblique. Nouveau Testament 7. Paris: Les Éditions du Cerf, 2018.

Reicke, Bo. *The Epistles of James, Peter, and Jude*. Anchor Bible 37. New York: Doubleday, 1964.

Rhoads, David, Dewey, Joanna and Michie, Donald. *Mark as Story: An Introduction to the Narrative of a Gospel*. 3rd edn. Minneapolis: Fortress, 2012.

Rhoads, David. "Performance Criticism: An Emerging Methodology in Second Testament Studies—Part I." *Biblical Theology Bulletin* 36 (2006): 118–33.

_____ "Performance Criticism: An Emerging Methodology in Second Testament Studies—Part II." *Biblical Theology Bulletin* 36 (2006): 164–84.

Ricoeur, Paul. *Time and Narrative*. Translated by Kathleen McLaughlin and David Pellauer. 3 vols. Chicago: University of Chicago Press, 1983–5.

Roetzel, Calvin J. *2 Corinthians*. Abingdon New Testament Commentaries. Nashville: Abingdon, 2007.

_____ *Judgment in the Community: a Study of the Relationship between Eschatology and Ecclesiology in Paul*. Leiden: Brill, 1972.

_____ *Paul: The Man and the Myth*. Minneapolis: Fortress, 1999.

_____ *The Letters of Paul: Conversations in Context*. 5th edn. Louisville: Westminster John Knox, 2009.

Roth, Dieter T. Review of B. Adamzciewski, "The Gospel of Luke: A Hypertextual Commentary." *Theologische Literaturzeitung* 1 (2018), 57–9.

Sandmel, Samuel. "Parallelomania." *Journal of Biblical Literature* 81 (1962): 1–13.

Schenk, Wolfgang. "Sekundäre Jesuanisierungen von primären Paulus-Aussagen bei Markus." Pages 877–904 in vol. 2 of *The Four Gospels: Festschrift for Frans Neirynck*. Edited by F. van Segbroek, C. M. Tucker, G. van Belle, and J. Verheyden. 3 vols. Bibliotheca Ephemeridum Theologicarum Lovaniensium 100. Leuven: Leuven University Press, 1991.

Schenke, Ludger. *Das Markusevangelium: literarische Eigenwart—Text und Kommentarung*. Stuttgart: Kohlhammer, 2005.

Schipper, Jeremy. "Interpreting the Lamb Imagery in Isa 53." *Journal of Biblical Literature* 132 (2013): 315–25.

Schlier, Heinrich. *Der Römerbrief*. Herders theologischer Kommentar zum Neuen Testament 6. Freiburg im Breisgau: Herder, 1977.

Schmithals, Walter. *Der Römerbrief: ein Kommentar*. Gütersloh: Gerd Mohn, 1988.

Schnackenburg, Rudolf. *Baptism in the Thought of Saint Paul*. Translated by G. R. Beasely-Murray. New York: Herder and Herder, 1964.

Schoedel, William R. *Ignatius of Antioch*. Hermeneia. Philadelphia: Fortress, 1984.

Schoeps, Hans Joachim. "The Sacrifice of Isaac in Paul's Theology." *Journal of Biblical Literature* 65 (1946): 385–92.

Schottroff, Luise. *Der erste Brief an die Gemeinde in Korinth*. Theologischer Kommentar zum Neuen Testament 7. Stuttgart: Kohlhammer, 2013.

Schweitzer, Albert. *Von Reimarus zu Wrede: Eine Geschichte der Leben-Jesu-Forschung.* Tübingen: J. C. B. Mohr (Paul Siebeck), 1906.

_____ *The Quest of the Historical Jesus.* Edited by John Bowden. Translated by W. Montgomery, J. R. Coates, Susan Cupitt, and John Bowden. Minneapolis: Fortress, 2001.

Scroggs, Robin and Kent I. Groff. "Baptism in Mark: Dying and Rising With Christ." *Journal of Biblical Literature* 92 (1973): 531–48.

Shaver, Stephen R. "A Eucharistic Origins Story: Part 1: The Breaking of the Loaf." *Worship* 92 (2018): 204–21.

_____ "A Eucharistic Origins Story: Part 2: The Body and Blood of Christ." *Worship* 92 (2018): 298–317.

Sim, David C. "The Family of Jesus and the Disciples of Jesus in Paul and Mark: Taking Sides in the Early Church's Factional Dispute." Pages 73–97 in *Paul and Mark: Comparative Essays Part I, Two Authors at the Beginnings of Early Christianity.* Edited by Oda Wischmeyer, David C. Sim, and Ian J. Elmer. Beihefte zur Zeitschrift für die neutestamentliche Wissenschaft 198. Berlin: de Gruyter, 2014.

Skoven, Anne Vig. "Mark as an Allegorical Rewriting of Paul: Gustav Volkmar's Understanding of the Gospel of Mark." Pages 13–28 in *Mark and Paul: Comparative Essays Part II, For and Against Pauline Influence on Mark.* Edited by Eve-Marie Becker, Troels Engberg-Pedersen, and Mogens Müller. Beihefte zur Zeitschrift für die neutestamentliche Wissenschaft 199. Berlin: de Gruyter, 2014.

Sleeper, C. Freeman. *James.* Abingdon New Testament Commentaries. Nashville: Abingdon, 1998.

Smith, Barry D. "The Problem With the Observance of the Lord's Supper in the Corinthian Church." *Bulletin for Biblical Research* 20.4 (2010): 517–44.

Smyth, Herbert Weir. *Greek Grammar.* Cambridge: Harvard University Press, 1984.

Soards, Marion L. *1 Corinthians.* New International Biblical Commentary 7. Peabody: Hendrickson, 1999.

Stackert, Jeffrey. "'This Is the Blood of My Covenant': The Markan Last Supper and the Elohistic Horeb Narrative." *Biblical Research* 62 (2017): 48–60.

Standaert, Dom Benoît. *Évangile selon Marc: commentaire.* 3 vols. Études Bibliques 61. Pendé: J. Gabalda, 2010.

Stein, Robert H. *Mark.* Baker Exegetical Commentary on the New Testament. Grand Rapids: Baker Academic, 2008.

Stuhlmacher, Peter. *Paul's Letter to the Romans: A Commentary.* Translated by Scott J. Hafemann. Louisville: Westminster John Knox, 1994.

Svartvik, Jesper. "East Is East and West Is West:' The Concept of Torah in Paul and Mark." Pages 157–85 in *Paul and Mark: Comparative Essays Part I, Two Authors at the Beginnings of Early Christianity.* Edited by Oda Wischmeyer, David C. Sim, and Ian J. Elmer. Beihefte zur Zeitschrift für die neutestamentliche Wissenschaft 198. Berlin: de Gruyter, 2014.

Tannehill, Robert C. *Luke.* Abingdon New Testament Commentaries. Nashville: Abingdon, 1996.

_____ "The Disciples in Mark: The Function of a Narrative Role." *The Journal of Religion* 57 (1977): 386–405.

Tarazi, Paul Nadim. *The New Testament Introduction: Paul and Mark.* New York: St. Vladimir's Seminary Press, 1999.

Telford, W. R. "Introduction: The Gospel of Mark." Pages 1–41 in *The Interpretation of Mark.* Issues in Religion and Theology 7. Edited by William Telford. Philadelphia, Fortress, 1985.

_____ *The Theology of the Gospel of Mark*. New Testament Theology. Cambridge: Cambridge University Press, 1999.

Theissen, Gerd. *The Miracle Stories of the Early Christian Tradition*. Translated by Francis McDonagh. Philadelphia: Fortress, 1983.

_____ *The Social Setting of Pauline Christianity: Essays on Corinth*. Translated by J. H. Schütz. Philadelpia: Fortress, 1982.

Theobald, Michael. *Der Römerbrief*. Erträge der Forschung 294. Darmstadt: Wissenschaftliche Buchgesellschaft, 2000.

Theophilos, Michael P. "The Roman Connection: Paul and Mark," Pages 45–71 in *Paul and Mark: Comparative Essays Part I, Two Authors at the Beginnings of Early Christianity*. Edited by Oda Wischmeyer, David C. Sim, and Ian J. Elmer. Beihefte zur Zeitschrift für die neutestamentliche Wissenschaft 198. Berlin: de Gruyter, 2014.

Thiselton, Anthony. *The First Epistle to the Corinthians*. New International Greek Testament Commentary. Grand Rapids: Eerdmans, 2000.

Thornton, L. S. *The Common Life in the Body of Christ*. London: Dacre Press, 1950.

Tobin, Thomas H., S. J. *Paul's Rhetoric in Its Contexts: The Argument of Romans*. Peabody: Hendrickson, 2004.

Tonstad, Sigve K. "Inscribing Abraham: Apocalyptic, the Akedah, and 'Abba! Father!' in Galatians." Pages 15–27 in *Galatians as Examined by Diverse Academics in 2012*. Edited by Heerak Christian Kim. Newark: The Hermit Kingdom Press, 2013.

Tooman, William A. "Scriptural Reuse in Ancient Jewish Literature: Comments and Reflections on the State of the Art." Pages 23–39 in *Methodology in the Use of the Old Testament in the New: Context and Criteria*. Edited by David Allen and Steve Smith. London: T&T Clark, 2020.

Tyson, Joseph B. "The Blindness of the Disciples in Mark." *Journal of Biblical Literature* 80 (1961): 261–8.

van de Sandt, Huub. "Why Does the Didache Conceive of the Eucharist as a Holy Meal?" *Vigiliae Christianae* 65 (2011): 1–20.

van de Sandt, Huub and Flusser, David. *The Didache: Its Jewish Sources and Its Place in Early Judaism and Christianity*. Compendia rerum Iudaicarum ad Novum Testamentum III.5. Minneapolis: Fortress, 2002.

van Henten, Jan Willem. *The Maccabean Martyrs as Saviours of the Jewish People: A Study of 2 and 4 Maccabees*. Supplements to the Journal for the Study of Judaism 57. Leiden: Brill, 1997.

VanderKam, James C. "The Aqedah, Jubilees, and PseudoJubilees." Pages 241–61 in *The Quest for Context and Meaning: Studies in Biblical Intertextuality in Honor of James A. Sanders*. Biblical Interpretation Series 28. Edited by Craig A. Evans and Shemaryahu Talmon. Leiden: Brill, 1997.

_____ *The Book of Jubilees*. Guides to Apocrypha and Pseudepigrapha. Sheffield: Sheffield Academic Press, 2001.

Volkmar, Gustav. *Die Religion Jesu und ihre erste Entwickelung nach dem gegenwärtige Stande der Wissenschaft*. Leipzig: F. A. Brockhaus, 1857.

_____ *Die Evangelien, oder Marcus und die Synopsis der kanonischen und ausserkannonischen Evangelien nach dem ältesten Text mit historisch-exegetischem Commentar*. Leipzig: Fues's Verlag (R. Reisland), 1870.

Wagner, J. Ross. *Heralds of the Good News: Isaiah and Paul "in Concert" in the Letter to the Romans*. Novum Testamentum Supplements 101. Leiden: Brill, 2002.

Watts, Rikki E. "Jesus' Death, Isaiah 53, and Mark 10:45: A Crux Revisited." Pages 203–15 in *Jesus and the Suffering Servant: Isaiah 53 and Christian Origins*. Edited by William H. Bellinger Jr. and William R. Farmer. Harrisburg: Trinity International Press, 1998.

_____ "Mark," Pages 111–250 in *Commentary on the New Testament Use of the Old Testament*. Edited by G. K. Beale and D. A. Carson. Grand Rapids: Baker Academic, 2007.

Watson, Francis. "The Two Roman Congregations: Romans 14:1–15:13." Pages 203–15 in *The Romans Debate*. Edited by Karl P. Donfried. Peabody: Hendrickson, 1991.

Welborn, L. L. "The Preface to 1 Clement: The Rhetorical Situation and the Traditional Date." Pages 197–216 in *Encounters With Hellenism: Studies on the First Letter of Clement*. Edited by Cilliers Breytenbach and Laurence L. Welborn. Arbeiten zur Geschichte des antiken Judentums und des Urchristentums 53. Leiden: Brill, 2004.

Werner, Martin. *Der Einfluss paulinischer Theologie im Markusevangelium: eine Studie zur neutestamentlichen Theologie*. Giessen: Verlag von Alfred Töpelmann, 1923.

_____ *The Formation of Christian Dogma: An Historical Study of Its Problem*. Translated by Brandon, S. G. F. New York: Harper & Brothers, 1957.

Whallon, William. "The Pascha in the Eucharist." *New Testament Studies* 40 (1994): 126–32.

White, Hayden. *Metahistory: The Historical Imagination of Nineteenth-Century Europe*. Baltimore: Johns Hopkins University Press, 1975.

Wiefel, Wolfgang. "The Jewish Community in Ancient Rome and the Origins of Roman Christianity." Pages 85–101 in *The Romans Debate*. Edited by Karl P. Donfried. Peabody: Hendrickson, 1991.

Wildemann, Bernd. *Das Evangelium als Lehrpoesie: Leben und Werk Gustav Volkmars*. Kontexte 1. Frankfurt am Main: Peter Lang, 1983.

Wiles, David. "Aristotle's *Poetics* and Ancient Dramatic Theory." Pages 92–107 in *The Cambridge Companion to Greek and Roman Theatre*. Edited by Marianne McDonald and J. Michael Walton. Cambridge: Cambridge University Press, 2007.

Wilk, Florian. "'Die Schriften' bei Markus und Paulus." Pages 189–220 in *Paul and Mark: Comparative Essays Part I, Two Authors at the Beginnings of Early Christianity*. Edited by Oda Wischmeyer, David C. Sim, and Ian J. Elmer. Beihefte zur Zeitschrift für die neutestamentliche Wissenschaft 198. Berlin: de Gruyter, 2014.

_____ "The Letters of Paul as Witnesses to and for the Septuagint Text." Pages 253–71 in *Septuagint Research: Issues and Challenges in the Study of the Greek Jewish Scriptures*. Edited by Wolfgang Kraus and R. Glenn Wooden. Septuagint and Cognate Studies 53. Atlanta: Society of Biblical Literature, 2006.

Williams, Sam K. *Galatians*. Abingdon New Testament Commentaries. Nashville: Abingdon, 1997.

Wimsatt, W. K. Jr. and Beardsley, Monroe C.. *The Verbal Icon: Studies in the Meaning of Poetry*. New York: The Noonday Press, 1954.

Wire, Antoinette Clark. *The Case for Mark Composed in Performance*. Biblical Performance Criticism 2. Eugene: Cascade Books, 2011.

Wischmeyer, Johannes. "Universalismus als Tendenz und Entwicklungsmoment. Die Frage nach Markus und Paulus in der historisch-kritischen Geschichtsschreibung des Urchristentums von 1850–1910." Pages 19–44 in *Paul and Mark: Comparative Essays Part I, Two Authors at the Beginnings of Early Christianity*. Edited by Oda Wischmeyer, David C. Sim, and Ian J. Elmer. Beihefte zur Zeitschrift für die neutestamentliche Wissenschaft 198. Berlin: de Gruyter, 2014.

Wischmeyer, Oda. "Konzepte von Zeit bei Paulus und im Markusevangelium." Pages 361–92 in *Paul and Mark: Comparative Essays Part I, Two Authors at the Beginnings of Early Christianity*. Edited by Oda Wischmeyer, David C. Sim, and Ian J. Elmer. Beihefte zur Zeitschrift für die neutestamentliche Wissenschaft 198. Berlin: de Gruyter, 2014.

_____ "Romans 1:1–7 and Mark 1:1–3 in Comparison: Two Opening Texts at the Beginning of Early Christian Literature." Pages 121–46 in *Mark and Paul: Comparative Essays Part II, For and Against Pauline Influence on Mark*. Edited by Eve-Marie Becker, Troels Engberg-Pedersen, and Mogens Müller. Beihefte zur Zeitschrift für die neutestamentliche Wissenschaft 199. Berlin: de Gruyter, 2014.

Witherington, Ben III. *Conflict and Community in Corinth: A Socio-Rhetorical Commentary on 1 and 2 Corinthians*. Grand Rapids: Eerdmans, 1995.

Index

A New Perspective on the Use of Paul in the Gospel of Mark
Cameron Evan Ferguson